PRICED OUT BY DESIGN

HOW AI, BIG DATA, AND CORPORATE LANDLORDS CRASHED OUR HOUSING MARKET, AND HOW TO FIX IT

JAMES M. NELSON

THE MAN BEHIND THE **REALPAGE** LAWSUITS

PRICED OUT BY DESIGN: How AI, Big Data, and Corporate Landlords crashed our housing market, and how to fix it.

The opinions expressed in this book are those of its author, underpinned by his extensive research. RealPage, Yardi, AppFolio, Experian, Greystar Real Estate Partners, and other industry participants, as discussed throughout the book, strongly oppose these views, asserting that they are simply good business practices.

For information about this title or to order additional books and/or electronic media, contact the publisher at email:
TheNewLandlord@mail.com.

ISBN (softcover) 978-1-7346418-2-0
ISBN (eBook) 978-1-7346418-3-7

Printed in the United States of America

Long live the American Dream!

May it inspire us

and guide us through the long nights,

by the lights

from above.

CONTENTS

Foreward: About the Book

Today, in 2026, we are facing an unprecedented housing crisis. With more than two-thirds of our workforce, including fifty-one million Americans, unable to afford housing, and nearly one-and-a-half million people unhoused and living on the streets, it's the worst humanitarian crisis since the Great Depression. Metropolitan areas like Seattle spend over a quarter of a billion dollars each year on crisis management for the unhoused. This total rises to billions of dollars at the national level. These numbers are unsustainable for taxpayers. Affordable housing and homelessness are more than just a catastrophe; they're an existential threat that demands our immediate attention, yet the crisis has been largely marginalized.

At the heart of the crisis, since 2012, metropolitan areas have experienced a dramatic surge in housing costs, affecting all income levels. In Metro Seattle, where we established a case study, between the years 2013 and 2018, rental rates skyrocketed by over 82%, coinciding with a 32% rise in homelessness. These trends have been observed in metropolitan areas all across America.

In a 2022 Congressional hearing, the housing industry argued that the rise in housing costs is due to a shortage of millions of housing units. Additionally, they claim it's also due to out-of-control construction costs. However, at the same time, a small law firm called Justice Catalyst Law filed a class-action lawsuit against a company named RealPage and the rental housing industry for price-fixing rental rates. By the middle of 2023, more than thirty similar lawsuits had been filed nationwide against RealPage and the housing industry. Then, in 2024, the Department of Justice joined the fray, filing a lawsuit against RealPage and the broader industry for alleged algorithmic price-fixing.

The skyrocketing housing costs have sparked a debate: Are they driven by a genuine housing shortage exacerbated by soaring building material prices, or are they the result of industry manipulation through algorithmic price-fixing? What exactly is algorithmic price-fixing?

Meet James M. Nelson, the man behind the RealPage lawsuits. To gain a deeper understanding of the housing crisis, Nelson, a former federal banking regulator with a degree in economics and over 40 years in the banking industry, conducted six independently funded economic impact studies on all aspects of the housing industry (see Bibliography). These studies, which required over 10,000 hours of work, were completed over a five-year period. This in-depth research is documented in more than 1,400 pages and 2.5 million words. It is supported by over 3,500 cited references from more than 10,000 pages of documents. Additionally, it includes nearly 500 quotes from industry insiders.

The six studies are summarized in a 400-page legal version that also includes a legal analysis titled "The New Landlord Powered by Big Data and Artificial Intelligence." This legal version, also known as a white paper, serves as the foundation for the legal cases against RealPage and the broader rental housing industry, alleging price-fixing. This legal version also underpins the book titled "PRICED OUT BY DESIGN: How AI, Big Data, and Corporate Landlords crashed our housing market, and how to fix it." The book presents the study in layperson's terms, making it accessible to a broader audience.

PRICED OUT BY DESIGN is not just a book; it's an exposé on the rental housing industry. It shines a light on the role of AI-powered revenue management technology, which artificially sets rental rates through algorithmic price-fixing. This practice has doubled the cost of housing and significantly contributed to the housing crisis. The book not only examines how this technology works but also features stories from both housed and unhoused tenants, highlighting its profound impact on their lives. These narratives remind us that, behind every statistic, real people are struggling to find and hold onto housing they can afford.

In early 2021, the author met with the senior management of the National Low-Income Housing Coalition and shared his research findings. Impressed by the depth and breadth of his work, they directed him to Justice Catalyst Law, a law firm, where he presented his research and became a consultant. This research is the foundation of the original lawsuit filed in October 2022 against RealPage, the owner and operator of the industry's pricing technology, for rental-rate price-fixing. Then, also in February 2021, this research, along with several other studies, was presented to the news outlet ProPublica, which broke the story in October 2022.

Then, in early 2023, the author was contacted by the law firm Scott + Scott and Hausfeld, LLP, which hired the author as a lead consultant. Eventually, they became the Co-Lead Counsel in the multi-district litigation (a legal maneuver where the thirty legal cases were consolidated into one class-action case) against RealPage. Additionally, in early 2023, the author was served with a Civil Investigative Demand (CID), a legal order similar to a subpoena, issued by the Department of Justice (DOJ), requiring the production and submission of this work. This work underpins the DOJ's 2024 lawsuit against RealPage for engaging in algorithmic price-fixing. It also serves as the foundation for various lawsuits against RealPage and the housing industry for price-fixing, including suits filed by state attorneys general. Additionally, it underpins the ordinances issued by the County of San Francisco and other jurisdictions prohibiting the use of this pricing technology within their areas.

The insights from the book are particularly relevant for housing policymakers, government agencies, legal professionals, academics, and advocates for affordable housing. It offers a comprehensive understanding of the housing crisis, highlights how technology has contributed to the issue, and outlines the actions society must take to address it. The book's findings and recommendations have the potential to significantly influence future housing policies and practices, making it a crucial read for anyone concerned about the housing crisis and interested in shaping the future of housing.

Join me on this five-year journey to uncover the truth about what is happening in the rental housing industry and in housing in general, as well as the causes of the skyrocketing housing costs that fuel gentrification and homelessness.

CHAPTER 1

Roosevelt's New Deal and the Origins of Our Housing Programs

Introduction

Since the adoption of President Roosevelt's New Deal in the 1930s, a significant conflict has arisen in America regarding how the housing market should function. And it all comes down to this fundamental principle: Who can provide better utility, in this instance, housing, to the consumer, "big business"—the free market system (private utility) or "big government" (public utility)? Before the New Deal, the Federal Government played no role in the housing market.

In this chapter, we discuss the origins of our housing program, the economic conditions that surrounded its creation, and the individuals who framed it. Reviewing this history offers a window into our current economy and political strife, as well as what may occur when history repeats itself. This historical context is essential for understanding our ongoing housing crisis.

Today, when it comes to financing the homes of our dreams, no other country offers consumers such a diverse range of options—a veritable smorgasbord of prices and terms. The thirty-year fixed-rate mortgage was revolutionary in its design, with its long-term amortization made possible by the government's guarantee of the loan.

However, this hasn't always been the case; for our ancestors, the lending policies and terms used to be quite different. Additionally, there are those among us who feel very strongly that "big government" should not play a role in our housing. They have been striving to convince you, the reader, that it's in your best interest to remove them from the process and place the program back into the hands of free enterprise—"big business."

The New Deal and the Origins of Our Housing Programs

The Roaring Twenties

In the 1920s, three prominent groups drove this era: religious reformers, wealthy investors, and the working caste. The defining principle of the caste system was entrenched in property ownership because only about a third of the population owned property. For the working caste, the Roaring Twenties, known as the Gilded Age, was marked by greed, opulence, and stark income inequalities. From America's early beginnings, the wealthy and propertied classes heavily influenced our laws. The police forces at the time were primarily focused on protecting property rights rather than human rights.

During this era, religious reformers, in collaboration with the wealthy investor class, emerged as a significant force in the nation's politics. Their influence was profound, as they worked with the government to care for the poor and disadvantaged. Most of the funding for their care came from wealthy oligarchs, who funneled it through churches.

The wealthy investors, who included industrialists and plutocrats such as Rockefeller, Carnegie, and Vanderbilt, controlled Congress and, leveraging their relationships with the religious reformers, handpicked the Supreme Court that has become known as the Lochner-era Court. Over the decades, this court maintained strong pro-business, anti-labor positions.

The court embodied outright judicial hostility toward labor and the working caste. For example, in *Lochner v. New York*, the Court ruled against labor unions seeking to set a maximum of sixty hours per workweek. In *Adkins v. Children's Hospital,* the court ruled against federal minimum-wage legislation. In *Hammer v. Dagenhart*, the Court held that it was up to the states to regulate over a million child laborers (indentured servant children (orphans) under the age of fourteen).

In other words, if the wealthy investors decided any legislation infringed upon their rights to economic sovereignty or hindered their ability to make unfettered private contracts, they called upon the Supreme Court to overturn it. Yet, the working caste considered these titans of industry beyond reproach and considered them exemplary role models for their children.

The downside to the Roaring Twenties was that about two-thirds of the population experienced varying degrees of poverty. The working caste was mainly comprised of renters, meaning there was no policing force to protect them from unscrupulous landlords. The housing conditions at the time were deplorable, especially for the lower-income earners who lived in the slums. However, the poor conditions affected all the renters as they lacked basic health requirements such as indoor plumbing, electricity, and health codes. Perhaps their rental housing is best explained by Herbert B. Swope, who discussed rental properties when he said, "They would not be continued if they were not profitable, and they are profitable only through operation on a dehumanizing method—through bleeding the tenant until all social justice is debased."[1]

The Financial Collapse of 1929

The financial industry's lack of oversight and regulation led to the 1929 American monetary collapse, a catastrophic event that shook the very foundations of the world. In the five years preceding the stock market crash, the stock market had increased by some 400%. In the preceding decade, the wealth of the top 200 firms doubled. By 1930, 130 corporations controlled over 80% of the nation's wealth. The consolidation of wealth and power was unprecedented.

Then, between September and November 1929, the stock market crashed, losing 90% of its value. The scale of the crash was also unprecedented; its effects spread to the banking industry, leading to the closure of about 9,000 banks within the first three years afterward. Nearly half of these—around 4,500—closed in 1933 alone, resulting in a loss of $140 billion in customer deposits.

As consumer confidence waned in the wake of the crash, the downturn in spending in investment-led factories and other businesses led to a halt in production. Even the once-great and powerful Detroit, along with its Ford Motor Company, lay idle. When President Roosevelt took office in 1933, twenty-eight states had no open bank within their borders. It was the worst economic downturn in the history of the industrialized world.

The 1934 Pecora Report—The Investigations into the Financial Crashes

In 1932, the American people suffered from the effects of the Great Depression and a great crisis of confidence in the American financial system and the wealthy elites. Americans demanded an investigation into the system's failure, transparency of the findings, and congressional action to address and nullify the deviant practices that had led to the economy's collapse.

President Herbert Hoover supported a groundbreaking 1932 congressional investigation into market manipulations he believed had contributed to the crash. The Franklin D. Roosevelt (FDR) administration continued the investigation, which came to be known as the 1934 Pecora Report, named for Ferdinand Pecora, the chief counsel to the inquiry.

Using the power of subpoena, Pecora obtained the records of the nation's largest financial institutions. He and his staff pored over thousands of internal documents to prepare for testimony. An astute prosecutor with a sharp wit and tongue, Pecora sensed that public opinion had turned against the captains of the financial industry. Shortly after the stock market crash, the investors earned a new nickname: "Bankster."

The enormous sampling of Wall Street banks included in the final 402-page report showed that the corruption on Wall Street was not limited to a few bad apples but permeated the entire institution and nearly every bank and person connected to it—they were all "banksters." The committee concluded that these actors determined who earned wealth and who made entire fortunes, often at the expense of working-class people. Below are a few of the critical findings upon a review of the 1934 Pecora Report:

- **Insider Trading and Conflicts of Interest with Governmental Officials**

The Report revealed the massive conflicts of interest between government officials and Wall Street titans. For example, Pecora uncovered J. P. Morgan's "preferred list of influential friends," which included U.S. presidents, Supreme Court justices, judges, governors, and members of Congress. These select few participated in stock offerings at steeply discounted rates and were granted access to untold wealth, provided they colluded with the corporation to secure unfettered access to its profits.

This malfeasance between government officials and Wall Street titans stands at the heart of the ensuing carnage—nearly a hundred million people would lose their lives during the chaos. Corruption, at the highest levels, will always cause the greatest damage to society—a lesson the American people should not have so carelessly forgotten.

- **Stock Manipulation**

In his investigation, Pecora discovered that Wall Street had been selling stocks that had been artificially inflated in value. Unscrupulous banksters sold overpriced stocks to working-class investors, reaping huge profits for themselves. Still, ultimately, the working class suffered significant losses. For instance, during Charles Mitchell's tenure as CEO of National City Bank (which later became Citibank), the bank colluded with the Anaconda Copper Company to defraud the public for over $150 million.

The scheme involved creating a joint account for almost 1.5 million shares of Anaconda Copper stock, which was valued at only four dollars per share due to the company's near-bankrupt situation. The bank then repackaged, aggressively advertised, and sold the stock through its National City affiliate, driving its price up to $128 per share. Three months later, the bank sold its stock holdings, and the stock plummeted to its original value of four dollars, causing significant losses to the working-class clients of National City Bank.

- **Failure to Disclose Risks**

One of the most pervasive findings was the failure to disclose risks. Pecora observed that Wall Street bankers made considerable efforts to conceal or exaggerate actual stock values and their associated risks.

- **Preferential Interest-Free Loans**

Pecora uncovered a harmful practice in which bank managers were taking interest-free loans for their own use. Banksters on Wall Street were lending themselves tens of millions of dollars from their clients' savings accounts and using that money to gamble in the stock market. This illicit practice allowed them to steal millions of dollars with no consequences. It's essential to note that this differs significantly from typical bank operations, where banks invest their customers' deposits. Instead, bank managers personally withdrew funds from their customers' accounts and invested them in the stock market. When the stocks did not perform well, the depositor suffered the loss, not the bank manager.

- **Tax Evasion**

Finally, Pecora revealed that the giants of Wall Street were guilty of massive tax evasion. Most interviewees responded that they "hadn't even filed their return in years." For example, Arthur William Cutten, a commodity speculator with a seat on the Chicago Board of Trade, had not paid or filed a tax return for years, despite earning more than $1 million in bonuses in 1929.

- **Summary**

However, the most significant finding of the Pecora report was that banksters had not really broken any laws because we lacked a system of rules to hold them accountable in the first place. Additionally, their investigation concluded that the Banking and Investment Banking Industries lacked clear boundaries and regulations to protect American consumers' bank deposits. To Pecora, the lack of adequate boundaries between the two industries directly correlated to the financial sector essentially falling off the financial cliff. Therefore, he recommended splitting the two industries and prohibiting their future intermingling—those that gather deposits from those that invest them.

The Pecora Report's findings created outrage and demand for Wall Street reform. Based on its recommendations, Congress created the Securities and Exchange Commission (SEC) and tasked it with regulating the stock market and protecting investors. Congress even adopted Generally Accepted Accounting Principles (GAAP), the U.S. federal accounting standard.

It also established appraisal standards and practices, which were the first line of defense against government and business corruption.

These guidelines standardized how assets were valued, and how credit was granted. Congress also created the Federal Deposit Insurance Corporation (FDIC), which provided regulations on deposit accounts and insurance. The Pecora Report's role in inspiring these reforms demonstrates the power of investigation and accountability in shaping a more just financial system.

The 1934 Pecora Report was intended to address the findings that Pecora himself had described in a 1933 article in *The New York Times*. Which read, "How men of might, not because of principle but because of economic power and wealth-have by the waving of a hand and adoption of a resolution taken millions and millions of the hard-earned pennies of the people and turned them into gold for themselves."[2]

These New Deal lawmakers lived through the most devastating financial collapse in history and responded by intensely scrutinizing the men and institutions surrounding that economic failure. Their courage in investigating the causes of the financial meltdown, their persistence in holding major players accountable, and their creation of new institutions and laws to protect against future calamities should be admired and emulated.

The Great Depression: Consequences of the Lack of Regulation

Unemployment peaked at nearly 25% of all households. Those who maintained their jobs experienced significant wage cuts. For instance, upper-middle-class professionals, such as doctors and lawyers, experienced a 40% drop in their incomes.

Before the New Deal, the older mortgage system was based on down payments as high as 50% and terms as short as three to five years (balloon loans), which would lead to massive defaults as the banking industry was no more, leaving them unable to refinance the mortgages. During the Depression, the average value of homes fell 40%, and the default rate jumped to about 50% of all mortgage holders. Worse still, delinquencies exceeded more than fifteen months in duration. In other words, half of the country hadn't been able to pay their housing cost for nearly a year and a half.

Nationally, many families in the Great Depression were too poor to afford even the cheapest housing. Some had been evicted, some had lost their homes, and some had nothing left after the market crashed. They moved to Hoovervilles, areas with makeshift shelters set up near cities. The name Hooverville was meant to mock President Hoover for his lack of response to the crisis.

Figure 1.1: Hooverville Seattle, 1935

Nevertheless, although it could be argued that the banksters had essentially taken their customers' deposits, leaving them unable to make their mortgage payments, foreclosures became rampant. Here's a case of how the process played out. In 1933, in Salt Lake City, Utah, the sheriff and several deputies were scheduled to conduct a sale on the steps of the county building. Six houses and a farm were scheduled to be sold following the foreclosures.

Hundreds gathered to try to prevent the sale from going through. Deputies turned a fire hose on them, slowing them only momentarily. The protesters quickly wrestled the hose from the deputies and turned it toward the building, flooding the ground floor. Finally, the police succeeded in dispersing the crowd with tear gas. That afternoon, the *Deseret News* ran an editorial expressing sympathy for those who were losing their homes but characterized the leaders of the protest group as "out and out communists."[3]

The same scenario played out across the entire country, underscoring the magnitude of the economic collapse. For instance, in Iowa, the governor put the entire state under martial law when a group of farmers attempted to hang a federal judge for selling their properties on the courthouse steps. Over half of the states operated under martial law. America was no longer the land of freedom.

Most federal relief efforts had been mired in political and legislative wrangling. Little aid or direction had reached the states or the public. Religious leaders grappled with how to respond to a crisis no one yet understood. Overwhelmed by the sheer number of those living in poverty, members and non-members fought to keep churches and charities open. For instance, according to Census Bureau records, over half of the elderly lived in extreme poverty, and thousands died of starvation.

The number of indigents soared, and offerings plummeted. Many charities closed their doors. By 1933, most churches were financially bankrupt. For example, the head of the Southern Baptist Convention acknowledged, "We are putting off the Lord's cause while we try to settle with our other creditors."[4] As coffers emptied, religious leaders began calling for help, but to whom could they call?

During the Hoover administration, the government invested billions of dollars in public-private partnerships (P3s) with the wealthy investor class. Still, the trickle-down economic theory failed, leaving the working caste in dire straits. P3s are contractual agreements between a public agency and a private entity that provide a utility to consumers. The working caste did not benefit, receiving only low wages, dangerous working conditions, and no hope for the future.

For two years, the working caste struggled to survive on meager resources while the government, judicial system, and monetary system were rife with corruption. The American attitude against government intervention fundamentally shifted as vast numbers of people were thrown into the streets. Losses or cuts in employment and the loss of their homes caused hundreds of thousands of middle-class families to experience their first real taste of poverty.

Roosevelt's New Deal

President Franklin Delano Roosevelt played a pivotal role in rebranding the Democratic Party as the party of change—the new Party of Lincoln—where all were welcome and equally protected under the law. He believed that adequate and affordable housing was not just a need but a fundamental right, and that it was a cornerstone of his policies. One of his popular 1932 campaign slogans best sums it up: "Human Rights before Property Rights."[5]

Following the devastating financial crash of 1929, the American people came together, saying they wanted a better choice than big business had proffered. The voters overwhelmingly decided that the Federal Government (big government—private utility) should participate and compete in the marketplace, including housing and other essential services, such as electricity, indoor plumbing, schools, infrastructure, and retirement programs like Social Security and Medicare.

When President Roosevelt took office, he believed the country's economic problems were so severe that traditional solutions and a weak bailout package would not be sufficient. Hoover's policies proved this. Therefore, the country needed to experiment with a new "go big or go home" approach. His advisors urged him to invoke the Emergency War Powers Act, which would grant him broad authority to issue executive orders. Congress delegated discretion to the executive branch to make the many decisions necessary to regulate the economy. "The millions who are in want," Roosevelt said, "will not stand by silently forever while the things to satisfy their needs are within easy reach."[6]

However, Roosevelt did not act alone. Instead, he went to great lengths to ensure that the American people were part of the decision-making process, collaborating with authorities from the legislative branches of the government. Then, Roosevelt called a governors' conference, in which he requested that the governors pass a resolution pledging their states' support for the emergency measures the president might undertake to correct the nation's economy, and they overwhelmingly approved it.

The Home Owners' Loan Corporation and the Federal Housing Administration

The New Deal created the Home Owners' Loan Corporation (HOLC) and the National Housing Acts of 1933–1937 to address the housing crisis. The HOLC was a government-sponsored corporation that provided long-term mortgage loans at low interest rates. HOLC led to the establishment of the Federal Housing Administration (FHA), which provided loan guarantees and insurance to encourage the construction of new homes and the repair of existing ones. But more than this, they provided the funding to refinance over a million homes, pulling them from the grasp of foreclosure. The innovative approach enabled homeowners to pay off old loans and taxes with a new mortgage, which was repaid over a thirty-year period while retaining ownership of their homes.

HOLC and FHA are where the U.S. Department of Housing and Urban Development (HUD) originated. HUD, a federal agency established in 1965, was created to address the nation's housing needs and to improve and develop the nation's communities. It oversees various housing programs, including those for low-income families, the elderly, and people with disabilities. It plays a crucial role in enforcing fair housing laws and promoting sustainable and inclusive communities.

Frederic C. Howe, the presiding head of that first Public Housing Conference in 1934, shared the beginning framework of what would become HUD's mission statement (its *Federalist Papers*, if you will): "We want, and we must have, attractive low-cost housing for those in the lower-income groups. The need for proper low-cost housing is not confined to the cities. But we do have a right to require that every child born into the world shall have an equal opportunity under the law with every other child. Every child is entitled to protection from the influence of vice and crime and physical degeneration."[7]

The program created the thirty-year fixed-rate mortgage, which was revolutionary in its design. The government guaranteed the loan, enabling its long-term amortization. In contrast to big businesses' approach to housing programs, HOLC estimated that homeowners should not pay more than 20% of their family budget toward housing. This modern concept, known as "cost-burdening," refers to a household spending more than 20% of its income on housing costs, which can lead to financial strain and housing instability. It also impairs their ability to save for retirement. A case study based in Ohio compared the percentage of area median income (AMI), which was $1,480 per year at the time, to calculate what constituted cost-burdening.[8] This understanding of cost-burdening was crucial in shaping the New Deal's housing policies and ensuring housing affordability for the American people, especially those in the lower-income groups.

Conclusion:

The New Deal legislation marked a significant milestone in America's history, enabling greater social mobility for the working class, the poor, women, and people of color. This historical significance helps us understand its impact on the present and connects us to the past.

Previously, government investments were largely for the benefit of the ruling class and wealthy elites, such as corporate America. However, the New Deal represented a shift toward greater investment in citizens, unlike any other government in the world's history. Thanks to the creation of the Home Owners' Loan Corporation (HOLC) and FHA, homeownership in America increased dramatically, from around 35% to almost 70% by 2005. It was at the heart of creating the largest middle class in American history.

The New Deal programs stand as a testament to big government's capacity to greatly improve the lives of the American people. Conversely, big businesses rarely (almost never) solve the challenges faced by the working class. However, their programs do result in substantial wealth transfers from the working class to the very rich. Therefore, in 1934, the stage was set for the ongoing battle that would rage across America: The roles of Big Government versus Big Business.

CHAPTER 2

How Artificial Intelligence (AI)-Powered Pricing Technologies Were Introduced to the Rental Housing Industry

Introduction

Have you ever wondered how prices for goods and services are established? For example, you go to the grocery store, and one day, a dozen eggs cost $2.49; a month later, they cost $7. Or you drive to the gas station, and one day, a gallon of gasoline costs $2.75, only to return two weeks later, and it's nearly $4.00. But of course, the big-ticket items, like housing, can increase by hundreds of dollars overnight.

For instance, the multifamily rental market in metropolitan areas has experienced a dramatic surge in prices since 2012. In Metro Seattle, where we established a case study, rental rates skyrocketed by over 82% between 2013 and 2018. These skyrocketing rates have occurred across the country, from Tucson, Arizona; to Houston, Texas; to Memphis, Tennessee; and New York City, New York. The word on the street is that these chaotic pricing swings are due to inflation.

Key Concepts:

What is Inflation?

We often hear a lot about inflation nowadays, but what does it mean? In economics, inflation refers to the ongoing increase in the general price level of goods and services within an economy over an extended period of time, with the adverse side effect of reducing the value of money. Historically, the underlying cause of inflation was sometimes understood but frequently unidentified or regarded as a byproduct of scarcities or shortages of crucial components within a supply chain. Worse still, political parties use the term inflation to confuse voters, blaming the other party for their financial woes. Regardless, economists, policymakers, and news pundits have often informed us that steep price increases are caused by inflation.

What is Price-Fixing?

However, today, these increases are not actually due to inflation. Instead, they stem from corporate landlords and other business leaders artificially raising prices through price-fixing. Price-fixing occurs when competitors offering a specific good or service stop competing for customers and instead work together to increase their profits.

But how can an entire industry "work together" to increase profits? For example, how can property managers in West Palm Beach, Florida; Trenton, New Jersey; Phoenix, Arizona; and Spokane, Washington, collaborate to enhance their profits by working together? In the new digital economy, including the rental housing industry, landlords utilize advanced, artificial-intelligence-driven revenue management technologies to manipulate the market and artificially drive up prices.

What is Artificial Intelligence (AI)?

AI, a buzzword in the current digital era, plays a pivotal role in the pricing process. This algorithmic technology, rooted in machine learning, has been in existence since the 1950s. Its primary function is to carry out specific tasks or repetitive functions, such as determining rental rates that humans once completed.

One of the most unique characteristics of this technology is its capability to gather vast amounts of data. Then, it uses this massive data to adjust prices in real-time by continuously monitoring market conditions. For example, the technology can accurately forecast the supply and demand of a product, thereby maximizing profits by limiting the available output of that product. For instance, by working together, corporate landlords can withhold a percentage of two-bedroom units from the market, creating the appearance of a shortage or scarcity, and then artificially increase rates significantly, thereby maximizing overall industry-wide profits.

What is Revenue Management Technology Software?

Revenue management, also known as yield or rent optimization software, is a technology system that is designed to automate pricing. The central concept is that the technology uses that vast amount of information to calculate and recommend pricing for the goods and services offered by a business, rather than the business determining the prices on its own.

What is an Industry-Wide Common Pricing Platform?

From beginning to end, the entire pricing process is intended to be carried out on a shared pricing platform (common pricing platform) utilized collaboratively by an entire industry to enable its revenue management technology to establish prices for that particular good or service. A practice that is opposed to individual business owners setting their own prices.

Introduction Continued

At its core, revenue management is designed to sell the right product (such as a rental unit, seat, or banana) at different prices (rates and fares) to different types of customers to maximize profits. Nevertheless, the prime directive of this powerful software is to maximize profits for its owners. In other words, this AI-powered technology was created to replace humans in the pricing process with a laser-like focus on maximizing profit.

But who wields the power of this technology in the rental industry, and what, if anything, has been its financial impact? Additionally, what are technology developers promising in exchange for the billions of dollars that landlords are investing? Furthermore, what are the potential effects of AI-driven revenue management on society?

Today, corporate landlords cooperate through the property management system or common pricing platform RealPage (hereafter referred to as the "Platform") to artificially inflate rental rates and maximize profits. At the heart of this expansive platform is an AI program designed to distort traditional supply-and-demand logic. This powerful AI, while providing near-perfect market information, is molded around toxic, racist, and greedy underpinnings that primarily aim to maximize profits by "pricing out" the bottom 15% of households based on income. This allegedly illegal practice is exacting a heavy toll on our society and costing billions of dollars from taxpayers as the government bears the burden of increasing numbers of unhoused people and their associated costs.

Despite the controversies, revenue management technology has proven to be a game-changer. It has the potential to double profits without incurring additional expenses, making it a cost-effective and powerful tool for business growth.

However, the ultimate success or failure of revenue management technology in maximizing profits depends on the number of competitors that employ it. In other words, the greater the concentration of users, the higher the profits it can generate. For instance, if a given market has 100 rental units and 87 are priced using this technology, the concentration of rental units on the common pricing platform is likely sufficient to control prices. Conversely, if only 25 units were priced on the platform, then the industry would lack adequate concentrations to control pricing. The effects of concentrations will be discussed more in Chapter 5.

The introduction of AI-powered revenue management technology ushered in the transition from an oil-driven/industrial economy to a data-driven economy, representing one of the most significant economic developments of the last 100 years. We are in the midst of the fourth economic revolution, which is seeing the lines between the physical and digital worlds merge ever closer. (The terms digital and technological are considered to have the same meaning and are used interchangeably throughout the pages of the book.)

This book, PRICED OUT BY DESIGN, details how corporate landlords implemented the data-driven economy in the rental housing industry. Its primary focus is how the industry uses AI to improve profits by implementing revenue management software—i.e., technology that has replaced humans in the pricing process. All the while, the use of the technology remains variably unchallenged or unregulated by any governing body.

The History of Revenue Management Software

However, to understand the full power of this pricing technology, we must first examine its origins and the objectives its creators sought to achieve. It all begins with revenue management software. Robert Cross, the owner of Manugistics Group, Inc., located in California's Silicon Valley, was at the heart of the revenue management movement. In the 1980s, he developed revenue management for the airline industry and is regarded as a pioneer in the field of technology. In

1984, he launched the software for Delta Airlines; the company saw $300 million in incremental revenue gains in the first year.

In 1997, he founded Talus Solutions, Inc. By 1999, they developed and managed three pricing and revenue management software solutions: Dynamic Pricing, Promotion Pricing, and Target Pricing. This early foundational technology is now used in just about every industry that deals with varying supply and demand levels and revenue management, i.e., Amazon, Ticketmaster, the grocery and petroleum industries, and the airlines and hospitality industries, to name a few. In 2001, Talus merged with the Manugistics Group, Inc., which owned the "Leveraged Intelligence" trademark.

Landlords can utilize this "dynamic pricing" software to set rent prices for tenants based on current supply and demand. When demand increases, landlords are advised to charge higher rent for available apartments. Conversely, when demand decreases, it suggests lowering rates, mostly.

In 1997, Cross published a book titled "*Revenue Management: Hard-core Tactics for Profit-making and Market Domination*," which offered a roadmap for effectively utilizing revenue management technology to gain market power and dominate an industry. The book's release would mark the beginning of the widespread use of revenue management technology. In 1998, Goldman Sachs invested $20 million in Manugistics to develop the pricing technology for use in multiple industries.

The technology revolutionized how industries create profits, not by adding services or improving products, but by eliminating unprofitable segments, such as labor-intensive services like ticketing, delivery, or luggage handling. The technology then recommends that the customer, rather than hired labor, complete those tasks, or the customer must pay a price for the service. In the digital age, nearly 40% of their revenue now comes from non-core services and junk fees. In this instance, the core service would be the airline ticket, and non-core services would include items such as meals, drinks, and fees for luggage or other services.

How Revenue Management Technologies Were Introduced to the Rental Housing Industry

In 1998, two notable multifamily companies, the Rainmaker Group and RealPage, were established to utilize the revenue management technology. In 1999, they approached Robert Cross to explore whether this software could be adapted for the apartment industry. After four months of analysis, they concluded that it was, indeed, applicable. Subsequently, in 2000, the Rental Housing Industry formed a consortium of forty-six companies to leverage the use of this technology and frame the industry around AI-driven revenue management.

However, in 2001, Silicon Valley encountered severe financial difficulties due to the dot-com bust, leading the Manugustics Group to shut down its multifamily division. Consequently, in 2002, Manugustics sold two licenses to its multifamily pricing algorithm. The first license would eventually be sold to the Rainmaker Group, which developed the Lease Rent Options (LRO) pricing algorithm. The second was ultimately sold to RealPage, which created its YieldStar Artificial Intelligence Revenue Management (AIRM) pricing algorithm. This transformative impact of technology has reshaped the rental industry, doubling profits without incurring any additional risk or expense.

The New Management Standard

The advent of revenue management necessitated changes to the traditional management structures of the old economy to accommodate and leverage the technology. The new management structure, referred to as "The Manugistics Standard of Non-Competition" (hereinafter, the Management Standard), was designed to promote collaboration over competition. This concept encourages companies to share data and insights, fostering a more cooperative and less competitive business environment.

In a 2002 interview, Manugistics CEO Greg Owens explained the company's fundamental approach to technology in the emerging data-driven economy. He emphasized that successful companies can no longer thrive in isolation. Instead, they must actively collaborate with their competitors, customers, suppliers, and subsidiaries to gain a competitive edge.

Essentially, the new data-driven economy's methodology fosters cooperation rather than competition within industries, with companies working together as if they were a single producer. This necessity of collaboration is at the heart of the Management Standard's domination campaign, which is a shift from the traditional competitive mindset. In this new economy, companies no longer compete on price; as we shall see, it would destroy the entire pricing structure, rendering the Management Standard and AI-powered technology ineffective.

Therefore, the industry allows revenue management technology to set its rental rates for them, thus avoiding direct competition. Yet, to make this possible, the process necessitates the cooperation of the data providers, the Platform, and its landlord members in adhering to the established rules of the group. Through the process, they disavow their competitive independence.

The Rental Housing Industry and Its Participants—Introducing the Characters

In 2017, institutional investors began pouring hundreds of billions of dollars into the rental housing industry for new construction. The massive investments have resulted in the industry undergoing a complete transformation to accommodate the enormous growth. The multifamily rental real estate market is a $12 trillion industry that generates over $100 billion annually, and property managers utilize a shared pricing platform (revenue management) supported by massive databases to manage those properties.

When considering the growth in the rental industry and the shift in ownership structures, we must ask: Who are the key actors driving this growth, and how have they impacted the overall multifamily industry? Perhaps more importantly, the part they each play in developing the industry's common pricing platform. We will now focus on the various participants and how the Platform leverages its working relationships, with a particular emphasis on the new "Management Standard" to enhance profits.

The Property Owners—Institutional Investors

Since 2015, a seismic shift in property ownership, particularly for multifamily communities, has been observed. Previously, these properties were predominantly owned by individuals or firms, who would then engage a property management company or manage the property independently. However, a new trend has emerged, with institutional investors increasingly dominating the multifamily housing market. This shift has led to profound changes in property management practices, construction strategies, and pricing models, resulting in a significant impact on the rental housing industry. By 2018, the top four multifamily property owners in the U.S. were all institutional investor-owned, as measured by the number of units.

These institutional investors provided the necessary capital for the development of the pricing technology. They recognized AI's potential to enhance operational efficiency and boost profits. Their support has been crucial in the widespread adoption of AI revenue management technology and the implementation of the common pricing platform in the rental housing industry. Chapter 4 will delve into the identity of these investors, their objectives, and the strategies they employ to achieve their goals.

The Builders

The 2008 Great Recession had a significant yet often overlooked impact on "local builders"—those who live and construct housing for their local communities. These builders have deep connections to their communities, obtaining loans from local community banks and sourcing supplies from local shops. Historically, nonprofit organizations relied on local builders to create low-cost, affordable housing that benefited their communities. However, during the housing industry crash from 2005 to 2008, the Federal Deposit Insurance Corporation (FDIC), which guaranteed (insured) their construction loans nationwide, declined to support them, leading to the bankruptcy and liquidation of most local builders. Very few local builders survived the Great Recession. Their assets were sold to national builders at significantly reduced prices—pennies on the dollar. At the same time, taxpayers covered hundreds of billions of dollars in losses through bailouts.

As a result, nonprofits seeking to build affordable housing are left with primarily only national builders to construct their units. National builders borrow money from Wall Street investors, buy their supplies from national chains, and aim to maximize their investors' profits with little regard for local communities. The lack of regard results in minimal financial benefits for the local community. In essence, all profits are shifted to Wall Street.

Worse still, the housing units they build don't meet local demand parameters. The primary reason? The national builder is also undergoing a revolution driven by AI platforms. Historically, housing demand determined the housing supply. But that is no longer the case today, thanks to AI's predictive capabilities and market analysis. It has resulted in builders constructing rental units at a very high cost and then selling the overpriced buildings to short-term investors, who fully lease up the new properties. Afterward, they sell the property to longer-term investors, such as pension funds. Although it generates substantial profits for the builders, this practice has flooded the markets with significantly overpriced properties that tenants can't afford. This practice has resulted in an oversupply of higher-priced units and a significant shortage of affordable housing units.

Not only are the units overpriced, but they also fail to meet the needs of renters. For example, nearly 75% of the units built between 2007 and 2018 are small studios or one-bedrooms. Why did the builders build these smaller units? Because they yield the highest profits per unit. However, this doesn't make much market sense. In Seattle, Washington, for instance, the median household consists of 2.6 people who require a two-bedroom unit. We discuss the construction industry further in Chapter 13.

The Property Managers

Property management companies are responsible for maintaining and managing properties to ensure they remain clean, well-maintained, and in good condition. These companies are also evolving. As ownership shifts to larger firms and investors, so do the contracts—hundreds of billions of dollars are up for grabs, with fewer and fewer players in the game. It has led to a new type of property manager that has replaced the traditional format with a "vertical trust organization," a structure that integrates various property management functions to provide better servicing arrangements for the new investor property owner and their demand to maximize profits.

Vertical integration is where a company controls multiple stages of its production process and supply chain. In other words, the same large property management companies in rental housing are also among the largest developers and builders. For example, as a builder, they construct the property, and then, as a property manager, they provide management services. An excellent example of this organizational format is Greystar Real Estate Partners (Greystar), the nation's largest developer, builder, and manager, managing nearly a million units of multifamily properties. They are also one of the largest property owners. Wall Street's Goldman Sachs has a 20% ownership stake in them, and BlackRock purchases its bonds. Greystar has over $53 billion in assets under management. Most of the top twenty-five management companies, which control 80% of the market nationwide, are equal to or greater in size.

The practice of vertical integration has sparked intense competition within the industry, leading to a winner-take-all scenario. Moreover, the new norm of property managers is to include investors in their ownership structure, which has further intensified this competition. However, the most significant change is the expansion of property managers' roles due to the advent of AI-driven technology. This technology has not only made renting on their platform easier than ever, but it has also redefined their responsibilities, making them more crucial than before.

The study concluded that national property managers, which are Wall Street-owned and funded entities that operate in more than one state, oversee over 82% of all rental units. The downside to these conglomerates is that they enter a community with the sole intent of maximizing profits for property owners, increasing housing volatility for tenants by about 70%.

Property managers played a crucial role in developing the industry's common pricing platform. The shift from individual landlords pricing their own units to a cooperative approach was facilitated through the use of their technology, specifically property management systems (PMS).

However, the property managers' primary goal is to maximize their property owners' profits. When they accomplish this goal, they are rewarded with lucrative income from management contracts; however, if they fail to maximize profits, the result is lost business. Therefore, each property manager is under immense pressure to perform.

The Property Management System (PMS) Providers

A property management system (PMS) is a centralized, cloud-based computer system that organizes, schedules, and performs the day-to-day functions and transactions involved in property management. For instance, AI-powered tools can now predict tenant turnover, optimize rental rates, and even suggest property maintenance schedules, thereby significantly improving the efficiency and profitability of property management.

Yet, just as Microsoft Office provides a seamless experience with its products—such as Word, Excel, and PowerPoint—the PMS works similarly, allowing users to access and move data, spreadsheets, and models across software and between users and competitors.

Property management systems are used to measure market share and pricing concentrations in the rental industry. In short, the PMS providers facilitate and drive the pricing process, i.e., the rental rate price-fixing through the industry's common pricing platform. For instance, in 2022, there were approximately forty-four million rental units in the United States. However, there are only three primary Property Management System providers: RealPage, Yardi, and AppFolio. Locally, they accounted for up to 95% of the market in Metro Seattle. The study concluded that PMS providers are concentrated in metro areas. Nationally, this group provides management services for thirty-three million units, or 75% of the national market. Thus, the PMS providers sit at the heart of the rental rate price-fixing schemes.

However, it's important to note that the Rainmaker Group, while not a PMS provider, plays a significant role in the industry by offering revenue management services. In Chapter 3, we will delve deeper into their functions, impact, and how they complement the services provided by PMS providers.

The Experian RentBureau

Experian RentBureau, a key player in the industry, provides crucial applicant data to the common pricing Platform. This data, which we will explore in more detail in Chapter 6, is a cornerstone of the rental industry. It guides decisions and influences strategies, making it a crucial part of the industry's operations and the implementation of a common pricing platform across the industry. Our research determined that Experian and property management system providers are the co-gatekeepers to housing. We will discuss how this data is collected, processed, and utilized to provide a more comprehensive understanding of its role in the industry.

The Industry Trade Associations

During the 1960s and 1970s, most pricing cartels were members of trade associations. Industry associations were charged with restraining competition by establishing rules governing their members' actions. A strong relationship with trade associations is one of the first clues for regulators to market manipulation.

The Platform has leveraged its relationship with various Industry Trade Associations to push the industry toward a common-pricing Platform. The process worked like this: During the algorithm's testing phases, the Platform and its landlord members evaluated their pricing technologies, and the trade associations reported the results throughout the industry. But they went beyond posting the results; they would push the entire industry to get on board or face financial ruin.

The book's chapters discuss multiple influential trade organizations that have profoundly affected the rental housing industry. For example, we discuss the National Multifamily Housing Council (NMHC) and its powerful ties to politics. In 2003, NMHC issued a joint study with PMS providers, prompting the industry to adopt revenue management pricing technology and utilize a common pricing platform.

How It Works

Take the Platform's abuse of fees, for example; multiple courts nationwide are ruling against its practice. However, court cases are costly to litigate, and the process typically takes years; for tenants, the entire process is cost-prohibitive, which is by design. In one such case, in 2018, a U.S. District Court in Texas ruled that the utility fees charged by Greystar's utility billing program were unreasonable and against current laws and regulations. They settled and paid a $2.7 million fine.

Unfortunately, when property owners and operators are found guilty in court, the case usually ends up in a settlement. However, the fines rarely deter the practice. For instance, a RealPage Utility Billing study was released during the adjudication process, revealing that property owners each year increased operating profits by $31 million using the program. The fine equates to an 8.7% penalty, which is seen as just the cost of doing business in the industry.

In rare instances where the tenant wins, investors and property managers often take steps to protect their interests. For example, shortly after the Texas utility litigation concluded, their legion of lawyers began working closely with the Republican Party and the Texas Apartment Association, a state-level trade organization. Together, they drafted legislation, testified at legislative hearings, and educated legislators about the benefits of Senate Bill 873. The new law limits the types and amounts of fines and penalties, making it nearly impossible for tenants to file grievances through the court system, thereby shielding them from future prosecution.

But it gets worse. The PMS providers have partnered with various state-level trade organizations and, frequently, the Republican Party to enact changes. For instance, in the State of Arizona, as well as many other states, they have pushed for the various states to provide tax-exempt status for rental properties. They push the narrative that the tax savings will be passed on to their tenants. However, that isn't the case. The pricing technology has been trained to convert these tax savings into profits. And this industry doesn't share profits with anyone. This process, known as tax-shifting, is discussed in greater detail in Chapter 9.

Conclusion

In conclusion, the advent of AI-powered revenue management technology has transformed and revolutionized the rental housing industry. This technology has fundamentally altered how rental units are priced, utilizing a common pricing platform that replaces human intervention with advanced algorithms. Chapter 3 thoroughly explores property management systems and their computer systems to help the reader gain a comprehensive understanding of the significant transformative process.

CHAPTER 3

How AI Technology Drives the Digital Operating Platforms

Introduction

Chapter 2 asked the question: How does an entire industry work together to increase profits? To answer that question, the chapter began by detailing who the participants in the rental housing industry are and their various roles in establishing the industry-wide common pricing platform. Chapter 3 will focus on their computer operating systems that enable collaboration and allow landlords to work together to maximize profits.

Historically, price-fixing occurred in face-to-face meetings or through gatherings of their representatives and collaborators. Today, however, the collusive process occurs within their technological or computer systems. It is called algorithmic price-fixing; hereafter, it is simply referred to as price-fixing.

We are entering the digital era, where complex business networks share technology, data, and insights to collaborate across industries and deliver seamless experiences for their clients. Traditional firms, especially those facing the imminent threat of competition, are undergoing a profound transformation to remain competitive and succeed in the new data-driven economy.

The AI technological revolution, which made its mark on the rental housing industry in 2002, has disrupted it and presented massive opportunities for those who embraced it early. AI-powered revenue management in the rental industry is a game-changer. It empowers property managers by enabling them to forecast demand, set optimal pricing, and automate routine tasks. However, those who were slow or resistant to this change were left behind.

Key Concepts:

What Is Proptech or Property Technology?

Proptech, short for property technology, encompasses all the technological tools and software utilized in the real estate and rental housing industries. Its primary objective is to automate tasks that were once time-consuming and labor-intensive by harnessing technology-driven solutions powered by machines. The automation leads to significant cost savings and a notable increase in efficiency for corporate landlords. For example, the digital system for maintenance requests enables managers to track them online, removing the necessity for paper and on-site labor to process them. Additionally, cloud-based lease document sharing minimizes the need for direct interaction with tenants.

The adoption of proptech has transitioned from being a trend to a necessity in the industry. As companies continue to introduce more real estate technology solutions each year, the importance of these tools cannot be overstated. The change in mindset between 2013 and 2019 was marked by over 100 mergers and acquisitions in the proptech space, with proptech deals exceeding $7 billion in value. The acquisition of RealPage and its technologies by Thoma Bravo for over $10 billion in 2021 further underscores the indispensability of proptech in the industry.

The Digital Operating Platform (DOP)

The entire algorithmic price-fixing process starts with their computer operating systems. Understanding these systems will help us grasp the subtle changes that have enabled this collaboration. Historically, a company's computer systems were primarily designed for internal operations and management. Each employee's computer was directly connected to the company's network, which provided the operating platform for running applications, facilitating communication and tasks, and storing large amounts of data.

However, today, everything has changed. The introduction of AI-powered revenue management technology has necessitated the handling of vast amounts of data related to their applicants, tenants, and properties. The effectiveness of AI is directly related to the quality and quantity of the data it processes. Therefore, the technology providers developed the Digital Operating Platform (DOP) to address this issue. This central software platform, replacing outdated standalone systems, combines automation and workflows to effectively streamline all business functions and synchronize data across various systems and businesses within a unified framework.

The DOP is a game-changer, enabling efficient data management and utilization. What sets the DOP apart is its unique features. It's not just a central software platform but a catalyst for collaboration. The enhanced collaboration has promoted shared progress and improved efficiency. The "Data Collection" in Figure 3.1 below symbolizes the collaborative nature of the DOP, with data collection and sharing happening in the background. Their jointly employed algorithms accomplish the data-gathering and sharing process.

In the rental housing industry, for instance, RealPage created a DOP, or "Platform," that facilitates a fluid relationship with other third-party data providers, enabling it to access and share the massive amounts of information required to establish pricing. It also facilitates seamless data collection and sharing, using algorithms to gather real-time information from thirty-three million rental units. It connects property management systems and landlords, underscoring its critical role in the price-fixing process.

Thus, to accomplish this, according to Figure 3.1, property management companies can collaborate by linking their computer systems to the DOP and by sharing data with their chosen Property Management System, "Your Customers & Markets," which also includes "Your Products, Services & Data." Additionally, on the Platform, other participating property management members join you—i.e., competitors—"Other Landlord's Products, Services & Data." For instance, on this platform, various property management companies, such as Greystar, Lincoln Property Company, and Equity Residential, among nearly all others, connect their systems and share data. Moreover, the third-party providers all plug into the DOP's "Third-Party Products, Services & Data." For example, Experian provides tenant data that meets the new Management Standards' requirements for its customers.

Figure 3.1: The Digital Operating Platforms

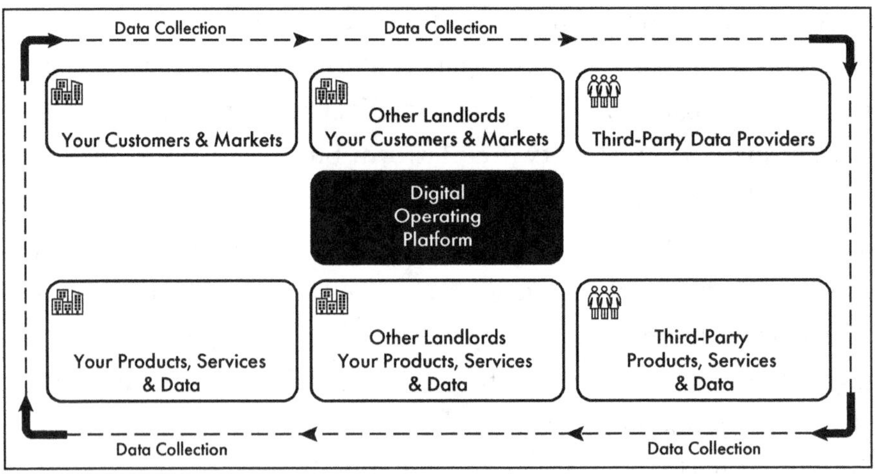

Historically, agents in different industries found it difficult to acquire information across boundaries; for instance, Experian has data on applicants that the landlords need. Conversely, landlords have data on their tenants that Experian needs. The DOP is further engineered to handle data sharing more efficiently with multi- or two-sided connectivity. It efficiently and conveniently brings together customers and service providers. For instance, the Platform and Experian have a two-sided relationship. This arrangement enables the Platform to obtain real-time data on its applicants from Experian, which is only possible through this platform as an intermediary.

To clarify this essential process, consider Walt Disney's 2016 film, "Alice Through the Looking Glass." In the story, Alice discovers a magical mirror that allows her to walk through its glass pane into the world of Wonderland. The Digital Operating Platform works similarly. It enables companies like RealPage to connect seamlessly with external systems. In essence, the DOP enables companies to reach through the "glass panes" of their would-be competitors' computer operating systems, creating a "Data collection & sharing loop," see Figure 3.1, where they access and share all the desired information and data in real-time.

The DOP created an environment where organizations that would typically compete to protect their proprietary data can access each other's information and processes as if they were part of their own systems. This innovative approach highlights increased collaboration and data sharing among organizations in our increasingly interconnected digital landscape.

The Digital Operating Platform in the Rental Housing Industry Is the Property Management System (PMS)

A Property Management System (PMS) is a unique Digital Operating Platform (DOP) designed for the rental housing industry. It provides a centralized cloud-based computer system to organize, schedule, and perform day-to-day functions and transactions, from processing applicants to filing business records to setting rental rates. The

Property Management System (PMS) is the backbone of the rental housing industry, enabling property managers to efficiently manage their properties and tenants.

The various PMS include four core components, each supported by a distinct module. Each module is critical and plays a role in the price-fixing process. Each element or module incorporates multiple technologies to achieve its function. Rule-breaking, including rental rate price-fixing, occurs within the Property Management System, primarily in the Revenue Management Module.

The Four Parts of the Property Management System (PMS)

Property Management Module:	Manages core property business processes, including accounting, budgeting, purchasing, facilities management, and document management.
Lease Management Module:	This module handles core leasing and marketing functions, including website management and syndication, applicant lead generation (encompassing all leasing-related activities), and applicant screening.
Resident Services Module:	Facilitates core asset management, providing and monitoring services such as utility billing, renters' insurance, and maintenance requests.
Revenue Management Module:	This module handles the rental pricing functions, including real-time yield management, revenue growth, benchmarking, and forecasting. It recommends the rental rates.

Today, every sector of the economy, along with its respective supply chains, has its own Digital Operating Platform or management system.

For instance, the hotel industry utilizes the Lodging Management System (LMS), which is similar to the Property Management System (PMS). The LMS is a software platform that automates all aspects of hotel operations, from reservations and credit card processing to housekeeping. It also includes modules for activity scheduling, ticketing, food and beverage sales, remote check-in, spa scheduling, and more.

In the Auto industry, they use the Dealer Management System. The Auto Insurance Industry uses the Arity Marketing Platform. But it doesn't end there. The grocery store and gas station industries also have their own management systems, which enable them to share data and insights and to use revenue management technology to set industry-wide prices. In short, each industry has its own DOP or pricing platform that is used collaboratively by the entire industry to establish industry-wide prices, as discussed more fully in Chapter 8.

Key Concepts:

What is the difference between a Single Stack and an Open and Connected Platform?

Nevertheless, the PMS has continued to improve through industry-wide collaboration. For instance, the rental industry evolved from stand-alone single-stack systems to open and connected operating systems. Single-stack software is a platform that encompasses all features and functionality within a single system or stack. All four parts (Modules) of the PMS system are developed, maintained, and managed by one provider. Historically, a PMS provided all the software solutions that property managers could utilize. For instance, if a manager chose Yardi, they would provide their single-stack software needs, including everything from core property management—such as accounting—to revenue management.

Open and Connected – This refers to a PMS platform that integrates third-party modules or systems into a single-user experience, comprising the four parts of the PMS system. The PMS provider is responsible for managing integrations with select providers. Consider how your iPhone and its App Store function.

In 2003, during the early stages of the industry's framing process, the National Multifamily Housing Council (NMHC), a primary industry trade association discussed in Chapter 2, conducted a significant joint study with RealPage and the Rainmaker Group (LRO). The results of the study propelled the industry toward revenue management technology, serving as a wake-up call and heralding the imminent arrival of technological changes. Additionally, the NMHC, in its quest to ensure investors maximize their returns, urged the industry to set aside their petty differences and focus on the bigger picture. As one industry insider aptly put it, RealPage and Yardi are the Coke and Pepsi of property management, underscoring the long-standing importance of integration in the industry.

The initiative involved replacing the traditional PMS single-stack platforms with an open, connected, agile platform featuring interchangeable modules, ranging from accounting software to comprehensive leasing platforms to revenue management. This adaptable platform enabled managers to focus on best-of-breed software that could be easily integrated into their property management systems. As one industry insider explained, the back office no longer dictates what you use in the front office. In other words, operators can use Yardi for their Property Management Module, accounting programs, and still connect to RealPage or LRO for their pricing (Revenue Management Module).

Undoubtedly, the **Revenue Management Module** was developed to play a pivotal role in the price-fixing process. It's essential to grasp its significance. However, to be clear, there were only ever two primary providers of AI-powered price-enhancing revenue management technologies (software): RealPage with its YieldStar AI Revenue Management (AIRM) pricing algorithm and the Rainmaker Group with its Lease Rent Options (LRO) pricing algorithm. The industry collectively developed these technologies, and the investor-sponsoring groups behind both competitors were the same, highlighting the industry's joint efforts in technological advancement.

YieldStar, like LRO, is an analytics algorithm classified as a "dynamic pricing" software tool. This approach enables the platform to adjust prices in real time based on market conditions. Also known as surge, demand, or time-based pricing, it can adjust prices multiple times a day to capitalize on market changes. The core principle of dynamic pricing is to sell the same rental units at different prices to various groups at different times, aiming to maximize revenue. It serves as a revenue-enhancing tool that aligns corporate strategies—such as pricing aggressiveness and discrimination policies—with pricing decisions, making the process more reliable.

Between 2003 and 2017, the two companies acquired nearly all of their competitors' pricing technologies. However, these acquisitions weren't all friendly. For instance, in 2011, Yardi accused RealPage in a federal lawsuit of hacking into its technology databases and stealing its proprietary technology and pricing strategies. RealPage settled the lawsuit by paying Yardi $2 million, but retained the licensing rights to incorporate the technology into its own technology programs.

Then, in 2017, a significant event occurred: with the blessing of Trump's Department of Justice, RealPage acquired LRO and merged the two platforms. The new combined algorithm is called "**Demand X**." This algorithm places greater emphasis on consumers (demand). It is three times more powerful than the original AIRM pricing algorithm. This acquisition had profound implications for the property management industry. It effectively consolidated pricing power in the hands of a single entity, potentially leading to a lack of competition within the revenue management module and to significantly higher prices for tenants.

White Labeling (Previously known as Private Labeling)

White-label software is unbranded software that a company leases or purchases from a vendor and then rebrands for resale to generate a profit. Due to its massive size, this technology, typically held in the cloud (data centers), has grown into an $180 billion industry since about 2010. This technology offers a world of possibilities: with little to no overhead, a landlord can quickly add new product features and attract new customers more promptly.

White labeling, a process that may be unfamiliar to some, is a concept where a developer or manufacturer creates a generic product or service, and the reseller or distributor (user) adds their unique touch to it. This customization includes their branding, logo, and other specific features. A classic example of this is Costco and its Kirkland Brands. Costco doesn't manufacture its Kirkland Brand; someone else produces the product, but their logo is placed on it and marketed as if Costco created it. In the technology industry, this process is known as white labeling. It allows the reseller or distributor to take ownership of the product or service and sell it to their customers as if it were their own without disclosing the original developer's or manufacturer's involvement.

Integrations

Software integration, a crucial aspect of the industry's operations, involves connecting one software application to another, typically via application programming interfaces (APIs). This seamless process underpins the industry's operations. It enhances efficiency and productivity, making it more agile and responsive to market changes. Additionally, integrations enable the technology owner to mass-market its products through white-labeling. For instance, RealPage and its pricing algorithms are compensated for their use, regardless of whether RealPage, Yardi, or AppFolio sells the white-labeled pricing product to a landlord.

Can the Revenue Management Module Be Terminated?

Of course, one of the questions we ask is whether the revenue management module can be terminated without interfering with property management. The short answer is yes. The PMS comprises various modules, with revenue management being just one of them. An excellent example of how these modules work is the Microsoft 365 suite of products. Just like a user can easily stop using Microsoft Teams without affecting other programs like Word and Excel, terminating the revenue management module should not affect the functioning of other modules within the PMS.

Summary of The Property Management Systems and Chapters 4-12 Objectives

The question we seek to answer is: With the changes in property management systems and their pricing strategies, where today landlords can now choose modules, and given the apparent lack of competition in the revenue management module, who is pricing those thirty-three million units?

Additionally, we aim to determine whether the three primary PMS providers operate independently as competitors or collaborate to improve profits. Specifically, does their practice of sharing data, technologies, and pricing strategies make them a pricing cartel? Or are the new methods simply good business collaborative practices?

But first, the entire industry is funded and controlled by investors. These institutional investors, such as BlackRock, are major players in the property management industry. They are not only financial backers but also strategic decision-makers who shape the industry's direction. Their decisions carry significant weight and can shape the industry's future. But who are they, and what do they aim to accomplish with this new AI-powered revenue management technology? Chapter 4 answers these questions.

CHAPTER 4

The Investors—The Wizards Behind the Wall Street Curtain

Key Concepts:

What are Nonbank or Shadow Bank Lenders?

Nonbanks are lending institutions owned and controlled by investors. However, they don't offer both lending and depositing services as banks do. They mostly rely on lines of credit from regulated commercial banks to fund their loans and investments. A program that the Glass-Steagall Act previously prohibited. In short, what's happening is that the banks that gather the deposits hand these taxpayer-guaranteed deposits over to unregulated investors in the form of high-risk loans that taxpayers, not the borrowers, guarantee. These loans are referred to in the industry as Warehouse Lines of Credit.

Investors prefer to use shadow banks as they are more likely to fund larger, more complex projects with significantly more risk than regulated banks. In fact, their investment sizes and the related risks have doubled since the 2008 Great Recession. They pose a substantial risk because they lack access to FDIC deposit insurance or other safeguards.

Data on their financial condition is less standardized and not widely available, making it hard to monitor them. In short, their financial statements do not comply with generally accepted accounting principles. Worse still, they are entirely unregulated. Federal agencies have little to no authority to monitor them or look into their practices. Today, they are responsible for trillions of dollars in mortgage-related debt that taxpayers guarantee. Yet, no one knows the types and quality of their loans.

The shadow banking system operates freely on Wall Street and in the housing market, with investors driving over two-thirds of all housing transactions through the unregulated nonbanking sector. The results are a significant issue for taxpayers. A similar banking scenario existed in 1928, despite all the warnings issued by our ancestors.

What is a Government-Sponsored Enterprise (GSE)?

GSEs are quasi-governmental organizations that enhance credit flow to specific sectors of the U.S. economy. Fannie Mae, Freddie Mac, and the Federal Home Loan Banks are GSEs that help bring capital (cash) to the housing market by purchasing those housing-related loans and providing federal guarantees. However, in the wake of the 2008 financial crisis, Fannie Mae and Freddie Mac suffered over $200 billion in losses due to poor lending policies driven by the investors. Yet, it was the taxpayers who funded their bailout. Congress established the Federal Housing Financing Administration (FHFA) to regulate and monitor the GSEs while they operate under receivership. The book "Stealing Home: How Artificial Intelligence is Hijacking the American Dream" provides more information on this topic.

What is Self-Regulation?

Industry self-regulation describes a scenario in which businesses within an industry monitor and ensure their own adherence to legal, ethical, and safety standards. Rather than depending on an external agency, such as a government regulator, to oversee compliance and enforce standards. However, similar to Hoover's trickle-down economics, it's a failed policy for consumers. In short, self-regulation is constrained by the moral hazard within an industry.

What Is an Institutional or Private Equity Investor?

An institutional investor is an organization that combines funds from large corporate clients and individuals to make investments. They are commonly called "Wall Street" because they control over 80% of all invested capital. Their members include pension funds, mutual funds, and insurance companies.

They also include private equity firms. Private equity firms, as they are commonly known today, employ highly destructive and overly aggressive investment strategies with the primary aim of maximizing profits at the expense of people. These firms often target high-risk investments, particularly in essential service sectors such as healthcare—specifically hospitals and nursing homes—as well as affordable housing. However, they are also heavily invested in technology such as RealPage, Yardi, and AppFolio.

They don't create a better product or service. Instead, their business model often involves stripping cash and equity from these organizations, resulting in significant financial gains for the firms at the expense of the communities they are meant to serve. In short, they employ a "smash-and-grab" investment strategy.

You may think you don't recognize these companies, but you do. Consider the firms that manage investments for your 401(k) retirement funds. These investors are considered major players due to the size of their investments. For example, as of 2022, BlackRock, the largest private equity manager, manages approximately $10 trillion in assets. That's three times the annual Gross Domestic Product (GDP) of Great Britain.

These investors, like their nonbank counterparts, are unregulated and strive for ever-increasing profits. However, since 2017, their premium investments have been focused on the housing industry. These investments have become the core component of the ultra-high-net-worth portfolio, making the sector the new choice for the wealthy and elite. By 2018, the four largest multifamily property owners in the U.S. were institutional investors, establishing them as the central figures.

Introduction

But who are the institutional investor property owners who currently own and control the apartment buildings, and what are their goals? Before the emergence of institutional investors in the late 1950s, the investors were primarily from the propertied class and the financial elite. This historical context connects us to the industry's roots. It underscores the significant shift in ownership and influence that extends beyond the housing market, shaping government policies and affecting broader societal dynamics. Before the New Deal, less than a third of the population owned property, with a majority being larger land and property owners.

However, this very small group that makes up the institutional investors can be recognized by their common operating strategies. For instance, the investor class firmly believes that the government's role is not to provide assistance to the people, despite the fact that people pay taxes to support the government. They are staunchly against social safety net programs for the working class, advocating instead for trickle-down economics. This economic theory involves the government providing significant tax breaks, bailout packages, or other resources to the largest corporations and businesses, with the intention that the benefits will trickle down to consumers. It is a failed economic approach invented by President Hoover as a means to enrich the wealthy, funded by the tax payments of the working class. Essentially, it's a wealth tax paid by the working class with the intention of redistributing tax revenues to the most affluent.

Another underlying economic principle that unites them is their views of wealth creation, which requires a balance between the wealthy and the impoverished. Because a large pool of cheap labor is necessary to create and sustain an affluent class. Historically, rich people have not valued labor as essential to the business equation. As a result, they have often resorted to using slavery and other forms of cheap labor to achieve their goals. This law of wealth creation has been in existence for a very, very long time.

Another underlying strategy that unites these investors is their determination to, at all costs, avoid paying their fair share of taxes. For instance, in 2012, Warren Buffett addressed critics of his "Buffett Rule." This rule means that no household earning over a million dollars annually should pay a smaller share of their income in taxes than middle-class families. However, for this statement, he was jeered by the wealthy conservatives as participating in "class warfare." He pointed out in that interview, "Actually, there has been class warfare going on for the last twenty years, and my class has won." "We're the ones who have had our tax rates reduced dramatically."[1]

But, in fact, it goes quite a bit deeper than this. The investors assert that the federal government lacks the legal authority to regulate them and considers such regulation unlawful. Further, the only real constraint to their business practices is the economic laws of supply and demand. Monopolies are considered the ultimate accomplishment. Monopolies create efficiencies, which, in turn, maximize profits.

A classic example of this business model is Purdue Pharma. The Sackler family owns this pharmaceutical company. They initially acquired an Opioid pain medication that was used mainly for cancer patients. However, by 1995, they realized that by readjusting the formula, it could be converted to OxyContin, a highly addictive drug. They achieved a near-monopolistic market share in the pain management industry, serving tens of millions of customers and generating nearly $2 billion annually. Additionally, their business model required mass production, regardless of the side effects. However, by 2005, that side effect had become the leading cause of half a million overdose deaths.

Yet, according to them, the government has no authority to prosecute them for the crimes they commit. Per their belief, the laws of supply and demand are the only factors that should determine their fate. In simpler terms, if their demand, i.e., the number of people using their products or services, decreases to the point that they are no longer profitable, they will then be forced to change their business model to return to profitability. Or face going out of business.

A similar example is the tobacco industry, which has caused over 100 million deaths due to the use of its products. The number of deaths is more significant than all of those of World Wars I and II and their holocausts, combined. To this day, tobacco use still claims the lives of over eight million individuals every year.

Another underlying principle of this group is their tendency to be driven by greed, a phenomenon known as moral hazard. Moral hazard is a financial concept that refers to the tendency to take risks when there are little or no consequences for those actions. It implies that if an individual or organization engages in risky behavior with the possibility of significant profits but without facing potential adverse outcomes, they are more likely to engage in that activity.

These master puppeteers have been around for millennia. They pass down their methods of market manipulation from one generation to the next, demonstrating how to expertly control governments and societies, and bend them to their will. In ancient times, the wealthy caste developed a philosophy: Indifference breeds wealth, wealth breeds power, and power breeds freedom. No price is too high for their wealth, power, and freedom.

From a political perspective, this group becomes more problematic when they form alliances in government and religion. This group is considered opportunistic and is known to take over political parties to control the government and appoint judges who are sympathetic to their cause of wealth creation.

After forming a coalition and placing their preferred lawmakers in positions of power, the alliance presents new laws for voting in legislatures or boardrooms. Think of the Republican Party's Project 2025, which is currently being discussed in the 2024 election. The voting members need only to approve the Project 2025 rules. The wealthy elites consistently win because they use their power to draft legislation that favors them and then manipulate the voting process to guarantee the desired outcome. To Fernand Pecora, the Chief Counsel to the congressional investigation into the financial crashes of 1929, discussed in Chapter 1, this propertied class, or as we refer to them today—the billionaire class— they are democracy killers.

The investors plan to reclaim power

In the late 1930s, the economic power and political influence of the investor class diminished. For the first time since the country's establishment, they were no longer in charge of the government. The Republican Party had virtually collapsed after the Great Depression, having been blamed for the crisis. President Roosevelt's New Deal, a bold and transformative policy, played a crucial role in challenging the investor class's control and in empowering the government to represent the people's interests.

We turn to a presidential speech to better understand how investors viewed the New Deal. President Herbert Hoover said during the 1932 presidential campaign, "This campaign is more than a contest between two men. It is more than a contest between two parties. It is a contest between two philosophies of government."[2] In short, Hoover and the Republican Party believed that our society is shaped by wealth and economic power, primarily benefiting the wealthy. After all, he crafted the philosophy of trickle-down economics. In contrast, Roosevelt and the Democrats believed that America was a society governed by laws created by the people and for the benefit of all its citizens.

Ultimately, the wealthy elites viewed the New Deal as an illegal power grab. To oppose President Roosevelt and the principles of the New Deal, the elites, investors, and the propertied class formed a conservative alliance in 1934. This alliance included Republicans, Southern Democrats, and business leaders who were unorganized yet vocal, as well as religious congressional representatives known as the Conservative Coalition.[3] This alliance, known as the Hoover Coalition, initially called the American Liberty League, joined forces with the America First Committee. These like-minded groups, representing the interests of big business and wealthy elites, opposed the New Deal and aimed to restore the investor class to power, placing it back in charge of the people, the working caste.

To accomplish this, they instituted a long-term plan to regain their former power. In the initial stage of the plan, Hoover assisted in uniting the party by forming a new Republican group called the Young Republicans. Hoover would spend decades rebuilding the GOP by establishing Young Republican Clubs on college campuses across the nation, their teachings centered on the philosophy that greed is good and monopolies are beneficial. The plight of the working class was even more severe, as Republicans claimed that their poverty resulted from their own moral failings. After all, the wealthy relied on a large, impoverished labor force to sustain their riches.

The second part of the plan aims to build close relationships with religious groups and establish numerous think tanks, such as the Heritage Foundation and the Cato Institute, which developed what is now known as Project 2025. Then, they organized legions of lawyers and lobbyists to attack the principles of the New Deal, funneling large sums of money to them. Additionally, they would leverage their relationships with large national trade associations and establish Super PACs within them, including the National Association of Realtors, the American Bankers Association, and the U.S. Chamber of Commerce, among others.

However, to achieve their goals, they would need to collaborate with Congress to ensure these groups were designated as "nonprofit" or tax-exempt. Rather than paying their taxes, they channel enormous sums of money into these tax-deductible organizations, effectively creating extensive tax-free empires to achieve their objectives.

In the third part of the plan, they destroy free enterprise and then the judicial system, putting themselves above the law and making it nearly impossible to hold them accountable for their crimes.

Their policy agenda is designed to fund only news agencies that promote their version of the truth, thereby undermining the very concept of truth. In 1987, President Reagan and the Republican-controlled legislature terminated the Fairness Doctrine. The post-World War II regulatory policy that required news agencies to present a balanced representation of differing viewpoints. The removal of regulation resulted in news media companies like Fox News, a company controlled by foreign agents, to be born and to flourish. Fox News has become the de facto propaganda arm of the wealthy investor caste. It retains the same design and misinformation tactics established in Nazi Germany during the 1930s.

Today, the billionaire class controls our news agencies, including the new world of influencers. Pushing ever harder to destroy truth itself in their quest to put themselves back in charge of the working caste. Conspiracy theories now dominate our airwaves and news media, including once-reliable news outlets such as *The Wall Street Journal*, *The Washington Post*, and *The LA Times*, causing chaos and blurring the lines between truth and fantasy for many citizens. Today, America no longer has a trusted news source.

It is often stated that the three pillars of democracy are truth, honesty, and integrity. Deception has the power to undermine a democracy faster than any military invasion. Ignorance, in particular, is one of the most destructive threats to democratic systems. When facts are ignored, those in power will impose their version of truth. Truth is then determined by the victors, not necessarily by the righteous or enlightened. Consider Kellyanne Conway and her "alternative facts." To this group, the truth is a matter of perspective, and their perspective is the only one that matters.

The History of the Investors

We will examine their practices over two periods to gain a better understanding of investor property owners and their plans. The first period begins with the New Deal in the 1930s. The second period starts with the emergence of revenue management technology in the late 1990s. In short, we examine their operating strategies during the Industrial Age versus the Technological Age.

Part 1: From the 1930s, The Industrial Age

Following the 1929 financial crash, the investor class grew restless. They started seeking economic opportunities in various sectors, including oil and gas. The industry we will focus on is real estate, and a notable company within this industry is the Trammell Crow Company (TCC). Founded by Trammell Crow (1914–2009) in Dallas, Texas.

In 1948, Crow pioneered a new type of career, and a new industry based on "speculative building." Speculative building is a practice where a licensed contractor builds a structure on their land without a specific buyer in mind, which was a departure from the historical approach of building properties to fill sales orders from highly qualified buyers.

This shift in the real estate industry allowed builders to construct housing units without a specific buyer in place, aiming for maximum profits. However, it also introduced significant risks and potential for massive losses. Crow obtained financing from the industrialists, the Rockefellers. First, he built warehouses. Then, he moved on to shopping centers and suburban offices, followed by giant downtown skyscrapers and market centers. Ultimately, the Wyndham hotels now specialize in multifamily and single-family construction.

By 1970, Crow had developed the Trammell Crow Company into a nationwide organization. *Forbes* in 1971 and *The Wall Street Journal* in 1986 referred to Crow as the largest landlord in the US. Historically, Crow has been one of the largest developers in the country. They would continue to become the most prominent apartment contractor in the U.S., building more units than any other company.[4]

We will now focus on politics and how investors leveraged their relationships in this field to advance their objectives. Following the tragic assassinations of President John F. Kennedy in Dallas, Texas, and shortly thereafter of his brother Robert, a leadership vacuum emerged within the Democratic Party, triggering a significant shift in the American political landscape. This shift moved away from the principles of the New Deal and toward the interests of the investor class and their chosen representatives—the Republican Party.

However, the Nixon coalition was mired in greed, racism, and corruption. By the late 1970s, the massive amounts of corruption within the Nixon coalition would cause its eventual collapse. However, after that, investors promoted a new economic movement known as Reaganomics, also referred to as supply-side economics. Supply-side economics is an economic theory that emphasizes removing regulations and oversight, granting businesses unfettered access to profits, and is pushed by the false narrative of trickle-down economics.

In 1978, the Reagan Coalition, including the wealthy class from the original Hoover Coalition, enlisted the assistance of the influential Conservative Coalition to restore their wealth-creation objectives. However, unlike in 1919, when the Coalition exploited public concern over alcoholism to push for Prohibition—an effort some historians believe was primarily aimed at dividing the working caste by splitting their vote, with pro-prohibitionists aligning with the wealthy elite. In 1978, the Coalition used abortion as a tool to once again drive a massive wedge through the heart of the working class and again split their vote, echoing their strategy from 1919.[5]

This movement brought back the Hoover Doctrine, and trickle-down economics was reborn and repackaged. The ideology was that large monopolies are better than smaller, individual, competitive companies, and the winner takes all, regardless of the consequences. The aristocracy had returned, bringing with it their policies of wealth creation, which led to devastating consequences of income inequality and significantly altered our economic landscape.

Then, as if orchestrated, Robert Bork, an influential antitrust scholar, wrote a notable book in 1978, The Antitrust Paradox. The book refers to Bork's argument that the antitrust laws, which were intended to promote competition and protect consumers, were actually harming consumers by protecting smaller, inefficient businesses. Additionally, he pushed the narrative that monopolies were a sign of a healthy economy. He concluded that as long as the massive profits generated by monopolies did not outweigh the harm to consumers, they should not be regulated.[6] Bork became the voice of President Reagan's conservative movement—and Reaganomics.

In 2012, Barak Orbach, a law professor at the Univ. of Arizona, published the book How Antitrust Lost Its Goal, reporting that Bork wrote: "Congress enacted the Sherman Antitrust Act as a consumer welfare prescription." He continued, "The Supreme Court adopted that sentence in 1979 as the stated goal in antitrust today. It's a big deal. A huge deal."[7] In 1978, the book The Antitrust Paradox sparked controversy due to its racist content. However, the ideology it presented had a more subtle but chilling effect on the principles of the New Deal. It dealt a significant blow to those principles, striking a dagger through its heart. Since then, the scales of justice have shifted toward a less free America, granting vast powers to the wealthy investor caste and prioritizing wealth creation at the expense of the working class and taxpayers.

But even worse, they also severely weakened the institutions established by our ancestors, such as the FDIC and the Securities and Exchange Commission, by systematically removing the regulations implemented to safeguard consumers and taxpayers. As a result, trillions of dollars were redirected to investors instead of reaching the intended recipients—the American people.

Part 2: The Investor Class Beginning with the Introduction of Revenue Management—the Technological Age

At the onset of the 2008 Great Recession, the Crow Empire, the largest single-family and multifamily housing contractor, was at the epicenter of the financial storm. Despite their strict policy against investing in speculative residential land, they were not immune to the chaos they created. The collapse of the oldest and largest real estate empire—the Crow Empire, known as the granddaddy of the construction industry and a titan of Wall Street—along with the downfall of their favored lending partner, the nonbanking giant Lehman Brothers and its $700 billion in assets, sent shockwaves throughout the industry. The effects of the combined collapses were profound. Vacancy rates soared, institutional investors defaulted on their billion-dollar loan portfolios, and real estate values plummeted. But the effects of their corrupt practices were more chilling still by throwing more than ten million Americans out of their homes and onto the streets.

The acquisition of the Crow empire by Coldwell Banker Richard Ellis (CBRE), the world's largest commercial real estate services and investment firm, was a significant event. Despite this, Crow was allowed to maintain its independent operations, a stark contrast to the liquidation of Lehman Brothers, which resulted in massive losses of hundreds of billions of dollars.

The Creation of the Industries' Common Pricing Platform and Its Pricing Cartel

In response to the financial crisis, independent and institutional investors collaborated to prevent a similar catastrophe from recurring. To accomplish their goals, the corporate landlords formed an investor group, composed of forty-six members, to frame the new rental housing industry around revenue management technology. The group included the top ten property managers by size, thirty other major landlords, as well as representatives from Experian, Property Management System (PMS) providers, and various other technology firms. This group collectively owned or managed approximately 5,000 apartment communities across the nation. The group's formation can be traced back to two sources. The footnotes in Camden Property Trust's 2000 Annual Financials and RealPages' financial reports provide details on the framing process. In essence, the consortium was formed to frame the industry around revenue management technology to maximize profits for the investors.

The investors' vision for the industry was further solidified through the implementation of the Management Standard, a framework designed to drive meaningful change. Their long-term goal was to develop a vertically integrated industry with a few dominant players at every level, from development and construction to property management. This strategic decision would shape the industry's future and profoundly impact all participants.

According to the Management Standard, they would also create a common pricing platform. On this platform, the investors demanded freedom. They sought independence from regulatory constraints and the opportunity to maximize their profits. The RealPage pricing Platform was always intended to be utilized by the entire industry to price their rental units using a common pricing algorithm (algorithmic price-fixing) based on massive amounts of shared private data, predicated on leveraging their relationships.

Calibrating the Pricing Algorithm

The first step in implementing the technology was to calibrate the pricing algorithm. Between 2005 and 2010, the industry collaborated to develop and test revenue management technology. The approach was simple: First, complete the tests, and then, second, release the results to the industry through its trade association's news outlets. See Chapter 2 for trade associations. However, the trade associations more than reported the results. They pushed the narrative that failure to adopt revenue management would result in financial ruin, similar to the situation in the home entertainment industry, as seen in the comparison between Blockbuster and Netflix.

However, institutional investors drove the rental industry toward revenue management technology. Leasing agents reported that property owners and managers faced increasing pressure from institutional investors to adopt the technology. From 2002 to 2010, the introduction of revenue management in the industry led on-the-ground leasing staff to feel that the technology was being imposed on them from above.

Framing the Rental Industry Around Revenue Management Technologies

To frame the industry, RealPage began hosting annual summits in 2002, inviting property management system (PMS) providers, corporate landlords, and industry executives to attend these events. These gatherings were designed to educate attendees about proposals that could improve profitability by collaborating, rather than operating independently as individual businesses. Senior management received training in the programs' theoretical and practical aspects. Beyond this, they received education on new technologies, business processes, best practices, and strategies to effectively leverage the Platform and enhance operations and profits. These summits were created to form a pricing cartel—a coalition of powerful entities working together to exert control and influence over the industry and their ability to increase profits significantly. Essentially, the rental industry was framed around revenue management technology and the new Management Standard.

Nevertheless, the success or failure of the industry's common pricing platform ultimately depends on pricing concentrations, the percentage of rental units employing the PMS, and its pricing technologies. Therefore, the question becomes: Could the industry persuade a sufficient number of independent landlords to adopt their property management systems and pricing algorithms? Chapter 5 provides the answer to this question, which would determine the future of the rental housing industry.

CHAPTER 5

The Rental Housing Pricing Cartel Obtains Monopoly Power Sufficient to Control Prices

Introduction

Centuries ago, the United States adopted a free market system. This economic framework is characterized by minimal government oversight and regulation, where market dynamics of supply and demand dictate the pricing of goods and services. In this environment, buyers and sellers compete to establish mutually beneficial prices, with buyers seeking the lowest prices and sellers seeking the highest prices. Sellers compete for consumers' business and can set prices based on demand levels; conversely, buyers retain the freedom to decide how to consume. However, what happens to consumers in a free-market system when sellers stop competing for business and instead collaborate with their would-be competitors to increase their profits?

Key Concepts:

What is the Sherman Antitrust Act?

According to the Department of Justice (DOJ), antitrust laws prohibit property owners and managers from engaging in conduct that unreasonably restrains competition by creating or maintaining monopoly power. They also prohibit attempts at monopolization and conspiracies to monopolize. Most claims involve behavior by an industry-dominant firm with significant market power. Most restraints challenged under the Sherman Act are subject to the rule of reason, which the Supreme Court described as "a fact-specific assessment of market power and market structure" aimed at evaluating the restraint's "actual effect on competition"—particularly its ability to reduce output and raise prices.

What is a Pricing Cartel?

A pricing cartel is defined in economics as a group of firms or individuals that collude to coordinate prices for a specific product or service. In short, it's when businesses agree to act together instead of competing against one another.

What are the Historical Measurements of Market Share and Market Concentration?

However, when businesses cease competing and instead collaborate to enhance their profits, a lack of competition can lead to the formation of monopolies. A monopoly denotes a market structure in which a single company, or a small number of companies, wield significant control over a product—including its production and pricing—and the ability to raise those prices substantially. This structure limits consumer options and hinders competition, potentially leading to unfair practices against consumers.

In economics, the historical terms "market share" and "market concentration" refer to the extent of dominance exerted by a few firms within an industry. In simpler terms, think of the U.S. soft drink industry, where Coca-Cola and Pepsi-Cola control approximately 70% of the market share. There is a direct correlation between market share and market power: the higher the market share, the greater the market power and the ability to artificially increase prices.

The primary challenge of monopoly power lies in its exclusive benefits for those involved in the monopoly, maximizing their profits at the expense of consumers. Monopolies create efficiencies for profit maximization but are known to deliver sloppy, ineffective, and sometimes downright dangerous products and services to consumers because they don't need to compete for business.

Consider the 2022 infant formula shortage, where industry owners and investors established monopolies that severely limited parents' choices and access. This shortage occurred because, over the past couple of decades, the industry has witnessed a significant concentration of production facilities. This situation arose because larger, more efficient companies acquired or merged with their competitors, resulting in the closure of many less efficient production facilities. As a result, only a few production facilities remained operational, which limited overall production capacity.

Consequently, when one of the major factories was shut down due to contamination in its production line, infant formula production in the U.S. was negatively affected, effectively bringing it to a standstill. Consequently, millions of infants were deprived of essential nutrition, leading to the tragic deaths of infants worldwide, all to enrich a handful of investors significantly.

In short, the process of market concentration was driven by investors merging with or acquiring their competitors. The method of creating market concentration is a critical step in creating monopolies, which enable fewer and fewer players to control markets and maximize profits for investors at the expense and detriment of their consumers. In the fourth and final step of this chapter, we will examine how concentrations were formed in the rental housing industry and their impact on markets and pricing.

One of the most significant downsides of monopolies is the lack of competition they create, which can lead to stagnant wages and substantial barriers to entry for new business growth. A great example of this was after World War II, when American soldiers returned home to find that monopolies still plagued the economy, making good-paying jobs scarce and starting a new business almost impossible, as companies with monopoly power often crushed new startup companies. This situation led to pressure on congressional leaders to act. They pushed the Department of Justice (DOJ) to use the power of the Sherman Antitrust Act, which authorized the government to act against trust companies with monopoly power and break them up.

In response to this challenging scenario, the DOJ took a proactive stance, initiating over 3,000 antitrust cases between the 1950s and the 1970s. This significant regulatory action played a crucial role in maintaining a competitive market. One of the most notable trust cases was the 1974 lawsuit against the Bell Telephone System (AT&T). By dismantling this monopoly in 1984, the DOJ opened the market to new players and paved the way for companies like Apple, which specializes in phones and technology, to emerge and thrive. The dismantling of this monopoly would set the new technological age, powered by big data and artificial intelligence, into motion. For instance, in 1984, Manugistics initiated its pricing algorithm with Delta Air Lines.

The antitrust actions greatly expanded the economy, and between 1960 and the 1980s, six million new small businesses—including Apple, Microsoft, Google, and other tech companies, as well as many firms across various industries—emerged, creating tens of millions of well-paying jobs. Now operating in a more open and competitive market, these businesses flourished, bringing a sense of empowerment and optimism. With new business growth and real wage growth, the middle class expanded significantly, allowing more citizens to create wealth and enjoy homeownership and the American Dream than ever before.

This historical context highlights the importance of open markets and competition in our economy, underscoring their significance. Therefore, free and open markets are the cornerstone of a prosperous and stable free-market economy. In an open marketplace, when sellers compete aggressively, it benefits both consumers and businesses by providing affordable options, higher-quality products and services, more choices, and increased opportunities for innovation.

What do Market Share and Market Power look like in the Digital Economy?

Today, in 2024, America is again plagued by monopolies; it appears that our economic cycle has come full circle. The buildup of monopolies resulted in less competition, stagnant wages, a severe lack of affordable housing, and skyrocketing rental rates. However, in today's data-driven economy, a monopoly looks quite different from those of fifty years ago. This market structure differs from the traditional concept of monopolies, in which a small number of companies control the market and set prices.

In today's digital economy, market share or monopoly power is often determined by a common pricing platform within an industry, rather than by individual companies themselves. Therefore, market power—the ability to artificially increase prices—is constrained by an industry's adoption of its common pricing platform. As a reminder, a common pricing platform is a technology platform designed for an industry to use cooperatively, enabling its revenue management algorithms to set prices for that industry. That is opposed to individual business owners setting their own prices. Therefore, instead of one or two large companies controlling prices, the industry collaborates on pricing, forming a pricing cartel that holds monopoly power.

Therefore, in the rental housing industry, market share and power are determined by the percentage of rental units priced on the common pricing platform. For example, if there were 100 rental units in a market and 87 were priced on the platform, the market share or power would be 87%. [As a note: the DOJ uses a technical process called the Herfindahl-Hirschman Index (HHI) to measure market concentrations.] However, the question remains: At what point is the concentration of companies using the industry-wide common pricing platform sufficient to control prices?

Today, algorithmic price-fixing occurs when a landlord outsources its pricing function (Revenue Management Module) to a third party, such as the RealPage YieldStar AIRM pricing algorithm, which has now been updated to Demand X. Suppose multiple competitors engage the same third-party agent to set their prices using an identical algorithm, knowing that their competitors also employ the same algorithmic price-setting agent. In this case, there is a risk that this practice would amount to "hub and spoke" collusion. This practice does not differ substantially from traditional price-fixing—it's still a cartel agreement between two parties, except that in the digital age, it occurs within their pricing technologies.

Pricing concentrations are further impacted by the various property management system (PMS) providers' white-labeling of their pricing technology. For example, our research found that Yardi and AppFolio's Revenue Management Module were more than likely using a white-labeled version of RealPage's pricing algorithm.

Determining if the RealPage Common Pricing Platform Has Created a Pricing Cartel

Today, the "Rental Housing Pricing Cartel" is an association formed through either a formal or informal agreement among landlords to control the housing supply, limit the number of applicants in the "qualified renter pool," enhance debt collections, and influence prices. Our goal in this chapter is to determine whether the rental housing industry has created a pricing cartel that utilizes a common pricing platform to enhance its profits by establishing monopoly power. This research is significant because it examines the potential impact of cartels' common pricing platforms on market power and on their ability to influence rental rates.

The Property Management System (PMS) and Its Revenue Management Module Measure Market Power.

We utilize property management system providers (PMS) to measure market share and pricing concentrations. In this text, the terms "PMS" and "Platform" have the same meaning and are used interchangeably. In short, PMS providers facilitate and drive the pricing process. Just a reminder, the algorithmic price-fixing allegations happened in the PMS and its Revenue Management Module. For instance, in 2022, there were approximately forty-four million rental units in the United States. However, there are only three primary PMS providers: RealPage, Yardi, and AppFolio. Combined, they hold a 75% market share nationally. As a result, we will focus on these three PMS providers to determine whether a pricing cartel with monopoly power exists.

National Market Share of the Primary PMS Providers

Property Management System Provider	Number of Units	National Market Share
RealPage	20 Million	46%
Yardi	8 Million	18%
AppFolio	5 Million	11%
Totals	**33 Million**	**75%**

In short, the success of the shared common pricing Platform ultimately depends on pricing concentrations, the percentage of rental units employing the PMS, and its pricing technologies. Chapter 3 further concluded that the merger between RealPage YieldStar and the Rainmaker Group LRO likely created a pricing monopoly due to the combined pricing algorithm. This chapter aims to determine whether the pricing algorithm for the revenue management module attracted sufficient participation to gain a substantial market share, thereby enabling it to influence rental rates. To address this question, this chapter describes the extensive Market Analysis conducted using the State of Washington as a case study; see Bibliography for details of the six studies.

To gain a deeper understanding of the housing crisis, we began our research by conducting a detailed rent analysis of the increase in rental rates for two Segments of the Washington State housing market from 2013 to 2018, as detailed in Figure 5.1 below. To accomplish this, we compared rents in three metropolitan areas where revenue management technology was deployed (King County (Seattle), Spokane, and Thurston County (Olympia)—Segment 1) to those where it was not used (Franklin, Yakima, and Walla Walla—Segment 2).

We verified the economies of both control groups and eliminated other contributing economic factors. In conclusion, we found no economic reasons for the sharp increase of 96.24% in rental rates in Segment 1, where revenue management technology is used, as shown on the left side of Figure 5.1 below, compared to the modest rental rate increase of 9.94% in Segment 2, where the technology isn't used, on the right side of Figure 5.1.

Figure 5.1:

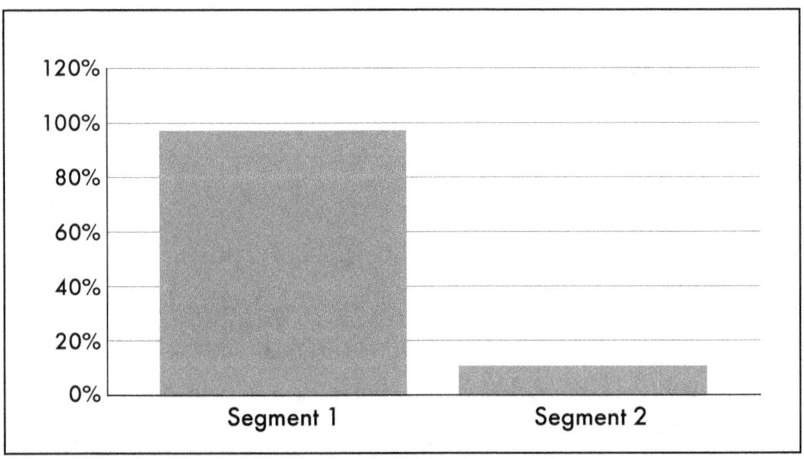

Therefore, in the second study, Market Share Concentrations in Multifamily Property Management Companies Using a Common Pricing Platform—Metro, Seattle, WA., referred to throughout this book as simply "Concentration Study," we completed the research to determine whether or not the common pricing platform attracted enough participation to gain sufficient market share, enabling them to influence rental rates. We use the Metro Seattle area as our case study; however, we found that most metro areas across the country are similarly impacted.

Step One: Define the Market to Be Tested

Our analysis of the Platform's market power and potential to artificially inflate rental rates includes a pivotal research document, the "Concentration Study." This study, which features the rental rates from Metro Seattle, Washington, in the top half of Figure 5.3 (below), is instrumental in establishing the correlation. In short, the first step in our research process was to establish a "defined market" and select the rental units for analysis.

This step involved selecting the rental units within three ZIP codes in downtown Seattle: 98121 (a residential area known as Belltown), 98119 (a residential area known as Queen Anne), and 98109 (a residential area known as South Lake Union). The data for these units was sourced from Apartments.com, a popular rental site, and provided by CoStar, a prominent real estate data provider. In essence, we followed the same process a prospective tenant would undertake when embarking on their house-hunting journey. The defined market, which includes the three ZIP codes, has 25,320 rental units and nearly 70,000 residents.

Step Two: For each Rental Unit, verify the landlord and their chosen Property Management System, and the Competitors in the Marketplace

After establishing the defined market, the next step was to verify the managers of each rental property, followed by determining their pricing methods. This important step involves categorizing properties as either managed by a third-party property manager using their chosen property management system (hereinafter referred to as "property managers") or self-managed.

This step involved a detailed investigation to identify the property manager for each rental unit within the "defined market." This investigation encompassed all properties with more than five units, including those classified as "mom-and-pop" rentals. This step, conducted with meticulous attention to detail, required a physical verification of each of the 25,320 rental units. This rigorous process was crucial in ensuring the accuracy and reliability of our findings.

The results showed that, in the defined market, 276 properties with 23,320 units were managed by 89 property managers using their chosen property management system (PMS) providers—RealPage, Yardi, and AppFolio—accounting for 92.10% of the market. Conversely, the remaining 2,000 units, or 7.9%, are self-managed. In total, 402 properties are managed by 215 competitors in our defined market.

The next part of the investigation focused on their pricing methods. In short, we determined that the verified property managers account for over 92% of the market and price 95.27% of their units on the common pricing Platform. To further enhance the depth and rigor of our study, we verified over 320,000 rental units in this market using the RealPage pricing Platform.

However, the 7.9% of self-managed properties posed a significant verification problem, as most of these properties are smaller (less than ten-unit buildings) and lack an online presence, thus limiting the ability to verify. The unverified group accounted for 10.37% of the market, or 2,626 units. Therefore, to adequately address this issue, we labeled these units as "unknown" and included them in the data set for analysis. In conclusion, on a combined basis of 25,320 units, 22,258 or 87.91% of all units were verified using the PMS and its pricing technologies to manage and price their units.

Details and Pricing Methods of Properties in the Defined Market

Number of Method of Pricing	Number Properties	Market of Units	Percentage
Using PMS Providers			
RealPage, Yardi, AppFolio	246	22,258	87.91%
Priced by Other Technology	4	436	1.72%
Priced by Unknown	152	2,626	10.37%
Totals	**402**	**25,320**	**100.00%**

However, given the 10.37% unknown, how concentrated is the pricing of rental units through the property management systems and their pricing algorithms? To answer this question, we turn to managed properties, which service 92% of the industry. We verified their pricing methods primarily because of their online presence.

Therefore, to provide more accurate market details, the study utilized a range (Figure 5.2) to estimate the percentage of rental units priced through the common pricing platform. The range, which is significant in understanding the dominance of these systems, starts with 87.91% combined (managed and unmanaged) for pricing their rental units. It extends to the 92% group of verified property managers who price 95.27% of their properties through the Platform. In other words, between 87.91% and 95.27% of all rental units were verified using the Property Management Systems and its revenue management module to price them. The Concentration Study revealed a significant concentration of rental units priced using these property management systems and their revenue management technologies, which may impact the market's ability to substantially raise rental rates.

Figure 5.2: The Concentration of Rental Units Priced on the RealPage Common Pricing Platform

Total All Units % Priced through the Platform	Range	Total Managed Properties % Priced through the Platform
87.91%	To	95.27%

Step Three: Establish a Correlation Between Pricing Concentrations, Market Power, and Unrestrained Rent Increases

The third step of the process, which is crucial in our research, was to establish whether or not a correlation existed between concentrations of rental units priced through the PMS provider's revenue management technology and the increase in rental rates. To demonstrate this correlation, we obtained and summarized the dates when property managers acquired the PMS technology, as shown in the bottom half of Figure 5.3. It was crucial to obtain the dates when the managers acquired the PMS and its algorithmic pricing technologies to establish the correlation.

We then compared this information with the top half of Figure 5.3, which describes the year-over-year growth in rental rates from 2013 to 2018. This comparison allowed us to discern any patterns or relationships between the adoption of PMS technology and changes in rental rates.

In 2014, in Metro Seattle, the Platform allowed the revenue management technology to push rents as hard as possible. The rental rates had skyrocketed 40.34% by the time the push ended. Therefore, to assess the integrity and strength of their market power, we focus on 2014 to evaluate the correlation between the two variables.

Figure 5.3: Metro Seattle Rental Pricing Data and Rental Units added to the Platform 2011–2018

Year	*2011*	*2012*	*2013*	*2014*	*2015*	*2016*	*2017*	*2018*
	Rent Analysis							
Annual Average Rent	$1,086	$1,069	$1,227	$1,722	$1,800	$1,940	$2,067	$2,245
Annual Rent Increase		-17	158	495	78	140	127	178
% Annual Rent Increase			14.78%	40.34%	4.53%	7.78%	6.55%	8.61%
% Cumulative Rent Increase		0.00%	14.78%	55.12%	59.65%	67.43%	73.98%	82.59%
	Pricing Concentration Analysis							
Total Units in Defined Market	25,320							
Units added by year		834	1,474	4,158	233	226	2,026	1,266
Total Units on Platform	12,039	12,873	14,347	18,505	18,738	18,964	20,990	22,258
% Increase by Year		3.29%	5.82%	16.42%	.92%	.89%	8.0%	5.01%
% Cumulative Units on Platform	*47.55%*	*50.84%*	*56.66%*	*73.08%*	*74%*	*74.9%*	*82.9%*	*87.91%*

Our research showed that in most major markets, once the technology reaches saturation, it's designed to push prices as high as possible to generate significant profits. After the initial surge, the algorithm aims to adjust rates as the market permits. However, there is always a "big push" in rental rates. For example, in 2014, as shown in the bottom half of Figure 5.3, there were 4,158 rental units in our defined market that were added to the Platform for pricing. This 16.42% surge resulted in a saturated market share of 73.08% at the time. Therefore, the Platform experienced a 40.34% increase in rates driven by its 73.08% market share.

To further establish this correlation, Figures 5.3 and 5.4 present a timeline of when the managers acquired the technology, as measured by their chosen PMS, thereby creating significant market power. Between 2011 and 2018, pricing concentrations increased from 47.55% to 87.91%, as indicated by the dots at the bottom of Figure 5.4. The chart also displays the timeline of rental rate increases, indicated by the rightward-arching dotted line labeled "Rent." Between 2011 and 2018, rental rates increased from $1,086 to $2,245 per month. The growth in pricing concentration is matched with the increase in rental rates to demonstrate the correlation.

Figure 5.4: Cumulative Concentrations of Pricing on the Platform Correlated to Cumulative Rent Increases Year-over-Year 2011–2018

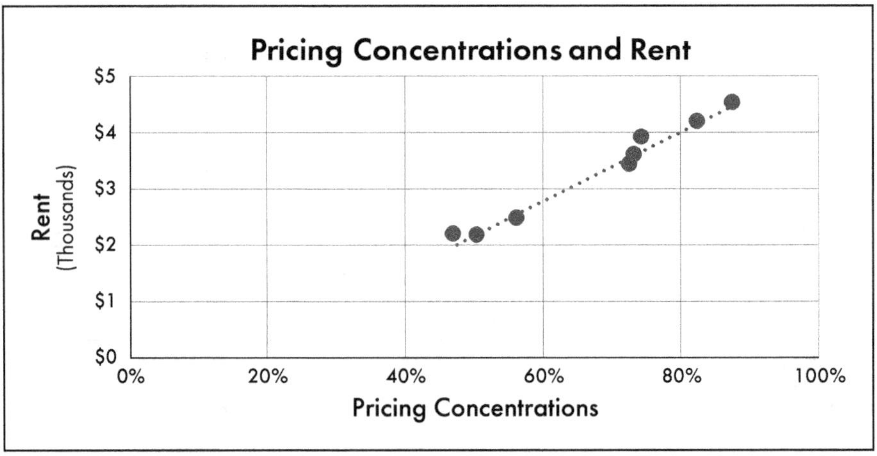

Our study found an undeniably strong correlation between the concentration of pricing units on this common pricing platform—accounting for 87.91% to 95.27% of all rental units—and the industry's ability to artificially increase rates. In simple terms, the high concentration of units priced on the industry-wide common pricing platform, managed and operated by RealPage, led to an 82.59% increase in rental rates in Metro Seattle.

Our study's findings are not just a discovery but a significant revelation that provides a clear takeaway for the reader. It highlights the potential impact of property managers' chosen property management systems, their utilization of the common pricing platform, and their ability to artificially inflate rental rates. Therefore, the author concludes that the industry has potentially formed a pricing cartel with monopoly power. The Department of Justice, using this research, agreed with this conclusion and filed an algorithmic price-fixing claim against RealPage in 2024.

Step Four: Property Management Concentrations and Interconnections

While important, the focus on pricing concentrations is not the sole determinant of market power. Concentrations in market share or power are further empowered by industry interconnections among property management companies. In short, industry interconnections and concentrations also affect market power. Understanding this impact is crucial, as having properties managed by fewer companies increases the likelihood of collusion and artificially inflated rates. Therefore, market power was further measured in the study's fourth and final step, highlighting the comprehensive nature of our research.

The analysis revealed a significant trend in property management concentrations following the 2008 economic downturn. The top ten property managers nationwide have experienced a substantial 169% increase in concentration as measured by the number of units they manage, underscoring the growing significance of this trend (2008–2018).

Locally, in the Metro Seattle area, the Concentration Study found that property management companies were highly concentrated. For example, Greystar, the largest, manages more properties than the bottom three-fourths of its 215 competitors combined. However, to truly comprehend the concentration level, the top fifty largest managers account for less than a quarter of the total competitors. Yet they hold nearly 90% market share. In stark contrast, the fifty smallest competitors also account for the same number of competitors. However, they hold only 1.47% of the market share, resulting in an 87:1 ratio between the top fifty and bottom fifty competitors. The top twenty-five managers have an 80% market share. This imbalance suggests that significant management concentrations exist, potentially leading to market manipulation and higher rental rates.

Interconnections and Interrelations within the Rental Housing Industry

Interconnections and interrelations refer to the connections and interactions between companies, their investors, customers, suppliers, subsidiaries, and other entities involved in commerce. For instance, institutional investors, such as private equity firms, play a significant role in shaping our housing market. They are a force to be reckoned with. Their influence, partly due to their common ownership of stock within their portfolios through a practice known as horizontal stockholding, is a key factor.

This term refers to the investment practice of many institutional investors who invest in more than one company competing in the same industry sector. In simpler terms, it means these investors own shares in multiple companies that directly compete with each other. For example, an investor could own stock in numerous property management companies (Greystar, Equity Residential, etc.) and providers of property management systems (RealPage or AppFolio).

This type of ownership has become the primary causal factor in the steep decline in the number of competitors and the level of competition. This common ownership reduces competition and may lead to higher prices for tenants. When investors acquire stock in companies competing in the same sector, it is in their best interest to merge those companies. Since market share gains typically come at the expense of other companies within the same investors' portfolios, it can be concluded that investors drive the market toward concentration, thereby significantly enhancing profits.

How Predatory Pricing Works Today—Mergers and Acquisitions

One consequence of AI-driven revenue management and its digital operating platforms is that, once companies within an industry connect to these platforms, mergers between firms become easier. The benefits of economies of scale have prompted firms to merge or buy smaller firms, thus creating monopolistic empires. We will now delve into the consolidations and interconnections that have emerged in the multifamily real estate industry.

Through their common ownership structures, investors facilitate mergers and acquisitions. Historically, when a firm sought to exert market power, it typically resorted to predatory pricing. By forcing the prices down, they would, in turn, put their competition out of business. Then, without competition, they would enter into a pattern of increasing prices, covering their losses during the predatory pricing period, and ultimately return large profits.

Today, however, Predatory Pricing has another meaning. For example, dropping rents is the last measure managers need to use, given their association with the Platform. Therefore, property managers and owners no longer need to lower prices and engage in price wars to maximize profits. The reason? They no longer view their competitors as rivals but as opportunities. Therefore, when they reach economies of scale that maximize profits, their investors encourage them to acquire or merge with their competitors. In this instance, those who can achieve the highest profits win the contracts or property, as the case may be.

We will now focus on the consolidation process and discuss how it was implemented. In short, it was the next step in the evolution of the rental housing industry and its use of revenue management. In June 2014, the Crow Empire, introduced in Chapter 4, urged Greystar to acquire Riverstone Residential Group. At that time, Riverstone was the largest management firm in the nation, providing property management services to the Crow Empire. As a result, the two largest management companies were merged, marking a significant shift in the industry's landscape.

In June 2020, after a series of other notable acquisitions, Greystar acquired Alliance Residential. At the time of the merger, Alliance Residential was the leading developer, second-largest builder, and eighth-largest manager of multifamily units. As a result of these acquisitions and consolidations, Greystar became the largest apartment property developer, builder, and manager of nearly a million units, making it the largest vertically integrated entity in the rental housing industry in our country's history. Not to mention, they are also one of the largest owners. The primary reason for the mergers was to benefit institutional investors by creating economies of scale and efficiency and generating substantial profits.

The Driving Force Behind Industry Consolidations and Its Interconnections

Continuing our discussion from Chapter 4, we delve into the industry's historical roots. Where did these consolidations and concentrations begin? In short, they began with Trammell Crow, known as the "Crow Empire," a figure often referred to as the "grandfather" of the industry due to his significant influence and impact.

The Crow Empire has established a highly influential network of senior managers, all of whom have previously worked for the empire. They hold significant sway over the top twenty-five property management companies nationwide. This influence allows the Crow Empire to shape the strategies and operations of these companies, further consolidating its power in the industry. These companies are culturally connected and deeply intertwined in their operations, technologies, and pricing strategies. Not to mention that they are also interconnected in their joint ventures used for property acquisition. This interconnectedness is a testament to the profound influence of the Crow Empire. Nationally, this group holds an 80% market share, which is even more concentrated than in the soft drink industry, where Coca-Cola and PepsiCo have a 70% market share.

However, the question remains: How dangerous are these consolidations and interconnections in the housing industry? To answer this, we look to the 2008 Financial Crisis Inquiry Commission (FCIC), a Federal Committee established by Congress to investigate the causes of the 2008 Great Recession—an economic crisis that gripped our country—and to explain its causes to the American people. Their report stated that the primary cause of the Great Recession was the "consolidations and concentrations in the financial industry."

Today, following the 2008 Great Recession, banks are more heavily regulated. As Chapter 4 explains, investors believe that these regulations are illegal. As a result, they have shifted the housing market away from regulated banks and into the nonbanking sector, where over two-thirds of all housing transactions currently occur. Worse still, these companies have become highly concentrated in their market share, much like the regulated banks before the 2008 financial crisis. Today, these same consolidations and concentrations have also spread into the housing industry, impacting property managers and their digital operating platforms. Unfortunately for the taxpayers, it gets worse still. This same economic structure existed in 1928 and was also considered a key contributor to the 1929 financial crisis.

How the industry has leveraged its relationships to gain political power

After Trammell Crow's retirement, his son, Harlan Crow, stepped into his role. Harlan has been in the news recently due to his controversial relationship with Supreme Court Justice Clarence Thomas. In 1998, at the start of the framing process, Harlan Crow sought to initiate an influence campaign involving the Supreme Court

Justice by funneling him millions of dollars in bribes under the guise of "gifts." This campaign was designed to sway the Supreme Court's decisions in favor of the property management industry and its use of algorithmic revenue management technology, further consolidating the Crow Empire's power.

Furthermore, Crow's influence extends across various sectors, encompassing not only the U.S. Supreme Court and property management industry but also attracting the attention of investors. Crow is the proprietor of CHC Investment Partners. This firm provides investment services to eighty-five of Forbes's top 100 most financially powerful individuals and entities.[1] These comprehensive services encompass real estate investments in the highly lucrative multifamily housing market, demonstrating the breadth and depth of Crow's impact on the investment landscape.

The Fix:

This section of the chapter will describe the steps and procedures needed to improve the rental housing industry and safeguard consumers from algorithmic price-fixing. The pricing algorithm uses four primary steps to manufacture the rental rates. Therefore, the methods and processes for monitoring and regulating the four steps will be detailed in Chapters 6-9 with a final summary in Chapter 12.

Conclusion: The RealPage Common Pricing Platform Has Sufficient Market Power to Control Prices.

This chapter concludes that the investors have orchestrated a significant shift in the rental housing industry, driving individual landlord participation in sufficient numbers to manipulate the market. The industry has coalesced into a pricing cartel, dictating prices for up to 95% of all rental units on a common pricing platform. The concentration of management companies and their interconnections within the Crow Empire reinforces this cartel's power, giving investors significant influence to manipulate the market and control the cost of housing.

It is evident that Robert Bork, the influential antitrust scholar detailed in Chapter 4, who President Reagan handpicked to shape Reaganomics, has successfully implemented the policy. As a reminder, the objective was to steer our economy once again toward a monopolistic structure that predominantly benefits the wealthy investor class. The tool at the heart of that policy is revenue management.

How Does the RealPage YieldStar AI Revenue Management (AIRM), now DemandX, Determine Rental Rates?

To adequately answer this question, we will examine their pricing algorithms and how they operate to generate such massive wealth. The Platform has sufficient market power to control prices. But how does it work? How do companies like RealPage, AppFolio, and Yardi work together to increase their landlords' profits? And what is the impact on the tenants? How has this market power affected them? After all, it is the residents or tenants of their properties who must pay that steep price for housing.

The role that advanced revenue management technologies, powered by AI, play in determining rental rates is detailed in Chapters 6 through 12. The pricing algorithm follows four steps to determine rental rates. These chapters will explore these steps in greater depth. Chapter 6 will primarily focus on the first step of their pricing process: their data-gathering campaign. Chapter 7 will detail how they combine the data obtained from Chapter 6 with their pricing and leasing technologies to select their tenants. Chapters 8 and 9 will delve into pricing steps two through four. The main question that Chapters 8 and 9 seek to answer is whether the free-market system, based on supply and demand, sets rental rates or whether landlords engage in algorithmic price-fixing that cheats the American people. Additionally, these chapters will discuss how their pricing program works.

Chapters 10 and 11 will detail the side effects and the intended and unintended consequences of revenue management on the tenants and society as a whole. The societal implications of revenue management are far-reaching, affecting not only individual tenants but also the overall housing market and social equality. Chapter 12 summarizes revenue management, its consequences, and its conclusions.

CHAPTER 6

In a Data-Driven Economy, Data Becomes the New Currency

Key Concepts:

Understanding Your Right to Privacy

The Platform requires massive amounts of timely data, and gathering it is the first step in its pricing process. Yet, getting that information may pose significant legal challenges. The Privacy Act of 1974 establishes the fair information practices that govern the collection, maintenance, use, and dissemination of information about individuals. The Fourth Amendment protects the right to privacy against unreasonable searches and seizures by the government. However, what happens when unregulated businesses like the Platform take over our housing program, which originated from the government? Should tenants expect any less of a reasonable right to privacy?

While the U.S. Constitution does not explicitly protect the right to privacy, some amendments do. The existence of numerous state-driven privacy laws to safeguard personal data from both government and corporate entities underscores the significance of this principle. Understanding your rights to privacy is more important than ever before, as Justices Clarence Thomas and Samuel Alito of the U.S. Supreme Court have called for its abandonment, suggesting that landlords' contracts should govern data collection. However, the Platform's extensive data-gathering campaign raises significant ethical concerns about tenants' privacy rights in the rental housing industry.

Introduction

There are approximately forty-five million renter households in the United States today, accounting for around 35% of the population. Historically, landlords would obtain a credit report from an impartial third party as part of the tenant screening process. However, more than forty-five million adults in the U.S. (19%) do not have traditional credit scores that landlords can use to assess their eligibility for housing. These individuals do not appear in conventional credit reports. Landlords must, therefore, consider other information, referred to as "alternatives," including a tenant's payment history for non-traditional credit items, such as rent, cell phone bills, utilities, insurance, and other recurring bills.

Additionally, fraud was a significant concern for landlords. For example, the digital age has also improved the ability of bad actors to abuse the system. There is a risk that some renters may arrive without the intent to pay rent, often through identity theft. Identity theft occurs when a completely fake identity is created. These individuals never pay any rent and then disappear after a few months of free rent, moving on to their next victim. In 2019, RealPage acquired a tenant screening algorithm specifically designed to combat the fraud problem and improve debt collections.

This chapter will examine the methods and sources employed to collect vast amounts of data. To facilitate data gathering, the Platform currently leverages its relationships with Experian and other third-party data providers, providing its members with a substantial advantage over those who do not use it, enabling them to access near-perfect, real-time data on their applicants, tenants, and properties. Real-time data is information that is collected, processed, and delivered almost instantly after it is generated, enabling immediate analysis and response. "Real-time" can mean milliseconds for some uses and seconds or minutes for others. Consequently, this allows them to make better-informed decisions about who to rent to—or, more commonly, who not to rent to—and how much to charge.

But at what point does this massive data-gathering campaign become an invasion of our privacy? Should corporate landlords and their PMS providers have unlimited access to this data? Here, we ask the question: Is this relationship, including the accessing and sharing of this data, legal or ethical? Should those gathering data be allowed to manipulate it and mold it to their benefit without oversight and regulation?

The 1934 Pecora Report identified one of the root causes of the 1929 financial crash as a lack of adequate boundaries between the banking industry's divisions—those that gather deposits and those that invest the deposits. Similarly, the relationship between entities such as Experian and the Platform poses an enormous threat to consumers. Therefore, should we consider separating entities such as Experian from the property management system (PMS) providers and their screening algorithms that landlords use to select tenants? The proposed practice would involve separating the entities that collect data from those that use it, thereby splitting the data collection industry from the data utilization industry.

Pricing Step 1: How they Gather, Access, and Share Data on their Applicants, Tenants, and Properties

The heart of the matter is that the Platform requires massive amounts of data to be cost-effective. For example, they need supply data on their inventory of properties and demand data on their customers, the tenants. The data they use comes from two primary sources, internal and external, and is stored in seven primary databases that are held in data centers.

The Sources of Data and The Flow of Data From the Landlord Databases

First is their internal data, which resides within the property management systems, such as the landlord's databases. The gathering process was designed to work as follows: Property Management Systems (PMS) providers integrate directly into their landlords' computer systems and databases on a nationwide scale and continuously export all the data needed to base forecasts and pricing. The Platform has comprehensive real-time access to the landlord's operating systems and all their information. This data, obtained from thirty-three million rental units nationwide, includes pricing strategies, actual rent prices, occupancy rates, and lease start and end dates—all relevant data for applicants, tenants, and properties.

The flow of data from landlords to their property management systems.

Step 1:	The landlords retain ownership of their data in their databases, but allow their selected PMS Providers unrestricted access. These PMS Providers integrate with the landlords' computer systems, enabling access to real-time data.
Step 2:	Once the three PMS providers have collected data from their landlords, they share the information on the 33 million units among themselves.
Step 3:	The three providers then use their common technologies to manipulate the data and make it usable, for instance, to create their forecasts.
Step 4:	The three providers share the combined manipulated data, including the recommended prices, with the landlords who initially supplied it.

Second is external data, which refers to information that resides outside property management systems, such as third-party data providers like Experian and market reports.

Where They Store Their Data—The Seven Primary Databases and Their Purpose

The goal of the pricing algorithm, often referred to as the "Optimum Mix Equation," is designed to find the highest-revenue combination of rents and ancillary revenues while maintaining the lowest possible occupancy. The equation is achieved by artificially balancing supply and demand, a concept that will be explored further in Chapter 8. The equation, a key component of the pricing algorithm, strives to strike the perfect balance between maximizing revenue and simultaneously maximizing vacancies. In short, they seek to maximize profits while providing the minimum required number of housing units. However, this task necessitates the collection of massive amounts of data. As depicted below, seven primary databases were created to facilitate the balancing process and power the pricing algorithm.

Their Seven Databases and Where They Store It

DATABASE 1:	RealPage: Historical Lease Records. 30+ Years containing 40 Million Records
DATABASE 2:	Experian: Comprehensive Current and Historical Tenant Data
DATABASE 3:	Finicity: Comprehensive Current and Historical Financial Data and Alternative Tenant Data
DATABASE 4:	RealPage: 20 Million Active Lease Records Maintained in Real-Time
DATABASE 5:	Current and Historical Apartment Sales Data and Market Trends Obtained from 200k Providers Containing $20 Trillion Volume of Sales Transactions
DATABASE 6:	Detailed Apartment Building Data on nearly 44 Million Rental Units
DATABASE 7:	Legal Database Containing every rule and regulation by area

Databases One through Four contain tenant and applicant information, including Guest Card applicant data, maintained in a subset of Database One. Databases Five and Six have information on the properties. Database Seven, the Legal Database, is tied to a legion of lawyers and includes every law, rule, and regulation affecting housing, broken down by each state, county, and municipality. This Database, a tool used to circumvent regulations, is pivotal in creating contracts prioritizing profit over the "spirit of the law." This misuse of legal resources, combined with the vast amount of data at their fingertips, has significantly altered the playing field in the rental housing market.

The Multi-Trillion Dollar Data Center Industry that houses the data

The data center industry is a rapidly expanding sector valued at over half a trillion dollars, with forecasts predicting it will reach seven trillion dollars by the end of 2029, highlighting its significant influence and importance. Currently, in 2024–2025, protests are intensifying over the industry's substantial consumption of electricity and water. However, the more pressing question is: What data is being collected, on whom, and what specific information is being gathered? And, for what purpose? Understanding this is crucial to grasping the ethical concerns involved.

The surprising answer is that tens of billions of records are generated daily solely to be sold to algorithmic pricing firms like RealPage, which then facilitate their price-fixing schemes. The RealPage Databases are stored in these data centers. But that isn't all. As we shall see, nearly every industry in our economy is designed to use these data centers. The primary purpose of this data collection is to feed their AI-powered pricing technologies.

The source and methods used to collect and share data on their applicants and tenants; databases 1-4.

The Authorization Behind Data Gathering—Their Contracts

Landlords throughout the United States gather extensive data on their tenants and often share it with others. When signing a new lease, tenants generally agree to allow access to all information provided during the application and any data collected during their residency. Consider the sensitive data you trust them with when applying for a lease, such as criminal background checks, bank account details, employment history, contact information, and even your mobile phone number with GPS tracking capabilities. However, the data collection continues beyond that point. Afterward, they engage in extensive data mining, a truly Orwellian program reminiscent of George Orwell's novel 1984.

Landlords justify their extensive data collection and sharing through the terms and conditions of their contracts. The troublesome sharing was made possible by adding a single sentence to the lease document, effective after 2006: "*If someone requests information on you or your rental history for law enforcement, governmental,* or business purposes, *we may provide it without prior notice to you.*" This seemingly harmless statement allows landlords to access and share the tenant's data with Experian, the Platform, and other parties for business purposes without requiring the tenant's prior knowledge or consent. Their data collection and sharing practices can severely affect your privacy and security.

Experian Data

Experian, mentioned in Chapters 2, 3, and 5, was one of the original forty-six framers of the rental housing industry around revenue management technology. In 2010, Experian purchased RentBureau, discussed below. According to the Management Standard, PMS providers and their member landlords must leverage their relationships with data providers to obtain data on their applicants and tenants, the customers. Experian supplies much of this data.

They have connected to the RealPage Platform through a two-sided arrangement with the PMS (DOP) to improve data access and sharing. This relatively new and unique platform enables them to access and share massive amounts of tenant data. Although Experian's initial goal was to gather tenant data during prescreening, its relationship now spans all stages of the tenant lifecycle. Providing daily updates on tenant information, including changes in their financial situation, such as taking on new debts like buying a car, employment status, pending legal issues, and overall creditworthiness. The landlords use Experian to prepare evictions, provide data, and support throughout the debt collection process. Afterward, landlords and Experian form a blockade to acquiring housing to enhance debt collections, as discussed in more detail in Chapter 10.

But it gets worse, for example, Experian has designed an AI-powered program to track all tenant-landlord debts indefinitely. In other words, Experian will monitor a tenant or former tenant indefinitely and notify the landlord of any financial changes to the tenant's situation. If a tenant gets a job, Experian prepares the paperwork for the landlord to garnish their wages. If cash is in a checking account, Experian will notify the landlord where to collect on that obligation. This process violates credit collection laws. However, this industry continues to operate without regulation or oversight. Experian and the Platform have become the co-gatekeepers to housing.

RentBureau—the Gamechanger (now Experian RentBureau)

The full benefits of AI revenue management technology in the rental housing industry were initially limited by the industry's inability to gather information about its tenants, its customers. Yet, according to the principles of the new Management Standard discussed in Chapter 2, landlords needed to collect information about their customers. Their ability to obtain tenant information was limited because, before 2005, there was no mechanism for the credit reporting industry to gather or provide rental tenant data. Consequently, RentBureau was created by the same investors who developed the Platform (RealPage and the Rainmaker Group) to obtain tenant information.

National Rental Data Exchange (NRDE)

The investors, through RentBureau, established the National Rental Database Exchange (NRDE) as a massive repository of tenant information. The success of this initiative relied on RentBureau's ability to build a network of landlords, both large and small, who would contribute rental data on their tenants. Like property management system providers, Experian integrates directly into its landlords' databases on a nationwide scale, pulling residents' rental histories every 24 hours.

In 2009, LeasingDesk, a subsidiary of RealPage, established a database that pulled tenant data records from NRDE. This initiative led to the creation of Database One, which now holds nearly forty million lease outcome records and continues to grow, highlighting the continuous expansion of tenant data. A lease outcome record contains all the information collected about a tenant during the duration of a lease, whether the lease lasts for a year or ten years.

Where they Collect Massive Amounts of real-time data—the Guest Cards

Guest card data refers to the information collected from prospective applicants who visit a rental community, either in person or online. This data includes the applicant's name, contact information, desired move-in date, preferred unit type, number of bedrooms and bathrooms, floor preference, and desired rent. Rainmaker developed an AI-powered leasing platform called Rainmaker ILM. This platform automates the guest card process across the entire rental industry by gathering data from various sources and entering it into landlords' databases with minimal human intervention. The platform has created a multi-billion-dollar industry that generates "qualified leads" on applicants and sells them to property managers. This discussion is completed in Ch. 7.

Alternative Data and Its Third-Party Providers

Landlords use various databases to obtain information about their tenants. Databases One and Four are accessed and shared with Experian, which, in turn, accesses and shares Database Two. Experian also links landlords to Finicity and Database Three to gather alternative tenant data, including a comprehensive financial picture.

The Alternative data they collect

Platform members claim to be recording a wide range of alternative data on their applicants and tenants. This practice includes online computer searches, social media posts and messaging, education records, driving histories, police records, all types and forms of insurance reports, medical records, and prescription drug usage. Additionally, the platform monitors and collects the tenants' online and offline purchasing habits. Not only that, but they also monitor and collect data from handheld devices such as phones and listening devices like Amazon's Alexa. They allegedly follow their tenants into private areas, such as bedrooms, bathrooms, workplaces, churches, and other sensitive locations, collecting a wide range of personal and private data. In short, wherever your phone travels, the Platform is listening and collecting massive amounts of data.

The $200 Billion Data Brokerage Industry

Their practices don't end there. The platform accesses and shares data from third-party data brokers that collect or purchase data from other companies. Most people need to be made aware of the existence of such companies. Still, the data brokerage industry has become highly profitable yet volatile and wholly unregulated, processing billions of records daily and generating $200 billion in revenue annually. The reader should consider this question: Would the frequent data breaches we hear about continue if there weren't a market to sell this information? Have data breaches become the modern equivalent of bank robberies that once plagued Wells Fargo and the Old West?

This data is obtained from the information users unknowingly share with digital companies whose services they use daily, such as Facebook, TikTok, or Amazon. For instance, Facebook processes over 500 terabytes of new data daily. These digital companies also gather valuable user information from the internet, both legally and illegally, and combine it with data from other sources.

The Financial Information They Collect

However, none of the information is more critical yet volatile than the collection of detailed financial information. Landlords acquire financial reporting directly from the tenants' financial institutions, which is referred to as Database Three. However, the pricing algorithm had to overcome a fundamental barrier: How to obtain the necessary financial data to power its algorithms from within the secured walls of FDIC-insured banks and NCUA-insured credit unions.

The Financial Data Exchange (FDX)

In 2018, the Financial Data Exchange (FDX) was established to play a pivotal role in the data-sharing process. This nonprofit industry trade association gathers comprehensive financial information from insured banks and credit unions. The data is then shared between these institutions, their non-banking counterparts, and data brokers. By leveraging the FDX, the Platform can access its tenants' financial records, which would otherwise be unavailable. Despite its nonprofit status, the FDX operates without a direct governmental regulating body or oversight, raising concerns about the potential misuse of this data.

Finicity is a Data Aggregator

Finicity, based in Salt Lake City, Utah, and a subsidiary of Mastercard, is a data aggregator in this emerging industry, providing landlords with an open banking platform. They connect with over 10,000 financial institutions, covering 95% of the market. Finicity's data aggregation AI software downloads all relevant data from the tenant's accounts to build data and analytics for the Platform.

To acquire and use massive amounts of detailed financial data, RealPage and Yardi became a Money Service Business.

What could be worse? In 2013, RealPage became a Money Service Business (MSB). Shortly after this, Yardi also became an MSB, meaning both Yardi and RealPage are now classified as financial institutions with unrestricted access to their tenants' bank accounts.

Conclusion on the Data They Collect on Their Applicants and Tenants

Property managers, however, fail to adequately disclose how they use their data against tenants throughout the tenancy process and forever after that. The data will be used in all future transactions without the option to opt out. This lack of transparency is a cause for concern, as your data may be sold or shared with other companies. Worse still, you would not be legally able to prevent it from happening, leaving you with no control over your information.

Unfortunately, it gets worse. Landlords can share this information with other landlords to block you from attaining future housing. They have repeatedly done this if they feel a tenant owes them back rent, fees, or eviction costs, regardless of whether these fees are accurate or legal. In short, the Platform and its third-party providers have assumed broad authorization and permission to access and share massive amounts of private, detailed tenant data. Yet, based on those inadequate disclosures, third-party providers such as Finicity claim they have been granted permission to access and share vast amounts of detailed financial information. This unfettered access to tenant data, along with a lack of transparency regarding its use, poses a substantial threat to tenant privacy rights.

But how could it possibly get worse? Today, AI-powered facial recognition technology is being unleashed upon the public. Consider, if you will, the methods, outcomes, and the potential for abuse of this biometric technology, especially when accessed with unlimited data by unscrupulous dictators or malicious actors. These are the technology and data-sharing processes that kept authors like George Orwell up at night, the author of the novel 1984.

How they Gather, Access, and Share Data on their Properties—Databases 5-6

We will now shift our focus to the supply side—housing inventories. Initially, RealPage utilized its own existing real estate data provider, MPF Research, to gather and report on real estate data. However, in 2017, they significantly improved their existing program. The first improvements were acquiring and integrating over forty-five popular IT software programs. However, not only did they acquire the IT technologies to improve data usage on their properties, but they also implemented them effectively.

They also created the ability to obtain massive amounts of data on those thirty-three million rental units and vast amounts of market data. To gather the data, they established relationships with nearly all apartment data providers, including Yardi and AppFolio, to receive and share all available data in real-time.

For instance, this is how the data-sharing process works: RealPage established a long-term data-sharing partnership with Real Capital Analytics (RCA). Since its inception in 2000, RCA has established a global reputation for providing the most timely and reliable transaction data, as well as valuable insights into market pricing, capital flows, and investment trends. Including over $20 trillion in commercial property sales transactions, which is linked to more than 200,000 investor and lender profiles. To allow the pricing algorithms to leverage the historical context of properties alongside current market trends, commercial property sales transactions are recorded and stored in Database Five. The new technology provides operators with deeper insights into their rental units. Their new and improved data reporting entity is called RealPage Market Analytics.

Database Six provides a comprehensive listing of nearly all of the forty-four million rental units across the United States. It gathers and maintains data on planned, new, and existing rental properties, including multifamily and student apartments. Using advanced technologies, it classifies and analyzes these rental units at the asset level based on various factors such as asset class, age, and specific competitive floor plans. This in-depth analysis offers enhanced insights that facilitate the creation of more effective opportunities for generating additional revenue.

Conclusion: The Data Gathering Process

The consortium that framed the industry provided the Platform with AI-powered revenue management technology and the seven databases, giving it massive amounts of data at its fingertips. It isn't that landlords shouldn't have access to the information needed to adequately screen their applicants. However, the abuse of the data-gathering and dissemination processes underscores the need for regulatory changes to empower and protect tenant rights and privacy.

All the data collected during their extensive process is stored in data centers, and this information will determine how much you will pay for rent. This stored data will also determine the costs of your next home and insurance, as well as expenses for auto and auto insurance. Furthermore, it will impact prices for everything from grocery trips to gas station visits and all in between. The free-market systems appear to be a relic of the Industrial Age.

In today's economy, data centers are at the heart of algorithmic price-fixing; they are co-dependent on each other—the pricing technology and the sources and storage of vast amounts of data. Without the storage capabilities, algorithmic price-fixing could not occur.

Today, AI revenue management sets rates for rent and nearly all products and services based on data stored in data centers.

The Fix:

Step 1: Data Sharing Must Be Prohibited

In short, property management system providers access and share all data; therefore, they work together rather than compete. This process of working together facilitates the landlord's price-fixing schemes. Hence, they should be prohibited from sharing individual property owner data with anyone. Each property owner should have their own data silo within their chosen PMS, where they use their own data to set their own rates. Furthermore, PMS providers should be prohibited from sharing data with other landlords or other PMS providers for any purpose or in any form. Additionally, landlords are prohibited from acquiring this data from anyone.

This recommendation includes prohibiting access to and the sharing of "Non-public competitor data," which means information not available to the general public, including actual rent prices, occupancy rates, lease start and end dates, and similar data. This step in correcting their unethical data-sharing schemes would make the algorithmic price-fixing process nearly impossible. The housing market would become fairer, again leading to increased competition among landlords for applicants and tenants.

Step 2: Break Up the Data Gathering Industry from the Data Usage Industry

Here, we answer the question: Based on a lack of adequate disclosure in the data-gathering process and the abusive methods built into their algorithms, supported by all that data, it appears that the Platform, its member landlords, and Experian have violated their tenants' right to privacy. The parallels between PMS providers and Experian, along with other third-party providers, have blurred the lines in the gathering and use of data, reminiscent of the inadequate boundaries in the banking industry in 1929. Consequently, the relationship between Experian and the Platform poses a comparable threat to consumers, underscoring the urgent need for action.

The Banking Act of 1933, also known as the Glass-Steagall Act, provides a roadmap for Congress's separation of commercial banking from investment banking. Therefore, following the 1929 financial crash and as a means to better regulate the moral hazard inherent in the banking system, the Act separated the two functions and industries.

Therefore, using Pecora's methodology as a first step, the use of Digital Operating Platforms to gather or share data and information must be prohibited. Additionally, this two-sided, digitally operated platform between Experian and other third-party data providers, and the Platform itself, should be broken up, and the data industry should be separated from the rental housing industry—i.e., the data users. Instead, truly disinterested third-party providers would develop and deploy credit-type reports to pre-screen their applicants. After all, cash is to the banking industry as data is to the data brokerage industry, concluding that data is the new currency and should be regulated equally.

CHAPTER 7

How the Lease Management Module Uses AI-Powered Technology to Select Its Tenants

Key Concepts:

What Does Affordable Housing Mean? And how is it measured?

Housing is affordable when it costs consumers no more than 30% of their income. Those spending more are considered cost or rent-burdened. According to HUD, to measure affordability, 100% of the national area median income (AMI) is about $70,000, making $1,750 (30%) or less spent on housing considered affordable. Nationally, that would make the purchase price of affordable homes under $300,000. However, the metro areas have become the most impacted. In Seattle, like many metropolitan areas, the AMI is approximately $100,000, which translates to a monthly rent of under $2,500 or a house price of under $400,000.

What is Gentrification?

Gentrification is a complex issue with various definitions that often sparks conversations about housing construction and the displacement of long-time residents. It typically occurs when land and older housing units are less expensive and can be demolished to make way for newer, more expensive housing units. This practice creates a high chance of profit due to the influx of wealthier wage earners who are able and willing to pay higher rates for their housing.

However, at its core, gentrification is the process of displacing long-time, less affluent residents from their neighborhoods. This stark injustice exacerbates the housing disparity between the haves and have-nots. The process has also disrupted the sense of community, where neighbors once cared for each other and looked after each other's well-being.

Today, one's educational and career opportunities are often determined by one's place of residence. Unfortunately, those living in lower-income areas face more disadvantages than their wealthier counterparts. Wealthier school districts typically have more funding and can offer a higher-quality education, which, in turn, leads to better career prospects and opportunities.

Introduction

When a family, whether a single person or a large group of eleven, begins searching for a new home, they typically conduct extensive planning and budgeting before making a final decision. Besides searching for a home, applicants have other important things to consider, such as finding new schools, selecting a place of worship, and choosing soccer, basketball, or other teams for their children. Moving is a very stressful and costly event in people's lives.

Being forced out of one's home and community due to gentrification—because one cannot earn sufficient wealth to keep up with rising rents—can devastate people's self-esteem. The loss of pride is a side effect that is rarely discussed. On the other hand, when minorities try to move into safer neighborhoods to provide better living accommodations and a safer living environment, their ability to pay doesn't necessarily guarantee that they can.

Therefore, when the Platform uses algorithms to pre-qualify and prioritize applicants, the question becomes: Is it the hard work and potential of the individuals that determine their future, or is it the pricing algorithm that ultimately makes the decision? And, does this approach foster communities based on data rather than on the hard work and efforts of its citizens?

Let's Meet Juan Julio Carlos

It was late in the evening; Juan Julio Carlos sat in his car, holding a letter in his hand. It was dark outside, and a chill hung in the air. He couldn't shake the feeling of unease as he thought about how to explain the contents of this letter to his wife and two children. They were looking forward to moving to a new, safe neighborhood with great schools and a promising soccer program. Their chosen apartment at 17 Cherry Tree Lane seemed perfect, with three bedrooms and two bathrooms. Despite the financial strain, Juan was recently promoted to a position with a significant salary increase. Still, he couldn't understand how the letter he held could be true.

Let's meet Juan Julio Carlos, a twenty-eight-year-old son of an immigrant farm laborer who grew up in a small multigenerational home with limited space. Working on the farm from a young age, he was determined to create a better life for himself. With hard work and determination, he obtained a college degree. He recently passed his state-required exams and earned his CPA certification.

Reading the letter, Juan Carlos was shocked to discover that his housing application had been denied due to a supposed felony conviction on his record. He struggled to recall any such event and felt fear and confusion creeping in. His recent work promotion could be in jeopardy if his credit report also showed the same information. Instead of feeling triumphant, Juan felt like his whole world was collapsing around him, all due to the impact of a revenue management technology he had never heard of.

As the sound of police sirens filled the background, he gazed across the broken concrete of the parking lot, where a shootout had occurred just weeks ago. He couldn't help but wonder how he would break the news to his wife, Christine, whom he had promised a safe and stable home for their children. On the other hand, it raises ethical questions about the possibility of having a felony record without being aware of it and whether such a record should be grounds for denying housing. It also prompts us to consider whether this is an error in Juan's credit report or if other motives are at play. Regardless, Juan Julio Carlos and his family are at a crossroads. But how could this have happened? And what, if anything, can he do about it?

The Origin of the Property Management System, Lease Management Module, and Its Technologies

In Chapter 3, we discussed the four components of the property management system. One of these components is the Lease Management Module. We will now examine this module, the technologies that power it, and its impact on the leasing process. Before doing that, let's explore the technology's origins to better understand its inner workings and processes.

In 1998, The Rainmaker Group established a strategic alliance with Manugistics, the original developer of the technology used in the airline industry. Their collaboration aimed to develop revenue management for the hotel and gaming sector. Manugistics provided a "white-labeled" version of the revenue management pricing algorithm. As a reminder from Chapter 3, this term refers to a product or service produced by one company but rebranded by another to make it appear as if it is their own. At the same time, Rainmaker contributed its technical expertise and staff to adapt the technology for use in the hospitality industry, specifically in hotels. The modified hotel revenue management algorithm was called "Revolution."

We will now explore how the hospitality sector prices and fills its hotel rooms. This understanding is essential because the Rainmaker Group developed the Leasing Module technology, which serves the entire rental housing industry, providing valuable insights into how it was initially designed to function. To reiterate, the digital operating platform used in the hospitality industry is the Lodging Management System (LMS), which, like the Property Management System (PMS), similarly has access to extensive internal and external databases containing vast amounts of information on its customers and properties, as discussed in Chapter 6. And the old saying, "what happens in Vegas, stays in Vegas," no longer applies in the digital age.

When Rainmaker entered the hospitality industry, it decided not to develop its own Lodging Management System (LMS) due to the time and cost involved. Instead, they integrated into the revenue management module of an existing company called Agilysys, which is the largest LMS platform in the industry and is similar to RealPage in the housing industry. This integration allowed their systems to exchange data and communicate seamlessly with other casino and hotel software applications.

They took the same approach when they entered the rental industry: instead of creating a PMS, they developed the pricing algorithm for the revenue management module. This process is representative of how revenue management technology was disseminated throughout various economic sectors, including insurance companies, grocery stores, and their supply chains, such as the marketing of eggs and the supply and distribution of gasoline.

In short, they developed revenue management for the hospitality industry and served some of the nation's largest resorts, from Las Vegas to the Jersey Shore. Their initial clients included Caesars Entertainment, MGM Resorts, Omni Hotels & Resorts, and Revel, among many other notable companies. They also served international clients, including The Palm in Dubai. By 2006, when they had expanded into multifamily, they provided revenue management and pricing recommendations to over 500,000 rooms in the hospitality industry.

However, unlike Manugistics, which manipulated ticket prices by controlling the airline industry's supply of flights and seats to ensure there was never an oversupply, they began by developing massive technology to manipulate demand, i.e., their customers. This entire massive pricing process, powered by AI, starts by calculating a consumer's future value. Then, it uses that data to pre-qualify and prioritize demand based on those who are able and willing to pay the highest rates.

Their theory is based on the premise that it includes a guest's theoretical future gaming value, as well as potential room rates and other ancillary revenue, such as spa use, entertainment shows, and dining. In part, their theory is underpinned because casino operators know who their loyal customers are and assign them a casino identification (ID). Non-gaming guests who do not have an ID are categorized as retail customers. Highly rated and frequent players are offered a comp or lower room rate. Conversely, retail customers would be charged amounts calculated to ensure their value or room rates are equal to the gamer's value, for instance, by adding the notorious "resort fees."

The Rainmaker technology was developed to identify its most profitable revenue sources by forecasting demand based on expected customer values and producing pricing recommendations that ensure rooms are always available for customers, offering the greatest contribution to profit. In other words, similar to the airline industry, they hold some rooms off the market for their most valuable customers, for instance, if one of its top gambling clients shows up without a reservation.

However, it was considerably more than this; the pricing software was designed to prioritize consumer demand. This unfair practice was achieved by utilizing massive databases of consumer information gathered from external sources, such as Experian, as well as internal sources, including the databases of their clients, primarily casino and hotel operators. This information was then used to determine which consumers were able and willing to pay the most for their services.

They aimed to shift the company's focus from increased revenue (occupancy and rate) to increased profitability. For instance, industry-wide, they reduced comp expenses by 35%, increased cash revenue by 4%, and automated the pricing process. As one prominent operator stated, since they installed the Rainmaker system (Revolution) in early 2006, they have reduced the number of stay-no-play and other low-profitability customers by 23%. In other words, they priced out the bottom 23% of customers—"priced out by design."

By pricing out the bottom 23% of income earners, the technology becomes unconstrained by the consumer's ability to pay and can then scale its rates for the highest-income earners and their willingness to pay premium rates, thereby significantly increasing its profits. Although it was a risky proposition, their clients willing to accept their pricing recommendations saw their net profits increase by 15%, resulting in tens of millions of dollars in additional profits and billions of dollars in increased property values.

The Leasing Platforms (Module) in the Rental Housing Industry

We will now focus on the rental housing industry and how it uses technology within the leasing module to select tenants to fill the landlord's vacant units. Historically, landlords independently sought out and obtained applicant leads for their rental vacancies, which was a time-consuming and often futile process. The result was that they frequently encountered situations where they struggled to find enough qualified applicants to fill their vacancies. Even worse for the landlord, the entire lead-generating process relied on chance—their options were restricted to applicants who walked through their doors and applied for their units.

Rainmaker developed the new leasing technology platform, Rainmaker ILM, designed to serve the entire industry through white-labeling. This platform has significantly optimized the demand-generating process. Unlike the older methods of chance, the new leasing platform efficiently seeks out and selects qualified applicants for its landlord members. This transformation, achieved by merging the leasing module with the revenue management module, has streamlined the entire lead-generation process, generating "qualified" leads more efficiently. In other words, Rainmaker has merged the Property Management Systems' Leasing and Revenue Management modules into a single, unified module.

Figure 7.1: The Rainmaker Group integrated the Lease Management and Revenue Management Modules into a single unified module.

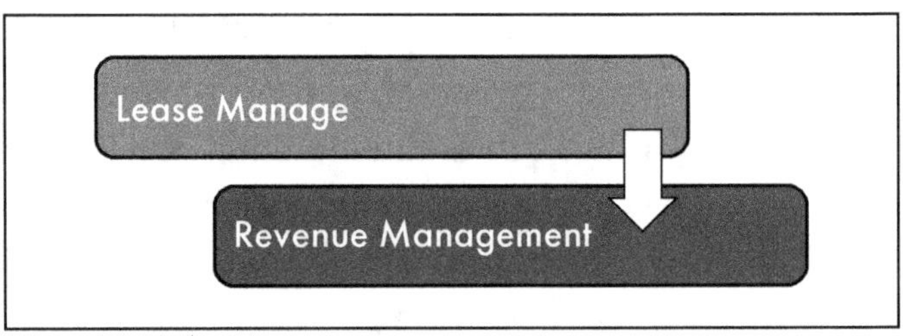

Then, in a groundbreaking move, Rainmaker revolutionized the rental industry further by introducing guest cards for pricing and lead generation (discussed in Chapter 6). Their pioneering platform not only automates the collection and entry of guest card data but also does so with remarkable efficiency, significantly reducing the need for human involvement. In other words, they collect guest card data from various sources and then input the information into the landlords' database on their behalf. However, it doesn't just provide leads more efficiently; it pre-qualifies them first to determine their ability and willingness to pay the highest rates. Similar to Rainmaker's technology used in the hospitality industry, it seeks to maximize profits by selecting tenants who are willing to pay the most for their services.

But it's more than this. The new leasing strategy is designed to efficiently fill landlord vacancies by seeking out and obtaining "qualified leads." A qualified lead is an applicant who can afford to make rent payments and is ready and willing to accept the landlord's proposed rent increases. Not only this, but the lead has also been prioritized by segments such as wealth, income, skin color, and other sociological characteristics. The entire lead-generating process was created to produce the type and quality of applicants the landlord has requested—thus, a "qualified lead."

This efficiency enables companies to make more informed spending decisions, lease properties more quickly, and set higher prices. Rainmaker's innovative approach has transformed the rental industry, creating a multi-billion-dollar sector that generates qualified leads and sells them to landlords, underscoring the significant impact of technology on the housing market.

How They Pre-Qualify Their Applicants by Ability to Make the Rental Payment

When the technology assesses an applicant's ability to afford rent, it uses data from companies like Experian and Finicity, including personal income information such as employment status and salary. Subcategories such as student loans versus credit card debts are considered when evaluating a tenant's overall financial strength.

This phase involves integrating the extensive amount of data gathered, as discussed in Chapter 6, with real-time consumer credit, demographic, and sociographic data. Their systems then use this information to pre-screen applicants and verify that they satisfy a specified minimum rent-to-income ratio. In the initial stage of searching for a home, before submitting a formal application, the technology pre-screens applicants based on their ability to pay the highest rates. This new practice differs substantially from historical legal methods, where the screening process occurred after the consumer signed an application granting permission to access and share their sensitive personal data.

Pre-Qualify by Willingness to Accept and Pay the Increasing Rental Rates

The pricing algorithm used by property management companies, powered by advanced revenue management and predictive analytics, represents a significant shift in the industry. With a high degree of accuracy, it measures a tenant's willingness to pay the proposed rent increase, predicting whether an applicant can and is ready to pay the increase, thereby producing the willingness factor. Consider the Revolution pricing technology created by Rainmaker in the hotel industry. This technology involves calculating a consumer's future value.

In a traditional free market, a store puts a price tag on a shelf, and you decide if it's fair. In the new Digital Economy, the price tag is looking back at you, determining how much you're willing to pay. The pricing algorithm doesn't evaluate the product's value; instead, it determines your breaking point. By examining all that data in Chapter 6, the technology can identify the highest price you're willing to pay before walking away. This technology has effectively replaced the Invisible Hand of the free market with a Digital Predator.

However, to truly predict a tenant's future value, the technology must first predict their willingness to pay the most for their services. Once the technology has established a "qualified" renter pool based on their willingness to pay rent increases, the pricing algorithm can predict how much to charge without incurring significant vacancy rates.

How They Prioritize Demand (Applicants) by Ability, Willingness, and Sociological Characteristics

Once the applicants have been pre-qualified based on their ability and willingness to pay the proposed rental rates, the program seeks to prioritize them by segments such as wealth, income, skin color, sexual orientation, political preferences, and other sociological characteristics. They will choose the applicant who can generate the most profit while remaining within the pre-selected risk factor.

However, by leveraging its relationship with Experian, a credit reporting company, the Platform maintains some measure of control over the number of tenants allowed in the applicant rental pool at any given period; the purpose is discussed more fully in Chapter 8. In other words, their forecasting tools dictate whether they increase or decrease the qualified renter pool by simply loosening or tightening their scoring models to achieve their desired outcome.

For instance, when they need additional tenants, they ignore certain white-collar crimes in their assessment, thereby approving applicants who might otherwise have been denied. In short, the scoring model allows property managers to deny an applicant housing one day because they failed the leasing score and then approve that same applicant the next day, simply because they can alter the integrity of the scoring model. This approach has significantly shifted the focus of competition among platform members. The only significant constraint on increasing rental prices is now the tenant's willingness to pay.

Landlords nowadays have access to Property Management System (PMS) providers who help them find the right tenant at the right price. This new practice means they no longer need to accept just any applicant who, by chance, walks through their doors. However, this raises ethical concerns as well. For instance, some PMS providers have been found to discriminate against certain classes of people based on their race, skin color, or other demographics.

For instance, RealPage, Yardi, and AppFolio have consistently been shown to falsely include criminal records or other incorrect credit information in the final credit reports of applicants whose landlords did not want them living in their apartment communities. The Federal Trade Commission's (FTC) investigation focused on these providers' specific "soft" matching practices for consumers with common last names. These "soft" matching practices involve associating a criminal record with an individual based on similarities in their name, even if they are not the same person. We discuss discrimination more fully in Chapter 11. In our example, Juan Carlos is a common name. The technology's ability to locate a criminal record on one of those commonly named individuals and effectively and conveniently apply that record to another similarly named person has altered the rental housing landscape.

The Results of Combining the RealPage and Rainmaker Leasing and Revenue Management Modules

Ultimately, Rainmaker's origins can be traced back to managing reservations in the hospitality industry, where the goal was to match them with the number of available rooms and fill them with consumers willing to pay the most for their services. Thus, correlating to the rental sector, they replace rooms with rental units. The tenant data was crucial to their pricing process, and they utilized guest cards to gauge demand. With the tenant data, the system could pre-qualify and prioritize that demand, ensuring it provides qualified leads to the landlord.

Conversely, RealPage's focus was on the rent roll, a document that lists a property's tenants, their rent amounts, and other relevant information pertaining to each lease. Harnessing the rent roll is where we trace their beginnings. The rent roll contains massive amounts of information, and harnessing its secrets has led to the development of YieldStar's powerful pricing technology. When these two methodologies were combined, they created a powerful leasing platform to manage consumer demand from all angles of the pricing process.

The Rainmaker component of the algorithm manages demand, starting with the applicant, by using guest card data that includes the applicant's preferences, budget, and other relevant details, such as the amount they can afford to pay. Then, once the tenant signed the lease agreement, YieldStar provided the platform to manage demand after that.

The combination of the two algorithms resulted in the Demand X pricing algorithm, which is three times more powerful than the original RealPage AIRM or Rainmakers' LRO. It provides a 360-degree view of demand—a near-perfect picture of their applicants in real-time. This comprehensive view allows for precise control over the rental process, from initial lead generation to ongoing management. It provides landlords with unprecedented insight and control over their properties.

The Role of Predictive Analytics

Let's explore how predictive analytics and revenue management data can help landlords effectively manage their rental properties, particularly in terms of rent increases and vacancies. This revenue management technology can forecast upcoming vacancies by predicting which tenants are likely to stay or go. For instance, it can, with a high degree of accuracy, predict which tenants are going to purchase a home or move to another apartment complex. This function is completed with the massive amounts of collected data described in Chapter 6, including data from handheld devices and listening devices, such as Amazon's Alexa.

For the tenants, the system predicts will leave, the technology—not the individual landlord—automatically launches a marketing campaign targeting the more lucrative, pre-qualified applicants to fill those units. This proactive approach ensures that those units are filled with qualified leads before they become vacant. In other words, the system selects a suitable replacement tenant well before any vacancy actually occurs. As Amy Dreyfuss, SVP of Revenue Management at RealPage, aptly notes about the Demand X algorithm: "It optimizes advertising spend with future exposure modeling to solve for vacancy before it even happens."[1]

Conclusion

The Property Management System Leasing Module focuses more on maximizing profits than on the hard work and sacrifices of people. At its heart, revenue management providers emphasize that landlords should no longer feel obligated to accept just any applicant who happens to walk onto their property. Instead, they can wait for the "right" applicant at the "right price" chosen by their predictive analytics from their qualified applicant pool.

This new practice was a stark reality for Juan Carlos and his family. Today, the technology in the leasing module assesses an applicant's ability and willingness to pay the highest rates, ultimately determining their eligibility for housing. In Juan's situation, despite his eligibility for better housing, the property owners at 17 Cherry Tree Lane, driven by discriminatory motives, did not want people of color with small children living there. Thus, to prevent them from entering the qualified renter pool, the leasing module technology added a felony record with a similar last name to Juan's credit report.

In short, although the system pre-qualified him as able and willing to pay the most for their services, their algorithms prioritizing applicants were created to eliminate minorities with small children from the qualified renter pool. The system acknowledges that Juan's felony record does not belong there. Yet it was trained to consider this practice because the technology can generate up to 2% in additional net profits, based on its understanding that people are willing to pay more to live among like-minded individuals who resemble them, resulting in millions of dollars in extra profits for landlords.

The technology's predictive analytics now guide the entire leasing process, ultimately determining who can rent a decent home in a safe neighborhood or who must live in unsafe areas or, worse, on the streets. This situation is reminiscent of the 2002 Tom Cruise blockbuster The Minority Report, a science fiction film in which a police division arrests individuals before they commit actual crimes based on predictions from a trio of psychics. However, instead of relying on psychics, landlords now utilize predictive analytics to predict the future behavior of their applicants and tenants.

Chapters 8 and 9 will complete the analysis of their pricing strategy.

The Fix:

White-labeled technology must be regulated. Users of the technology, their applicants, and tenants must be informed about the technology's original creator and its ties to other technologies and databases. Additionally, the Fair Housing Laws must be enforced (see Chapters 8-11). In addition, the collection and sharing of tenant data must be prohibited as discussed in Chapter 6. The pool of qualified renters must be restricted from using tenant and applicant data without the tenants' or applicants' explicit prior consent.

CHAPTER 8

When Are Rising Prices Not Inflation? When There's Algorithmic Price-Fixing

Introduction

Property Management Systems and its revenue management technology, originally YieldStar AIRM, have now combined with Rainmakers' LRO to create the RealPage "Demand X" pricing algorithm. The new algorithm is three times more powerful than the original program. It is designed to employ four primary steps to manufacture rental rates for its member landlords, who control up to 95% of the rental market in metro areas and 75% of the national market.

The Four Steps to the Pricing Process

Step 1:	Involves conducting a comprehensive and truly massive data collection campaign on their applicants, tenants, and properties.
Step 2:	It consists of four parts, including data processing, benchmarking, and forecasting. During this phase, the algorithm seeks to balance housing supply with consumer demand using the data gathered in Step 1. Then, the system uses the common data and technology to set the rent prices.

Step 3:	Known as Yield or Rent Optimization, it utilizes the Economic Occupancy Pricing Strategy to increase income by 35% above the listed or advertised rental rate.
Step 4:	The industry-wide common pricing platform determines rental rates through a recommendation process generated by the Property Management System (PMS) provider's pricing algorithm.

Chapter 6 details Step 1 of the pricing process; Chapters 8 and 9 will complete the discussion of the pricing algorithm's four steps. However, since the third step is such a large and complex process, involving hundreds of components, it will be explained in detail in Chapter 9.

Additionally, this four-step pricing process functions similarly to other revenue management systems used in various sectors of the economy, such as the egg production and marketing, and the automobile fuel distribution industries. Understanding how revenue management systems generate price recommendations can help legal experts, regulators, and policymakers better understand them. This understanding can guide them in ensuring these systems are used ethically and transparently, fostering a fair housing market and economy for all.

Let's Meet the Johnson Family

Hunter and Carol Johnson, the parents of two children, are Millennials who met in high school in a small suburban community outside Reno, Nevada. Hunter, the oldest of four children, was twelve years old when his father, a schoolteacher, was tragically killed by a drunk driver. His mother, struggling to make ends meet, worked multiple jobs to support the family, often earning just minimum wage. As a result, they always struggled financially.

He never saw college as a realistic option, so he began working while still in high school to help support his mother's living expenses. He started at a big-box home improvement store, earning minimum wage. Recently, he was promoted to a shipping and receiving clerk, earning an annual salary of approximately $40,000. Despite his desire to follow in his late father's footsteps and attend college, the long hours at work and lack of resources make it challenging for him.

On the other hand, Carol grew up in a military family, and cooking was her passion. Like many military families, she grew up moving from one military base to another, which made it difficult for her to obtain a good education. Worse yet, she had few close friends. So, when they met during their junior year of high school, it was love at first sight. The two formed a very close relationship, a family bond.

Unfortunately, she became pregnant in her senior year. She was unable to obtain her high school diploma. However, she attended an alternative school where she acquired her GED. She works in the deli department of a big-box superstore and earns about $30,000 per year. Together, they earn around $70,000 per year, which is the average family income in America in 2018.

The primary issue in America today is the economic disparity between income groups. While upper-end wage earners earn significant amounts of money and are financially comfortable, lower-wage workers, who make up about 66% of the workforce, earn less than $20 per hour or $70,000 per year. This gap highlights ongoing challenges in income inequality. This economy is known as the K-shaped economy. In this structure, the upper-wage earners' segment is thriving, as indicated by the upward arc of the K. Conversely, the lower-wage earners' segment is weakening, as noted in the downward arc of the K.

Despite their financial challenges, the Johnsons are determined to give their children the opportunities they never had. They are a hardworking family striving to provide a better future for their children. They currently reside in a modest two-bedroom apartment. Still, they dream of moving to a better neighborhood with improved educational and career prospects for their children. Recently, Carol's father passed away, leaving her a few thousand dollars in his will. With that money, Hunter and Carol want to move into a three-bedroom, two-bathroom apartment at 1164 Morning Glory Circle, unit 67. Their experience with the impact of revenue management on their housing search is a stark but typical example of the societal implications of this technology.

When the Johnsons meet with the property manager, they are unaware of the enormous amount of information the landlords already have on them, so much so that it would shock the reader. When people begin their search for a rental apartment online, they may not realize that they are entering a world of Big Data powered by Artificial Intelligence. From the moment an applicant types the word "apartment" or "housing," AI begins tracking their movements. In fact, AI algorithms are trained to monitor applicants and direct them to properties that AI manages without the applicant's knowledge. According to an industry study completed by the Lincoln Property Company, this practice can result in up to 50% more applicants being directed to these AI-managed properties.

When a tenant shares their housing budget, it's likely the landlord already knows. This knowledge is because the pricing algorithm, a key player in the process, understands the tenant's financial situation, including their debt or rent-to-income ratios, in real-time and can predict how much they can afford and are willing to pay.

We will review the family budget prepared by our applicant. Industry experts consider the numbers in Figure 8.1 below to be an average budget for a working-class American family. In this example, the advertised rental rate is $2,400. Figure 8.1, on the left side, shows the family budget based on the stated rental rate. It reveals that 41% of the total income is dedicated to housing, creating a financial burden because it exceeds the 30% income-to-housing-cost rule. The Johnsons anticipated that the budget would be tight. Still, they believed they could manage it, a belief that many can understand.

Figure 8.1: Family Budgets Influenced by Stated vs. Effective Rates of Rent

Annual Income	$70,000	Example 1	Stated Rate of Rent		Example 2	Effective Rate of Rent
	Monthly Expenses	Annual Expenses	Percent of Income	Monthly Expenses	Annual Expenses	Percent of Income
Housing	$2,400	$28,800	41%	$2,890	$34,680	50%
Transportation	438	5,250	8%	438	5,250	8%
Food	770	9,240	13%	770	9,240	13%
Utility Bills	301	3,612	5%	301	3,612	5%
Phone	105	1,260	2 %	105	1,260	2%
Child Care	245	2,940	4 %	245	2,940	4%
Ongoing Education	66	788	1%	66	788	1%
Clothing	109	1,313	2%	109	1,313	2%
Health Insurance	700	8,400	12%	700	8,400	12%
Other Insurance	153	1,838	3%	153	1,838	3%
Student Loans	306	3,675	5%	306	3,675	5%
Health & Fitness	58	696	1%	58	696	1%
Term Debts	250	3,000	4%	250	3,000	4%
Totals	$5,901	$70,800	101%	$6,391	$76,691	110%

However, Figure 8.1 on the right side, which reflects the actual cost of the rent based on management's Economic Occupancy Pricing Strategy, shows that the landlords will collect an additional $490 per month over the advertised rate, bringing the total rent to $2,890. In short, after selecting a property unit, tenants are presented with a stated rate, such as the $2,400 in Figure 8.1.

However, the rental contract, when offered for review, may not immediately reveal the numerous hidden costs. Property managers are skilled at locking tenants into contracts, often without the tenant fully understanding the potential fees and charges associated with them. During the fee discussion, costs such as parking fees, pet fees, early termination fees, annual renewal fees, account fees, and many other undisclosed fees are skillfully brushed over or hidden.

If a tenant objects to these add-on fees, the sales manager is trained to overcome the objections and close the deal. For instance, if a tenant questions parking fees, the manager may respond in a demeaning manner, focusing on the tenant's lack of education, as Hunter experienced in front of Carol. The second part, or the extra $490, will be discussed in detail in Chapter 9. This chapter explores how the technology was used to determine the advertised rental rate of $2,400.

Step 2 of The Pricing Process: Data Processing, Benchmarking, and Forecasting that Results in Balancing Housing Supply with Consumer Demand. Then, the system uses the common data and technology to set the rental prices.

In addition to the pricing algorithm's four-step pricing process, Step 2 of that process also uses four parts to artificially manufacture rental rates. Understanding each of the four parts is crucial to grasping how the technology, rather than the individual landlord, determines rental rates. In this section of the chapter, we will begin with a brief summary of the four parts, followed by a thorough review of the components of Step 2.

The Theory of Profit Optimization versus Revenue Generation

The technology is designed to maximize profits rather than increase revenue at each part. Understanding the distinction between profit maximization and revenue generation is crucial. Revenue generation focuses on increasing revenue or cash flow regardless of whether or not the practice is profitable. For instance, borrowing money can generate cash flow or revenue, but it doesn't generate profit. Conversely, profit optimization aims to increase profits by renting fewer units at significantly higher prices while adding substantial amounts of junk fees. In short, profit optimization doesn't focus on increasing cash flow by raising occupancy at lower rates; it focuses on maximizing the profit generated by each unit, regardless of whether or not it's occupied. We will now focus on the four parts of the rental rate manufacturing process.

Summary of Step 2 and Its Four Parts

- Part I - How the Pricing Algorithm Maximizes Profits. This section explains how the pricing algorithm, a powerful tool in landlords' hands, maximizes profits through a three-part revenue-generation process.
- Part II: How the Revenue Management Pricing Algorithm Adjusts and Manipulates Market Variables to Maximize Profits. Individual landlords wield a significant amount of control over their pricing strategies. The system empowers them by providing a series of steps in which each landlord selects from a menu of variables that enable them to manipulate the market.
- Part III. Data processing, benchmarking, and forecasting that result in balancing housing supply with consumer demand. This phase of the pricing process comprises three distinct steps. The first step encompasses data processing and benchmarking. In contrast, the second involves forecasting the supply of rental units in relation to projected consumer demand. In the third step, the goal is to balance the housing supply with consumer demand.

- Part IV. How the Pricing Algorithm Sets the Rates of Rent. Once the technology has balanced the market, the next step is to set the rental rates. In this step, the technology, rather than the individual landlords, determines the highest rent rates that will maximize profits. Understanding this process is crucial for tenants, as it directly affects the rates they pay.

Step 2 of The Pricing Process Part I: How the Pricing Algorithm Maximizes Profits Using The Three-Part Revenue Generation Process

Revenue management is a technology system that automates pricing by allowing technology to determine rental rates instead of individual landlords. For instance, before the advent of revenue management technology, landlords determined rental rates by conducting a rental survey, which involved calling their competitors and asking them to disclose their rental rates. This process was very time-consuming and lacked accuracy. The result was that rental rates changed rarely, perhaps only once or twice a year.

With the advent of the internet, employees can now search for comparable properties and their advertised rent rates. Still, these rates may lack details such as additional fees or discounts, making them unreliable. As a result, landlords have recognized that the older pricing method is prone to flaws and errors, leading to the industry losing billions of dollars annually. Today, corporate landlords maximize profits by implementing the pricing algorithm's three-part revenue generation process.

The Three-Part Revenue Generation Process

In addition to the four-step pricing process, in Step 2 Part I, revenue management technology employs a three-part approach to enhance profits. Part one involves artificially inflating rental rates based on market power, as explained in Chapter 5. For example, let's examine the case of Hunter and Carol Johnson, who were initially offered an advertised monthly rental rate of $2,400. How was that rate determined? Where did it originate? More importantly, did the free market system play any role in its establishment?

The second and third parts of revenue generation, which are also Step 3 of the pricing process, are elaborated on in Chapter 9, specifically, Rent Optimization. Once again, this chapter examines how the advertised rental rate of $2,400 was determined.

Step 2 of The Pricing Process: Part II, How the Revenue Management Pricing Algorithm Adjusts and Manipulates Market Variables to Maximize Profits.

Revenue management is a complex process that involves forecasting the supply (housing units) and demand (applicants), managing lease expiration, and considering factors such as seasonality to determine unit pricing. We will now focus on some economic factors that influence rental rates, starting with seasonality.

Seasonality in the Pricing Process

Seasonality refers to periods of time when consumer demand fluctuates. Consider the airline industry and how the sharp increase in demand for flights during the holiday season significantly drives up prices. In the student housing industry, for example, at the beginning of the school year, there is often a surge in prices for college student housing due to high demand among students. Surge pricing occurs when the supply or amount of housing is known and is limited relative to consumer demand. However, the ability to manipulate supply and demand allows landlords to maximize profits.

Nevertheless, the situation is more complex than it appears. The system is aware of the precise number of students seeking housing. It then assesses and prioritizes them based on factors such as income, race, and other sociodemographic criteria, including their willingness to pay the highest rates. At the same time, the system has perfect information about the quantity and types of available housing units. Therefore, the landlords can significantly maximize profits by balancing supply and demand. Then, they can generate more profits by intentionally withholding properties from the market, thereby creating scarcity. The continuation of this process will be expounded upon in greater detail in Part III below.

The Optimum Mix Equation.

Property managers use pricing algorithms to achieve an "Optimum Mix Equation." This formula determines the optimal balance between the highest possible rent price plus ancillary revenues, matched against the lowest possible occupancy, resulting in maximum profits. Ancillary revenues refer to non-rent fees and charges added to the advertised rate to increase the effective rental rate, as discussed in Chapter 9.

Historically, property managers have faced the dilemma of choosing between increasing occupancy or raising rent to maximize profits. For instance, it is common industry knowledge that raising rental rates lowers occupancy. However, the pricing algorithm was designed for this task. It's designed to identify a sweet spot that balances rent growth and occupancy levels, thereby avoiding the negative impact where one of the objectives does not cannibalize the other. This process is effectively and conveniently completed through their Objective.

The Sustained Occupancy Rate Objective (Objective)

It's important to note that price-fixing is not the same as pricing all similar rental units, such as two-bedroom apartments, at the same rate. Instead, the algorithm sets the highest possible rate for each unit based on its economics and location compared to its competition. However, it's actually quite a bit more than this. Today, the rate differential depends on the particular landlord's profit goals. Meaning that a rental rate of $2,400, rather than a possible rate of $2,250, is determined by the profit the landlord demands, typically a sliding scale ranging from 3% to 7% above open-market rent rates.

The landlord's profit objective significantly influences the pricing algorithm, which is designed to maximize profits. The landlord sets their Objective, which serves as the starting point for the pricing process. It informs the algorithm about the intended profit level and the aggressive profit-taking style they desire to employ. The entire process is efficiently automated, functioning much like a thermostat in your home. When you set your home thermostat to seventy-five degrees, the technology adjusts the temperature to maintain optimal comfort levels by distributing either heated air (consider increasing rental rates) or cooled air (consider decreasing occupancy) to reach the desired temperature.

The Objective operates similarly: To increase occupancy, the rate is set high, nearing the maximum 100% mark, such as 96 or 97%. Conversely, the setting is lowered to 89 or 90% when the aim is to increase rents. However, the recommended Objective setting is around 94%, allowing the pricing algorithm—not the individual landlord—to balance supply and demand in the marketplace. More than 90% of all landlords use the 94% setting, allowing the algorithm to manage the pricing process effectively for both individual landlords and the entire rental industry.

Setting the objective may seem straightforward, but there's a catch. It involves strategically manipulating the supply of rental units by removing some of them from the market, while claiming they are "economically occupied." In simpler terms, this means that a tenant with a signed lease may not actually occupy the unit. The study found that a landlord's profitability is directly correlated with the number of units withheld from the market. For landlords to increase profits, more units must remain unoccupied but reported as "economically occupied," a process detailed in Chapter 9. When considering the duration that a unit remains off the market, the technology recommends an extended "hold time" once the unit becomes vacant. Therefore, it's more about the strategic number of days a unit is kept off the market rather than the number of units.

Step 2 of The Pricing Process: Part III, Data Processing, Benchmarking, and Forecasting that Results in Balancing Housing Supply with Consumer Demand

This phase of the pricing process comprises three distinct steps, all of which are completed by technology. The first step involves data processing and benchmarking, where advanced algorithms are used to analyze market data. In contrast, the second step involves forecasting the supply of rental units relative to projected consumer demand, a task that is more accurate when predictive analytics are used. In the third step, the goal is to balance housing supply with consumer demand, a task made possible by sophisticated software. Before delving into these steps, the historical principles of supply and demand will be explored, followed by an analysis of how the economic concepts of elasticity and inelasticity influence the pricing process.

Understanding The Historical Principles of Supply and Demand

Demand is an economic concept that describes consumers' ability and willingness to buy goods and services at a specific price. In the rental industry, the supply of available rental properties is matched with demand to determine rental prices. When there are more homes available than renters, rental prices tend to decrease. Conversely, when there are more renters than homes, rental prices tend to increase.

Understanding Price Elasticity

Elasticity, an economic term, measures how sensitive the quantity demanded of a good is relative to its price. This measurement goes a bit deeper than just people buying more of a good when it gets relatively cheaper and less when it gets relatively more expensive. Elasticity refers to the degree to which demand for a product changes in response to a price change. Some goods, considered luxuries, are very price-sensitive—think high-end jewelry or expensive restaurant food. When these goods get more expensive, people can very easily cut back on their consumption.

On the other hand, in economics, a good is considered inelastic when its demand does not change significantly in response to changes in price. This concept of elasticity depends on meeting two specific criteria. First, there are no reasonable substitutes. Second, the good is a necessity. A classic example of an inelastic good is gasoline. For the most part, at least in the short run, there are no reasonable substitutes. It is also a necessity for most people. Thus, when gasoline prices rise, demand for gas will fall, but only by a small amount. People still need to travel in their daily lives. The converse is also true. When gasoline prices fall, gasoline demand will rise, but only by a small amount. People can only put so much gasoline into their cars. Housing is also considered inelastic—there are no reasonable substitutes, and it's a necessity.

Their pricing algorithms are more than passive players when it comes to elasticity. Just as they use market share and technology powered by massive data resources to manipulate supply and demand, they also manipulate price elasticity. This practice is more difficult for some luxury rental units. Still, for most units within their overview, manipulation of elasticity is a critical element of their overall pricing strategy. We will now turn our attention to the three steps outlined in Part III.

Part III- Step 1: Data Processing and Benchmarking

The pricing process involves utilizing business intelligence (BI), a form of artificial intelligence (AI), to analyze data obtained from

Step 1 in Chapter 6. The process begins with data aggregation, which summarizes a large dataset for high-level analysis and interpretation. Various strategies and methodologies are used to analyze vast amounts of data, transform it into actionable insights, and make the information usable. This process involves compiling data from multiple sources—the seven databases—and organizing it into a simpler, easy-to-understand format.

This process is unique because the three primary Property Management System (PMS) providers all utilize white-labeled technology to complete the benchmarking and forecasting processes; in other words, their technologies operate in the same manner. Therefore, they use the same data and employ the same technologies to analyze it.

Part III- Step 2: Forecasting

After analyzing the data, the company uses its forecasting tools to automatically optimize profits. The heart of their pricing algorithms lies in their ability to forecast based on all available data. Their theory holds that they can maximize profits when supply and demand are in balance. Therefore, they aim to control the number of applicants allowed in the renter pool to equal the number of available rental units, first by prequalifying them and then by prioritizing them. Simply put, if there were 99 available rental units, there should be 100 applicants.

This depth of understanding provides a framework known as supply and demand forecasting, which plots a forward-looking unit supply alignment with prospective demand to allow them to balance the known supply of properties, by adding or removing units, against forecasted demand, thereby balancing the market and maximizing profits.

Part III- Step 3: Balancing Supply (rental units) with Consumer Demand (tenants)

The Platform's claim that it can consistently raise rents in a balanced market is not just a statement; it's a fact. The process arises from their unique pricing algorithm program, "Continuous Optimization Through Connected Intelligence." This program allows it to manipulate supply and demand by controlling consumers' reactions to price changes for rental units, thereby demonstrating its significant influence on the market.

How The Technology Balances Housing Supply

The process begins by determining the total housing inventory by gathering information from Database Six, which lists all available sources. But it's more than this. For instance, in the construction pipeline for their new inventory, they use satellite imagery to more accurately predict when those units will be ready to hit the market. This knowledge gives them an accurate picture of the total available supply. In short, the technology has a near-perfect picture of the available supply of housing units, right down to a unit's views.

To better understand their practices, we turn to a 2018 DOJ court case that settled an algorithmic price-fixing claim against the airline industry. The DOJ suit alleges that the airline defendants illegally signaled to each other how quickly they would add or remove new flights, routes, and extra seats. In short, they increase profits by controlling the supply of flights and seats, ensuring there is never an oversupply. In short, the technology creates the appearance of a shortage of seats.

Our research has concluded that landlords hold rental units off-market by extending a unit's "hold time" once it becomes vacant, using a process similar to that used by the airline industry. The algorithm signals the predetermined extended hold period to the participating landlords and is integral to balancing the supply.

This practice is widespread. Nationally, on any given day, the platform withholds what amounts to hundreds of thousands of rental units from the market, up to or exceeding half a million units. Additionally, locally, the Seattle Concentration Study, Chapter 5, concluded that what the Platform did during the 2013–2014 period was to take an already bad housing market situation (low vacancy and high demand) and create massive amounts of profit by making the housing situation worse still by withholding over 9,000 units from the market—even though a severe housing shortage existed. This practice artificially drove rental rates up by over 40%.

How The Technology Balances Consumer Demand

By leveraging its relationships with Experian and other data providers, the Platform maintains some control over the number of tenants allowed in the "qualified" applicant rental pool at any given time. In other words, their forecasting tools determine whether they increase or decrease the renter pool by adjusting their scoring models to match the numbers and types of available rental units.

This part of the process is made possible by the pricing algorithm's direct integration into the landlord's databases, which provides access to that real-time data. Thus, it begins with their leasing platform's internal data, where guest card information attributed to the LRO methodology is stored in Database One, along with the twenty million active lease records of RealPage. Then, from Database Four, the lease transaction data covers the forty million lease outcome records, providing a historical record of those tenants. However, it goes much deeper than this. Then, the leasing platform technology adds external data, such as real-time consumer credit, demographic, and sociographic data.

Then, they incorporate that data with their technologies and software programs, improving the accuracy of models used to calculate the depth of demand by price point. Once the system has verified the amount of money the tenants are able and willing to pay, the applicants who don't fit their supply availability are eliminated from the "qualified" renter pool, which is accomplished by simply adjusting the scoring model.

The process of removing tenants who don't fit their model produces what is called "qualified demand." Qualified demand is the set of applicants and tenants with whom the pricing algorithm will rent properties. The tenants who are left out of the qualified pool and priced out of housing are discussed in Chapter 10.

In this step, the Technology Balances Supply and Demand

The system will then balance housing supply with qualified consumer demand to ensure the correct rental units are available. However, we point out that this manipulative process can only be carried out by accessing and sharing massive amounts of data on their applicants, tenants, and properties. This process enables the technology to know precisely how many people are searching for housing, the size and type of housing they are seeking, how long they plan to stay, and the amount they are able and willing to pay.

Additionally, balancing the market can only occur when the variable, housing supply, is known and controllable, which they have apparently accomplished because rental units that are in excess of the newly developed qualified renter pool are held off the market.

Think of it this way: Accessing and sharing data on applicants, tenants, and properties provides their users with an enormous advantage, with the same effects as "insider trading"—an illegal practice on Wall Street where people involved in a pending transaction use inside knowledge before the general public to purchase stock in that transaction. This inside knowledge enables the technology to manipulate supply, as it knows the qualified number of applicants seeking specific housing types. This knowledge allows the Platform ample time to withhold or to add particular rental units to the market to match qualified demand—it's a balancing initiative that's constantly in flux—between qualified demand and housing supply.

Figure 8.2: The Pricing Algorithm is Designed to Balance Supply with Demand

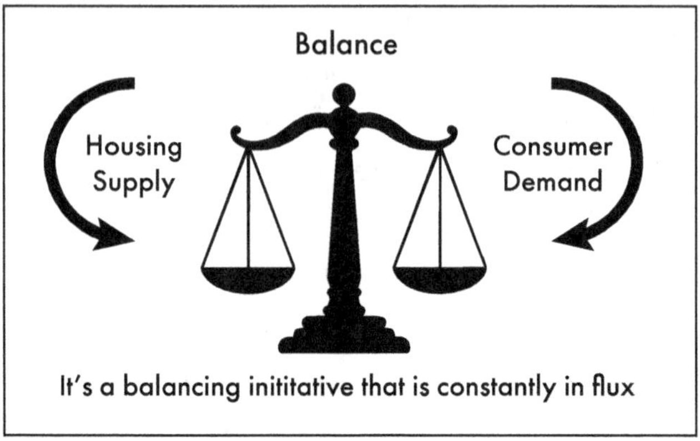

In short, maintaining a balance between the available rental units and the number of qualified prospective applicants means that more of those "pre-qualified" applicants—those able and willing to pay the most for their services—will view property listings, even if the stated rent rates are higher than they would typically want to pay. In our example, the Johnsons wanted to keep their rent under $1,750, but upon researching the market, they realized that their rent would be significantly higher.

How Technology Manipulates Demand to Maximize Profits

In short, when applicants begin searching for an apartment, they can see that most similar units are similarly priced. In the end, the applicants resign themselves to the higher rental rates. Thus, to a certain degree, the algorithm has manipulated elasticity or the reaction of the change in price to demand for rental units, i.e., increasing the rate and its acceptance. In this case, the applicant viewed the proposed rental rates and accepted them as market rates, based on normal historical supply and demand principles, which highlights the platform's successful manipulation of demand.

Further, to achieve the technology's goal of balancing the market. The algorithm was created to operate on a principle similar to that in the childhood game "Musical Chairs." In this game, players walk around a row of chairs while music plays. When the music stops, the players try to sit down in a chair. However, the number of chairs is always at least one less than the number of players. The player who does not find a chair when the music stops is eliminated from the game—or, in this instance, housing.

Additionally, revenue management creates a competitive environment in which tenants compete for available housing. This practice leaves tenants feeling fortunate when they find suitable accommodation, even if it creates a financial burden. In our example, Johnson's income-to-rent level increased to 41%, creating a financial burden.

Step 2 of The Pricing Process: Part IV, How the Pricing Algorithm Sets the Rates of Rent

Once the technology has balanced the market, the next step is to set rental rates. However, the rent-setting process may differ from what you might typically expect. In fact, it's based on the highest-income earners in a given region, i.e., a ZIP code—the information in each of these steps is broken down by area or sub-market, such as a ZIP code. The algorithm relies heavily on Experian and Finicity for this information. These data sources provide detailed financial information about individuals, including income levels, which is crucial for identifying the highest-income earners in a sub-market.

So, what does this mean for Hunter and Carol Johnson? To better understand the process of setting the rental rates, we refer to a study focusing on new households and their income levels in the Seattle metropolitan area. Between 2006 and 2016, 60% of new households had an annual income of $125,000 or higher, while 18% earned $50,000 or less. The remaining 22% earned between $50,000 and $125,000. In short, the initial price-setting process aims to establish a baseline by focusing on a 30% rent-to-income ratio for the highest-income earners, specifically those earning more than

$125,000 per year. From this starting point, they will push the rental rates accordingly.

According to the Rainmaker Group, the technology, once implemented in an area and having obtained market power, is designed to create an initial push in rates. Consider Chapter 5, where the Platform's rates increased by over 40% between 2013 and 2014. That initial push is based on the highest income earners in a sub-market.

As a result, the Platform will increase rents as much as possible. Still, it will be constrained by the 30% income ratio of the 60% group, the region's highest income earners, who are able and willing to accept the new rent price. Then, if they need more applicants, they repeat the process with the remaining 22% group, which includes the Johnsons, as well as those making less than $125,000 but more than $50,000. In Johnson's case, the highest-income earners in this region, outside Reno, earned $96,000, resulting in a rental rate of $2,400. Thus, Johnson's income of $70,000 pushed them to a 41% rent-to-income ratio, creating a rent burden.

Nevertheless, the entire pricing process is made possible due to the Platform and its members' overly close relationship with third-party data providers like Experian and Finicity. In short, the only real constraint to increasing rental prices appears to lie in the tenant's ability (or lack thereof) and willingness to make the rental payment increase. The knowledge of this constraint, combined with all that tenant data, and combined with the algorithm's primary directive of maximizing profits, sheds light on the immense value of the relationship and the co-interdependency for success among its member landlords, the Platform, Experian, and the other data providers.

See Chapter 9 for Step 3 of the Pricing Process: Rent Optimization

Step 4 of the Pricing Process: The Rental Rate Recommendation

In the fourth step of the pricing process, known as the Rental Rate Recommendation, the Platform and each PMS provider within the cartel employ a sophisticated recommendation process, heavily reliant on advanced technology, to set the rental rate. For instance, the pricing algorithm claims that once it balances the market, it can calculate the right price at the right time for every unit in the portfolio. The final step of the process involves generating recommendations that optimize profit rather than revenue.

Today, the responsibility for setting rental rates depends on who provides the recommendations: The property operator or the pricing technology. Property operators must decide whether to create their own rental surveys, perform their own applicant screenings, or rely on technology to handle these processes conveniently and efficiently. This approach contrasts with historical methods of setting rents, where landlords relied on trial and error and their own judgment to determine rates.

To better understand the price-setting process, the technology calculates each unit type's rent performance daily relative to its competitive peer group in the submarket. However, it will not set rents lower than the minimum historical position. Thus, once a price floor has been set, the system simply won't recommend price decreases. In the final step in the process, the database is updated each night, providing property managers with a matrix of rent recommendations for new leases and renewals for up to 95% of all apartment units.

The rate-setting process allows property operators to accept or reject recommendations. However, a key question we sought to answer was: Whether or not they could reject those recommendations.

The answer is not likely. Property management contracts are incentive-based, meaning that the compensation of property operators is directly tied to their profits, creating a significant conflict of interest.

The Concentration Study, detailed in Chapter 5, provides examples of how the Platform artificially inflates rents, providing context to the property managers' conflict of interest. One example detailed in the Concentration Study was a 226-unit property that generated an additional $1.98 million in profits, resulting in a baseline bonus of approximately $59,000 (a 3% management fee) for the property manager. The typical property manager oversees around 200 properties, meaning that by simply accepting those pricing recommendations, the manager earns an additional bonus of about $12 million each year. The likelihood of an operator walking away from that much wealth is very low in a risk-versus-reward scenario. Over 90% of the landlords accept the rental rate recommendation.

Rent Syndication

The Rainmaker Group developed Rent Syndication Technologies, which automate the publication of rental rates across multiple Internet Listing Services (ILSs). This tool ensures that prospective renters see the most current pricing, saving staff valuable time by eliminating the need for manual updates. Consider the various sources of online rental rates. For example, when applicants search for an apartment, they can explore multiple sources for this information. They might check sites like Zillow, Redfin, or Apartments.com, which display the same information and rates. The results are not a coincidence. This white-labeled technology, developed by the Rainmaker Group, establishes and disseminates rates across the entire industry. To maximize profits, it first optimizes those rates before publishing them. In other words, it is powerful evidence that RealPage, as the price leader and now the owner of the technology, sets the rental rates for the entire rental market.

Conclusion

In conclusion, the technology recommended a rental rate of $2,400 to the landlord for the Johnsons. The landlord accepted the algorithm's recommendation, and the Johnsons had to pay the artificially inflated rate. Theoretically, the overall free market plays a minimal role in determining rental rates. Just how prevalent is the pricing recommendation process nationally? To answer this question, we turn to the Rainmaker Group. When RealPage acquired it in 2017, it was one of the world's largest providers of revenue management, spanning multiple sectors and issuing over a billion pricing recommendations daily.

Figure 8.3: The Revenue Management Technology is designed to maximize profits for the Landlords.

The Fix:

Step 1: Members of the rental housing cartel must be held accountable under the Sherman Antitrust Act (Chapter 5).

Heavy fines must be imposed to deter the violation of the Act. Any entity found to have violated the Act after being warned must be held accountable. The entity and its owners must be banned from the industry or renting any property for at least five years.

Step 2: Prohibit intentionally holding rental units off the market.

Laws must be enacted to prohibit the practice of holding rental units off the market. Heavy fines and taxes should be assessed in an amount sufficient to deter the practice.

Step 3: The processes creating qualified applicants should be prohibited by law.

CHAPTER 9

How Landlords Use the Economic Occupancy Pricing Strategy to Increase Profits

Key Concepts:

The Difference Between Physical Occupancy and Economic Occupancy

Historically, landlords relied on physical occupancy to assess and report their occupancy and vacancy rates. However, the new AI-powered pricing algorithms are no longer constrained by the past. Instead, they now utilize the economic occupancy method. But what's the difference?

Physical Occupancy refers to the percentage of units tenants currently occupy with a signed lease agreement. It is calculated by dividing the number of rented units by the total number of units and multiplying by 100. For example, if there are 100 units in a building and five units are vacant, then the physical occupancy rate would be 95%, and the vacancy rate would be 5%.

Conversely, Economic Occupancy is the Gross Potential Rent (GPR), which includes ancillary revenues, a ratio of what a property could earn if it were fully occupied at the going "market rent" versus the actual amount collected. For instance, if a property's gross potential rental income for a given month is $100,000, but only $92,000 is collected, it is 92% occupied, resulting in an 8% economic vacancy rate.

In other words, physical occupancy is calculated based on occupied units, whereas economic occupancy is calculated based on revenue-generated calculations; however, a tenant with a signed lease may or may not be occupying the unit. Today, all revenue management technologies utilize the economic occupancy methodology in their pricing strategies.

This methodology has completely transformed the industry. Take the multifamily data reporting industry, for example. When data reporters release their market reports, do they disclose their methods and inform their readers of any changes? For instance, is the vacancy rate 5%, or is it actually 8%? After all, when using this methodology, the sum of one plus one may or may not always be two.

Introduction

Historical Perspective—The Truth in Lending Act (TILA) and the Stated or Advertised Rate of Rent versus the Actual or Effective Rate of Rent

The rental housing industry's Economic Occupancy Pricing Strategy, often touted as a novel concept, has deep roots in the banking industry, dating back to the Roman Empire. For instance, the 1960s saw a heated debate over the banking industry's stated versus effective interest rates. Lenders would typically advertise a stated interest rate for a loan program. However, the actual or effective interest rate was often significantly higher than the advertised rate. For example, if a bank offered a $1,000 loan at 5% interest rate, the customer would pay $50 in interest during the first year. However, if the bank charged a $250 loan fee, the effective interest rate would be 30% instead of 5%, leading to $300 in interest and charges in the first year, rather than just $50.

At its heart are the abusive processes used to increase the actual or effective rate of return over the stated or advertised rate. For instance, banks would pay large incentives to their bankers to sell those loan products; however, the incentive amount was directly tied to the *yield spread* or the increase between the advertised and effective rate of return. Yield spread is the difference between an advertised rate and the effective rate that is actually paid. Understanding yield spread is essential for assessing the actual cost of renting or determining the true cost of a product or service.

For instance, if a bank aimed to achieve a 5% return on its investment, it would advertise that 5% rate and loan product. Subsequently, their management would motivate themselves and their bankers to sell that loan product by incorporating various fees and charges, resulting in an effective rate of, let's say, 11%. The bonuses paid to management and bankers were tied to that 6% margin over the advertised 5% rate. This practice resulted in widespread fraud and abuse.

Before 1968, consumers were faced with a complex range of credit terms and interest rates. It was challenging to compare loans because they were rarely presented in the same format, and lenders made great efforts to conceal the actual cost from consumers. In 1968, Congress outlawed this practice through the Truth in Lending Act (TILA).

The legal battles concluded that lenders failed to adequately disclose fees, charges, and actual costs, with parallels to today's property managers who use similar tactics. However, until now, the pricing strategy lacked the AI-driven power to adequately harness its ancillary-generating potential—today, it's designed to increase the effective rental rate spread over the advertised rate by more than 35%.

Step 3 of the Pricing Process: Yield or Rent Optimization

Once a landlord has signed a lease agreement with a tenant, the next step is to maximize the revenue earned from that lease. However, specific additional steps are needed to do so. In this chapter, we'll build on our discussion from Chapter 8 about how landlords determine their rental rates. We'll focus on the third step in their rent-setting process: Rent Optimization.

This step uses the Economic Occupancy Pricing Strategy to increase the actual rate of return above the advertised rate. The Johnson Family from Chapter 8 provides a clear example of being advertised a rental rate of $2,400 but ending up with housing costs of $2,890, as shown in Figure 9.1, leading to severe rent burdening. The process of increasing rents was intentionally designed.

Figure 9.1: Combined Effective Cost of Rent and Yield Spread

Beginning Rent - Stated Basis	*$2,400*
Added Fees and Charges	
Parking Fees	$225
Pet Rent	$75
Appliances-Washer/Dryer	$85
CAM-Utility Billing Charges	$75
Renters Insurance	$30
Sub-Total Ancillary Charges	$490
Effective or Actual Cost of Rent	$2,890
The Yield Spread	*20%*

Revenue Management Requires the Landlord to Set an Asset-Specific Strategy

Several studies have discovered that landlords who own properties in neighborhoods undergoing gentrification tend to increase rents or remodel the property to provoke evictions. They may also clear their buildings through no-cause evictions to charge higher rents. This strategy is not accidental; it starts with the property itself. Revenue management emphasizes the need for property managers to adopt an asset-specific strategy for each property. Maximizing profits, however, may involve various approaches, as the technology system offers custom engineering to ensure that each property is managed to optimize its profitability.

Additionally, each property has unique laws and regulations. Database Seven can help maximize profits by finding ways to work around them. But it's actually quite a bit more than this. This technology not only provides the information needed to circumvent the law but also informs the landlord about the likelihood of local governmental entities enforcing it. In other words, the technology allows a landlord to assess whether choosing to circumvent a law is likely to expose them to any legal repercussions.

Think about how you file your taxes with a service like TurboTax. As you fill out the return, you can review the risk assessment of certain expenses against the chance of an IRS audit. The pricing technology works similarly. After all, for several years, the Rainmaker Group used TurboTax's (Intuit Inc.) technology platform to develop its pricing software and related technologies.

A few examples will be used to better explain the process of setting an asset-specific strategy. For instance, in Utah, doing nothing to maximize profits might mean including language in the lease document that limits or waives any liability to the property owner—Liability Waivers. In one such case, an arsonist started a fire at an apartment complex in Ogden, Utah. As a result of the fire, tenants suffered property damage and personal injuries.

The property manager based their perceived lack of liability for the fire damage on the Liability Waivers included in the lease agreement. However, according to the court case, the property manager failed to ensure that apartment units had functioning fire detectors and alarms and could not provide adequate access to firefighters.

On appeal, the court ruled that, due to gross negligence, the liability waivers in the lease were unenforceable. Additionally, we have also seen builders force customers into restrictive arbitration and non-disclosure agreements in the construction industry, forbidding them from publicly discussing their cases or repairs.

Another example could involve choosing a leasing strategy to maximize profits, which might mean doing nothing and allowing the property to fall into disrepair. Undoubtedly, the most egregious example of doing nothing and letting the properties fall into disrepair is military housing or lower-end properties in military housing.

In 2001, President George W. Bush implemented the failed Hoover Private-Public Partnership with the Department of Defense (DOD) and created the Military Housing Privatization Initiative (MHPI). In short, Bush turned Military Housing over to the members of the rental housing cartel.

A 2018 *Reuters* report, based on interviews with more than 100 families, concluded that the DOD is as secretive about privatized military housing as it is about its accounting for sensitive weapons systems. Fifteen private management companies partner with the Armed Forces to manage some 200,000 on-base housing units. Yet two decades after the military's housing privatization program began, the Pentagon says it hasn't calculated how much money these property managers receive each year, in the form of government-subsidized rent payments for military families.

However, the *Reuters* study estimated that the privately controlled housing ventures on U.S. bases would receive an estimated $3.9 billion annually in DOD rent stipends, known as Basic Allowance for Housing. Yet, their report found that U.S. Marine families battle rats, mold, and powerful corporate landlords. Worse yet, when military families face vermin and other home health hazards, they have few weapons to fight back. A primary reason is the granting of vast powers to landlords through military contracts on U.S. bases.

Military families are suffering from illnesses with lifelong implications due to poor housing conditions. Despite filing reports and requesting remediation, their pleas are often denied or ignored. Shockingly, housing company representatives and, at times, military command allegedly collaborate to suppress their complaints. Many families fear retribution or negative impacts on their service members' military careers. This dire situation leaves families with little or no recourse. They are unable to withhold rent for poor conditions, mismanagement, or noncompliance with lease terms. The studies have revealed a crisis in Military Housing.[1] Yet, property management companies continue to profit from billions of U.S. tax dollars, providing minimal benefits in return.

The Three-Part Revenue Generation Process: Continued from Chapter 8

Property managers prioritize fee collection because it results in additional management fees. For instance, landlords can charge tenants excessive fees in states like Minnesota due to a lack of a clear definition of "reasonable" written into the law.

After establishing the leasing strategy, the focus shifts toward increasing income or the yield spread. This strategy is achieved through three essential parts. The first part involves artificially inflating rental rates based on the alleged cartel and price-fixing discussed in Chapters 5 and 8. In the case of the Johnsons, it's the $2,400 rental rate. The second part involves the practice of charging excessive amounts of junk fees to artificially inflate the actual rent rate. The third part involves transferring many operating costs directly to tenants, thereby increasing the landlord's yield spread and the tenants' rents.

Part Two of the Revenue Generation Process: Increase Revenue

In the second part, the technology increases income through aggressive revenue management, which is designed to "mine" the lease contract. This step in the pricing process focuses on generating a massive amount of ancillary revenue in the form of junk fees. The lease was developed as a fee trap, with hundreds of points where they can artificially increase revenue. For example, pet rent, utility billing, late fees, overdraft fees, early termination fees, trash removal, pest control, and application fees are a few of the hundreds of points where the system can boost ancillary revenue. We will now focus on some of the more common, larger-dollar programs the landlords have employed to increase the yield spread.

Parking Fees and Costs

Parking has become a big-ticket item for property owners, as parking in most metro areas remains in short supply. A 2013 study conducted in Seattle found that the average monthly parking fees totaled over $225. For instance, in the case of the Johnsons, they were charged an additional $225 per month, as shown in Figure 9.1.

Pet Rent and Fees

Pet fees and deposits vary but typically range from $200 to $500 per pet. Landlords may also charge a monthly pet rent of $25 to $100, typically equivalent to 1% to 3% of the monthly rent amount. In the case of the Johnsons, they were charged an additional $75 per month, as shown in Figure 9.1.

The "Opportunity" to Collect Non-Rent Fees—A Case Study in New York City

Revenue management can have significant adverse effects, particularly when it circumvents rent control laws. In parts of New York City, for instance, landlords in low-income neighborhoods have employed various strategies to evict rent-stabilized tenants from their homes, despite legal protections. The rent control laws also prohibit adding junk fees to the rent. Therefore, the technology established a new category of expenses called non-rent charges to avoid those regulations. These fees may cover costs for amenities such as air conditioning, washing machines, dryers, and dishwashers, as well as legal and damage fees. Building improvements, which include items such as improving the parking lot, are included in some cases.

The prevalence of these fees, primarily designed to circumvent rent control, underscores the urgent need for heightened regulation and oversight by state agencies. A recent study in one of New York City's most impoverished communities revealed that 81% of tenants had been charged non-rent fees, averaging $671.13 on their most recent rent bill.[2] For instance, in the case of the Johnsons, they were charged an additional $85 per month per Figure 9.1.

How they Increase Profits through the process of financing their Properties

Driving the yield spread higher using aggressive methods is more than just charging fees. Some of those hundreds of points are incredibly complex. For instance, one of the more lucrative ancillary revenue sources is circumventing taxpayer-subsidized rental units for citizens who qualify for low-income housing. When landlords hold rental units from the market in their balancing scheme, the question becomes, which ones should be left empty?

To answer the question, we will focus on how metropolitan areas have turned to HUD-sponsored programs to create affordable housing. For example, cities like Seattle entice contractors by providing special financing terms under HUD's Multifamily Tax Exemption Program (MFTE). In this program, taxpayers—not property owners—guarantee the property debt. In other words, if the apartment complex does not perform well and falls into foreclosure, it is the taxpayers who bear the loss on their loans. Additionally, the program aims to incentivize builders and property owners to construct apartment units in areas struggling to acquire affordable housing by waiving most of the property's taxes.

Tax-shifting

However, these taxes are not discretionary; they fund essential city services, including police, schools, firefighters, and infrastructure. In short, the city waives most of the property taxes and passes them on to other taxpayers who are already paying more than their fair share. The process is known as "tax-shifting." Tax-shifting occurs when the city waives the collection of tax revenues on certain properties. However, the city still needs to collect those tax dollars; therefore, it raises property taxes on other properties. In short, if a city needs to collect \$100 in taxes, it will collect \$100 from someone.

Rent-Restricted Units for Low-Income Families

In exchange, the owners must set aside 20% of their rental units and accept discounted rental rates based on tenant eligibility requirements (a 30% rent-to-income ratio), thereby creating taxpayer-funded rent-restricted units. For an excellent example of this program, we turn to Metro Seattle, which has provided tax exemptions for over a billion dollars in new apartment construction annually since 2015, resulting in the waiver of over \$137 million in annual taxes.

In 2019, the state of Washington completed an audit to assess the program's effectiveness. The audit revealed a staggering injustice—over a quarter of the rent-restricted units were overcharged for rent. Even more egregious, many rent-restricted units have been illegally used for vacation rentals, allowing landlords to charge significantly higher rates. The investigation also revealed that landlords had kept many of those rent-restricted units off the market for extended periods of time as part of the platforms' economic balancing scheme.

The audit findings are significant because many rental units intended for the less advantaged and unhoused—those who need affordable housing the most—are not being used for that purpose. The result is that these companies are increasing their profits by utilizing the MFTE program while providing minimal benefit in exchange for the cities' $137 million annual investment in affordable housing.

Conclusion: How they Increase Profits through the process of financing their Properties:

So, we ask the question, why don't these financing programs work as intended? In short, the same national conglomerates that manage the rental units are vertically integrated within their organizational structures, meaning they are also the nation's largest builders. For example, as previously discussed, Greystar is the nation's largest apartment developer, builder, and property manager. This vertical operating structure enables the Platform to maximize profits through a scheme where the builder (Greystar) contracts with the city (Seattle or New York City) first to waive its property taxes on the property. Second, Greystar, now in the role of the property manager, violates the MFTE agreement by renting only a few of those units to qualified low-income tenants.

This violation occurred because Metro Seattle, in breach of the MFTE rules, failed to verify the data provided by landlords on the MFTE program. Database Seven was aware of this breach and recommended cheating the MFTE program to maximize profits. In other words, the technology recommended violating the MFTE program because the city of Seattle was not likely to enforce the policies.

Early Termination Fees and the Landlord's Duty to Re-rent the Rental Unit

Imagine a tenant undergoing a significant life change, such as embarking on a new job in a different city, experiencing family separation due to a death or a divorce, purchasing a new home, or facing financial challenges. The COVID-19 pandemic was a stark reminder of this example. Terminating the lease contract early can result in a much higher financial burden than expected. For instance, ending the lease one day early can lead to fees totaling tens of thousands of dollars.

Aggressive Leasing Tactics

Property managers employ aggressive tactics during the leasing process to ensure tenants remain bound by the contract. They accomplish this by imposing high early termination fees, such as the typical fee of over $7,000, regardless of whether it's day one or day 364. This fee traps tenants in the lease agreement, even when they can no longer afford it, and forces them to pay the hefty fee or risk becoming homeless.

This practice also makes it nearly impossible to purchase a home. The single-family housing market, discussed in more detail in Chapter 13, is experiencing a shortage of affordable housing. Finding a home is very difficult. However, finding a home and correlating the purchase date with the lease's end date is nearly impossible. The result binds the tenant to that rental unit at significantly higher rates and for a more extended period than the tenant may have desired. In essence, revenue management fosters a society of renters, directly opposing the New Deal's goals of achieving the American Dream, which is centered on homeownership.

Meet Jane and John, along with their two toddlers.

Let's meet Jane and John, a couple living in Olympia, Washington, with their two toddlers. They rent a two-bedroom apartment, and their story begins on what appears to be an ordinary day. However, this day would soon turn their lives upside down. On this seemingly ordinary day, John never made it to work. But how could one auto accident on one ordinary day produce so many unintended consequences?

Jane, a stay-at-home mom, now has to deal with her corporate landlord. Our research found that in Olympia, like most metro areas across America, over 82% of all rental units are managed by national conglomerates whose only agenda is to maximize profits for their Wall Street investors. Jane's problem is that they signed a two-year lease at $3,200 per month two months ago. She is now liable for the remaining twenty-two months' rent, which exceeds $70,000. Here is what Jane will face from her corporate landlord. All the while, her life is in shambles, and she can no longer afford her rent. This personal story illustrates the significant impact of revenue management on tenants, such as Jane and her now-deceased husband, John.

In Washington State (most states have similar laws), under the Landlord-Tenant Act, the landlord must make a reasonable effort to re-rent the units rather than charge tenants the remaining rent due under the lease. If the landlord re-rents the property quickly, the tenants would only be responsible for the time the unit was vacant. Therefore, the question becomes, what is a **reasonable** effort?

Point 1) What is reasonable? The landlord's use of economic occupancy, a program that intentionally holds property off the market to maintain high rental rates, violates the Washington Landlord-Tenant Act. This conflict between the Act and the economic occupancy strategy is clear, and the use of this program suggests that landlords are not making reasonable efforts to rent their properties. As a result, Jane remains responsible for the hefty sum of $70,000.

But is the practice illegal? To better understand the term "reasonable," we again turn to the State of Minnesota, where rental tenants sought to establish a class-action lawsuit over massive abusive fees. In this court case, the judge ruled that the law did not specify the definition of **"reasonable."** Therefore, the judge ruled that the law does not prohibit a landlord from charging tenants fees and does not require those fees to be equitable. This ruling sets a precedent for similar cases in other states, potentially allowing landlords to continue imposing high fees on tenants without legal repercussions.

Point 2) How Landlords Circumvent—"Reasonable." Most lease contracts today prohibit the subleasing or re-leasing of the rental unit. Therefore, to lock renters into the agreement, the new lease contains an overly high early termination fee, usually two or more months' rent; in Jane's case, it is $9,600. There is also a fee of over $2,000 for drawing up the new lease documents.

Additionally, suppose Jane isn't careful about following all the rules hidden within the lease contract. In that case, she might be required to pay for all remaining months of the contract. Hence, at the very least, Jane would still have to spend nearly $11,600 to terminate the lease agreement, even though there is a waiting list to fill the rental unit, and the landlord will not miss a month's rent. With the early termination fees, landlords use the Act against tenants who become locked into higher rents and for extended periods.

One of Jane's primary problems is that landlords have been left to self-regulate. Additionally, the use of AI-powered revenue management technology remains variably unchallenged or unregulated by any governing body. In the end, the landlord will collect the maximum allowed by the contract, regardless of any implied agreement under the Washington Landlord-Tenant Act—it's designed to circumvent the intent of the law.

Part Three of the Revenue Generation Process—Decrease Expenses

We will now focus on the third part of revenue generation. In this process, expenses are reduced through operational efficiencies, and others are charged directly to the tenants. Previously, owners were responsible for covering the maintenance costs of their properties and the expenses for any vacant units, which were factored into the rent. These costs are commonly referred to as Common Area Maintenance (CAM) and cover the charges the landlord incurs for property maintenance, repairs, operations, management, and insurance.

Rather than lumping all costs together under one transparent, stated rental rate today, landlords break this down into other fees to bait and switch renters. This practice parallels the advertised and effective interest rates that bankers used. It's not that the landlord shouldn't include maintenance costs in the rent. It's that they are separating these out on purpose to be sneaky about higher rates. We will now focus on some of the more common programs the landlords have employed to transfer their operating expenses to the tenants.

Utility Billing

The Utility Billing industry has expanded significantly in recent years to become nearly a $10 billion industry. But what exactly is this quickly growing industry? A Ratio Utility Billing System (RUBS) is a process used by landlords to determine a tenant's utility consumption based on factors such as square footage, number of bedrooms, and/or the number of occupants. They can operate this program because most apartments receive one bill for services, and property managers are the only parties involved in distribution.

How the Program Works

The process is relatively straightforward. The property owner sells the utility meters and utility distribution system within an apartment complex to a holding company, typically comprised of the same property owners. The holding company then purchases electricity, water, or both from utilities and resells them to tenants at a price markup of up to 40% over the actual costs. In other words, what would typically be a $200 utility bill for a tenant becomes $275. For instance, in the case of the Johnsons, they were charged an additional $75 per month, as shown in Figure 9.1.

The question arises: Is this even legal? Once again, under the law, it becomes a matter of reasonableness. Buried deep in the many pages of the lease document, the landlords charge the inflated utility billing based on recommendations from Database Seven. Where do the managers get the authority to charge these fees? Simply put, the algorithm adds this one sentence to the lease document: *"Resident may be paying for part of the utility usage in common areas or in other residential units as well as administrative fees."* Once the tenant signs the lease, they become responsible for thousands of dollars in charges, regardless of whether or not they are aware of the terms.

Renters Insurance

Another example of shifting operating expenses to the tenant is through liability insurance, also known as renters' insurance; however, before RealPage, this wasn't the case. This practice was a program they developed to increase the effective rental rates. Today, over 90% of apartment communities require residents to provide liability insurance, typically with coverage of $100,000 or more. However, none of that insurance covers the tenant; it only covers damage to their apartment building unit. In the case of the Johnsons, it's unit 67. Suppose the tenant wants insurance to cover their personal belongings. In that case, they must purchase additional insurance, and yes, their PMS provider will also sell that to them. For instance, in the case of the Johnsons, they were charged an additional $30 per month, as shown in Figure 9.1. This fee is used to pay the landlord's insurance costs on their apartment building.

In Conclusion, the Pricing Algorithm, not the Individual Landlords, Sets the Rates of Rent.

In conclusion, the pricing algorithm employs a unique four-step pricing process. Each step of this process is essential for setting the rental rates. At each stage of the process, for their member landlords, the pricing algorithm utilizes the same data, technologies, and methodologies in the rental rate manufacturing process, all of which are executed by the algorithm rather than the individual landlords.

Therefore, it's the pricing algorithm, not the individual landlords, that artificially manufactures rental rates using the three-part revenue generation process. In other words, the information from the seven databases, combined with their legion of lawyers and every rule and regulation, results in the algorithm engineering the fee mixture to ensure the most profitable method is created, thereby maximizing profit.

It begins with part one of the revenue-generating process, where technology manipulates various economic factors within the market, balancing supply and demand. By utilizing technology to select tenants who are both able and willing to pay the most for their services, landlords can intentionally withhold 3 to 5% of their rental units from the market. This strategy creates a misleading sense of housing scarcity, allowing landlords to charge significantly higher rates.

Furthermore, the technology enhances the pricing process by artificially raising the base rent to maintain a rent-to-income ratio of at least 30% based on the highest earners in the market. By working together as a pricing cartel, the landlords can maximize profits. We will complete this discussion in Chapter 12.

In the second part, the technology, rather than the individual landlords, optimizes revenue by mining the lease contracts and charging excessive junk fees. In the third and final stage of revenue generation, landlords pass numerous operating expenses to tenants through additional forms of junk fees, all the while increasing the advertised rate of rent by up to 35%. In our example in Figure 9.1, the spread was 20%; however, if the Johnsons are compelled to break the lease, the early termination fees would increase the spread by over $7,000, bringing it to over 35%. By following this approach and the three-part revenue generation process, landlords can effectively double their profits. While it may seem counterintuitive to withhold rental units compared to traditional pricing strategies, our research confirmed their claims of doubling profits, all the while renting significantly fewer units. The free market system plays no role in the rate-setting process.

Let's refocus on the Johnsons. Hunter, Carol, and their two children's situation is truly heartbreaking and, unfortunately, all too familiar in today's America. The sudden unplanned addition of $490 in rental costs, as shown in Figure 9.1, has pushed the family into a category referred to as severe rent burdening. They will now spend 50% or more of their income on housing. This practice means they can cover only 90% of their household expenses and must cut their family budget by 10% (see Figure 8.1).

The artificial increase in rental costs has left the family struggling to maintain their standard of living. They cannot meet their living expenses and must cut essential services, such as health insurance, medical services, and healthy food choices. Their only other option is to increase their consumer debt by using credit cards to manage their cash flow. How prevalent has the practice of subsidizing cash flow become? In July 2024, national credit card usage in the United States reached an all-time high, exceeding $1.1 trillion.

As their landlords continue to tack on additional fees to their rent, the Johnsons are forced to work overtime to keep up with rising housing costs. However, the extra income from overtime doesn't solve their financial struggles, as it results in higher tax withholdings and even greater living expenses. As a result, their once-happy marriage has been strained by the weight of financial responsibilities, leading to blame and tension between them.

However, the greatest tragedy is the harm it causes their children. Due to the weaponization of pricing technology in revenue management, the Johnsons' financial struggles have not only depleted their savings accounts and blown up their family budget, but their financial situation has also had a detrimental impact on their children. The increased housing costs left no money to cover the cost of the improved educational and sports programs that should have benefited their children. After all, this was the primary reason for the move.

Instead of paying tuition for a great soccer program or funds for the math club, those funds had to pay bloated utility bills or parking costs to their already obscenely wealthy landlord. This practice is a stark example of the injustice that many families face due to the cruel side effects of the landlord's abuse of revenue management technology. Their new home at 1164 Morning Glory Circle did not improve their living conditions; instead, it became a spiraling money pit that cursed their once-happy family.

It's a tragic story of a family facing overwhelming financial strain—a family suffocated by the landlord's willful and unregulated price gouging, which includes the addition of fees, and lots of them. This situation is pushing the new working-class family into becoming a vulnerable population, which is a typical scenario in today's world.

Chapters 10 and 11 will further discuss the impact on tenants, while Chapter 12 will provide a final summary of the pricing technology.

The Fix:

Step 1: Establish the Truth in Rental Housing Act (TIRHA).

In 1968, Congress enacted the Truth in Lending Act (TILA) to better safeguard homeowners from dishonest lenders. However, the time has come to ask why tenants aren't equally protected from unscrupulous landlords. Therefore, our study recommends establishing the Truth in Rental Housing Act (TIRHA), which would reflect the practices within TILA to ensure fairness and better protect applicants and tenants from the exploitation of their pricing algorithms and the substantial fee structure inherent in revenue management.

Similar to the successful Truth in Lending Act, the proposed Truth in Rental Housing Act would mandate standardized disclosure of the actual charges and costs associated with a lease. This uniform standard for presenting rental terms would enable individuals to more easily compare and shop for the best rental rates, empowering them to make informed decisions about the actual cost of housing.

Additionally, the process for collecting fees must be further regulated. For instance, tenants must be given a warning and a cure period before a fee can be charged. For example, if a tenant misses a rent payment, the landlord must issue a warning and allow a five-day period to cure the missed payment before charging a late fee. This step helps prevent the implementation of a "gotcha" pricing strategy.

Step 2: Establish a Regulatory Agency to Monitor Rental Properties

Additionally, our research has uncovered a significant lack of oversight in the rental housing industry. To address this, we strongly recommend establishing a Regulating Entity. This new entity would be responsible for providing oversight and enforcing regulations in the $12 trillion Rental Housing Industry and its forty-four million rental units, ensuring the rights and safety of tenants.

CHAPTER 10

My Brother's Keeper

And Cain talked with Abel his brother: and it came to pass, when they were in the field, that Cain rose up against Abel his brother, and slew him. And the LORD said unto Cain, Where is Abel thy brother? And he said, I know not: Am I my brother's keeper? And he said, What hast thou done?

(Genesis 4: 8-10)

Introduction:

At the heart of the problem is a housing crisis of urgent proportions. By the end of 2018, nearly fifty-one million Americans—43% of households in the U.S.—found themselves unable to afford housing within their monthly budgets. This group, which accounts for two-thirds of the labor force, earns less than twenty dollars per hour and $70,000 per year, a figure significantly below what is required to survive in the modern economy.[1] This segment of the population is rapidly expanding due to the widening income inequality driven by greedy investors. Their shrinking paychecks make it increasingly challenging to cover their monthly expenses, leaving them vulnerable to exploitation.

The Correlation Between Market Power, Unrestrained Rent Increases, and Homelessness

We continue the discussion from Chapter 5 and the Seattle Concentration Study, which found a direct correlation between the 87.91% growth in pricing concentrations on the Platform and the 82.59% increase in rental rates in Metro Seattle.

The 2017 Zillow Study on Homelessness

We will now focus on the 2017 Zillow Study—"Dynamics of homelessness in urban America," a blockbuster that linked skyrocketing rents to homelessness. In short, the Study found the skyrocketing homeless rates in the larger metropolitan areas alarming. In addition to the rising counts of homeless, rental costs in these same cities are also significantly increasing. In summary, it was discovered that a 5% increase in rent correlates to a defined number of tenants being priced out of housing and into the streets—in Seattle, this translates to 258 people—in Los Angeles, it's 2,000; in New York, it's 3,000.[2]

The Zillow study included the Seattle Market. Therefore, this study aligns with our Seattle Concentration study from Chapter 5. Even more so because, in 2014, Zillow and RealPage entered into a data-sharing agreement similar to the one between Real Capital Analytics and RealPage detailed in Chapter 6. In other words, the data and information Zillow used in their research originated from the RealPage Databases, providing an apples-to-apples analysis.

The question we seek to answer in this section of the chapter is whether the Platform is responsible not only for artificially increased rents but also for the exploding homeless population, as detailed in the Zillow study. In other words, are the Platform and its participating landlords responsible for those skyrocketing rents? If so, then are the Platform and its participating landlords also responsible for the skyrocketing homeless population? This issue of accountability is crucial in addressing the homeless crisis. By understanding the

Platform's role in the crisis, we can better advocate for immediate attention and action.

Maximizing Profits Means Pricing Out the Bottom 15% of Tenants.

To gain a deeper understanding of the homeless crisis, we will continue our discussion from Chapter 4, where we explored how the industry collaboratively conducted pricing strategy studies to design the pricing algorithm. One set of studies, including three of the largest property managers, found that maximizing profits required pricing out 15% of the entire rental population. This practice was similar to the approach that the Rainmaker Group found in the hospitality industry, where their technology necessitated pricing out the bottom 23% to maximize profits for the hotel owners.

As a striking example of how the homeless population is being created, we examine the financial statements of Camden Property Trust. This Texas-based company owned and sold the YieldStar pricing technology to RealPage for collaborative industry development. However, not before releasing the initial 80-page revenue management in multifamily housing study, titled "Follow the Leader." This study offered a strategy for landlords to optimize profits by establishing the Rental Housing Pricing Cartel, which would dominate the rental housing industry.

Camden CEO Ric Campo revealed the harsh reality of the pricing algorithm's programming. He stated: "His tenant turnover rates increased around fifteen percentage points in 2006 after implementing YieldStar." Meaning that fifteen out of every one hundred tenants were priced out of their homes. Yet, despite a 15% displacement, overall same-property revenue growth came in at 7.4% within the same year. For Camden, that's over $10 million in additional net profits. He continued: "The trick now is to make sure you keep the right heads—those who are willing and able to pay the rents you push—in the right beds while letting those who won't walk."[3]

The Platform members concluded that driving out financially disadvantaged consumers was necessary for their plan. To optimize profits, the pricing technology deliberately excludes lower-income consumers from the market. For example, in the hospitality industry discussed in Chapter 7, the system is designed to exclude the bottom 23% of income earners. Similarly, in housing, it aims to exclude the lowest 15%. By excluding lower-income consumers, the technology is free from affordability constraints. This enables the pricing algorithm to set prices aimed at the highest-income earners and their willingness to pay premium rates. Although this approach carries certain risks, operators who follow these guidelines doubled their profits, as evidenced by higher rental rates.

The outcomes have created a new class of people, "the priced-out," those who, based solely on their financial ability alone, can no longer afford the cost of housing in their budgets. The principle of driving out 15% of the population is referred to as the "15% tenant elimination rule—priced out by design."

The Seattle Market Study Concludes a Correlation Between Market Power, Unrestrained Rent Increases, and Homelessness

The rental rates referenced in this section are sourced from Chapter 5, Figure 5.3, as shown in the top half of the chart. They are specific to the Seattle market but similar to those in other metro areas. This discussion aims to establish a correlation between the 82.59% increase in rental rates and the 32.11% escalation in Seattle's homeless population that occurred during the same period.

To better understand the relationship between pricing strategy and homelessness, we have developed a chart labeled Figure 10.1. This chart is constructed to accurately gauge the correlation and demonstrate how the various components of the landlord's pricing strategy directly impact tenants and homelessness. It is intended to be viewed as a sliding scale that illustrates the direct impact on homelessness from each 5% increase in rent. Specifically, for every 5% rise in rent, housing costs increase proportionately, ultimately resulting in 258 individuals being displaced and experiencing homelessness.

The central part of the chart, "Priced out into Homelessness by Year," illustrates the increasing number of people who are forced into homelessness due to their inability to afford housing costs. The trend began in 2013 with 763 individuals and reached its peak in 2014 with 2,082 individuals. By 2018, during this five-year period, the number of people unable to afford housing and forced to live on the streets had risen by a staggering 4,262 men, women, and children.

The lower section of the chart illustrates the percentage increase in rental rates. In 2013, there was a 14.78% rise; in 2014, the increase was 40.34%; and in 2018, it was 8.61%. Overall, the chart shows a total rental rate increase of 82.59%.

Figure 10.1: Sliding scale, Correlation in Unrestrained Rental Rate Increases, the Percent of Family Budget to Housing, and the Number of People being Priced out of their Housing—Homeless

		Priced out into Homelessness by Year						
		2013	2014	2015	2016	2017	2018	Combined
	Housing Cost Burden							# priced out of Housing to the Streets
Growth by Year	111.34%							4,262
2018	111.34%						444	
2017	103.98%					338		
2016	96.20%				401			
2015	88.42%			234				
2014	83.71%		2,082					
2013	44.78%	763						
2012	30.00%							
	Cumulative % Rate Increase	14.78%	55.12%	59.65%	67.43%	73.98%	82.59%	82.59%
	Annual Increase	14.78%	40.34%	4.53%	7.78%	6.55%	8.61%	

Additionally, the left side of the chart highlights the percentage of income tenants allocate toward housing, commonly referred to as "housing cost burden." In 2012, the housing burden was 30%. By 2018, it had increased to 111.34%, a direct result of the percentage increase in rental rates. For example, in 2012, a tenant paid $1,069 in rent, which was 30% of their income. In 2018, that same tenant would have paid $2,245 in rent, which was 111.34% of their income. With rental rates continuing to rise, the number of individuals unable to afford housing and becoming homeless is expected to increase. The rising rental rates have significantly harmed tenants' overall financial stability and their ability to remain in the qualified renter pool.

The chart in Figure 10.2 below shows the timeline of rent increases resulting from the Platform's market power. On the left side of the chart, you can see the "Total Rent $." In contrast, the bottom of the chart shows the year-over-year increase in homeless count, represented by "Total Homeless # (number)."

Figure 10.2: Cumulative Rent Increases Correlated to Cumulative Homeless Increases YOY 2011–2018

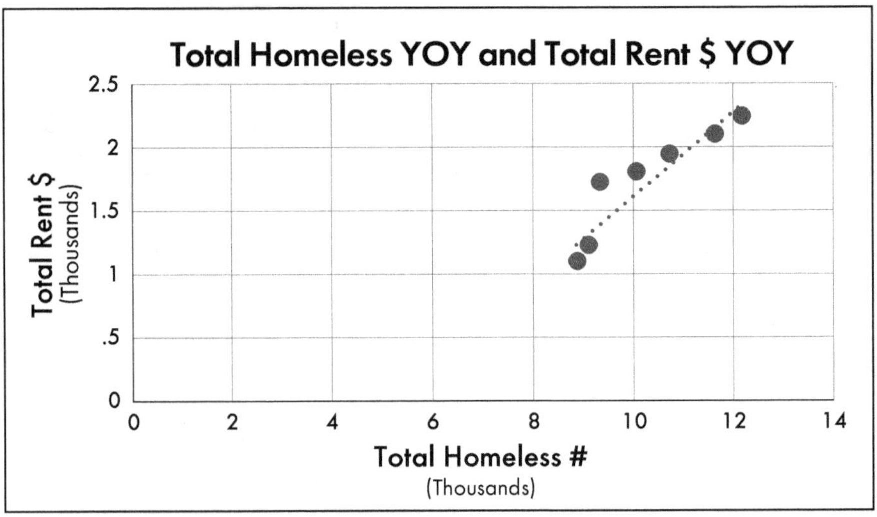

Between 2011 and 2018, the pricing concentration of rental units on the Platform grew from 47.55% to 87.91%. That market power proportionately increased rental rates from $1,086 to $2,245, as represented by the rightward-arching dotted line. This data underscores the substantial impact of the Platform's market power on rental rates. During this same period, the homeless population grew from 8,922 to 12,112, as represented by the dots (for the years 2012–2018). The chart shows a very strong correlation between the year-over-year growth in rental rates and the corresponding increase in the homeless population. In fact, the strength of this correlation is as robust as the correlation between the concentration of rental units priced on the common pricing platform when compared to the growth in rental rates, according to Chapter 5, Figure 5.4.

To further assess the theory that a correlation exists between the market power of the Platform and its ability to raise rental rates, as well as its direct correlation to the increase in homelessness, we continue to use the year 2014 to evaluate this correlation. In 2014, as shown in the center of Figure 10.1, the platform pushed rental rates as high as possible to maximize profits, resulting in an increase of over 40%. Therefore, if a correlation were found to exist, then a significant number of people would, by necessity, have been priced out of their housing. The assumption is based on the 15% tenant elimination formula. In other words, a similarly large percentage of the population must have been evicted. And they were, as it turns out, in 2015, over 35,000 people became homeless in Seattle for the first time, concluding a likely correlation. In 2015, King County (Seattle) declared a state of emergency over the homeless crisis. Since the 40% surge in rates, Metro Seattle taxpayers have been forced to pay nearly a quarter of a billion dollars each year to manage the ongoing crisis.

The price of the Platform's enormous success is directly related to and correlated with gentrification and homelessness. In conclusion, there is little remaining doubt that the Platform is the primary cause of homelessness. The pricing algorithm functions exactly as intended. The foundational industry-wide studies concluded that pricing the poorer 15% of tenants out of housing was necessary for the plan. Regarding their struggling tenants, property managers were instructed by their PMS providers to "get used to the turnover" and "view turnover as a good thing."

In conclusion, a correlation between pricing concentrations that created market power, unrestrained rent increases, and homelessness—the "priced-out" was determined to exist. Therefore, the rise in gentrification and homelessness is a byproduct of the programming of pricing algorithms.

Let's Meet Aaron Carter

Aaron Carter was born in 1981 into a family with a proud military tradition. As the youngest of five siblings, he spent his formative years in rural Washington, south of Seattle. Described as a good-looking young man with a reserved and well-behaved demeanor, he veered away from soccer—a sport his mother encouraged him to pursue at age ten—in favor of video games, notably the 1992 hit "Mortal Kombat."

During high school, he actively participated in the Reserve Officers' Training Corps (ROTC) and scouting, achieving the prestigious Eagle Scout rank and graduating in 1998 as a member of the National Honor Society. He was awarded an ROTC scholarship and began his college education. Aaron was recognized as a bright young man with a promising future.

Then, on September 11, 2001, a terrorist attack struck the U.S., killing about 3,000 of our citizens and injuring about 6,000 others.

In response, on September 20th, President George W. Bush addressed the Joint Session of the 107th Congress. He said: "My fellow citizens, for the last nine days, the entire world has seen for itself the state of our Union—and it is strong. Tonight, we are a country awakened to danger and called to defend freedom. Whether we bring our enemies to justice, or bring justice to our enemies, justice will be done. Our war on terror begins with al Qaeda, but it does not end there. It will not end until every terrorist group of global reach has been found, stopped, and defeated."[4]

In early 2002, Aaron answered President Bush's call to serve in the Marine Corps and defend his country. During his boot camp training, he formed strong bonds with three other young men who shared his passion for protecting their nation from the threat of weapons of mass destruction. However, the harsh realities of war proved to be vastly different from the video games of their youth. Nevertheless, they persevered, motivating one another to excel and consistently surpassing their commanders' expectations. In 2006, all four chose to reenlist for another four-year term.

In October 2009, an ambush at their outpost caused his injury and the tragic loss of his three comrades. This pivotal event significantly altered his life, leaving him with a constant sense of being engaged in guerrilla warfare. Subsequently, in early 2010, a diagnosis of Post-traumatic Stress Disorder (PTSD) was confirmed, accompanied by severe night terrors. Subsequent assessment revealed the presence of schizophrenia, a mental health condition stemming from exposure to or involvement in a severe, distressing event.

Medical professionals at the Veterans Affairs Administration (VA) prescribed potent medications to manage his symptoms. In June of the same year, following a decision made by his sergeant, he was granted an honorable discharge and awarded the Purple Heart. At the time, he was twenty-nine years old.

Returning home would bring Aaron face-to-face with a fresh set of challenges. The world he left behind was not the same as the one he returned to, and neither was he. Departing for war as a mere boy, he returned home a shattered man. His relationships with his family suffered greatly, especially with his father. This formidable military leader struggled to comprehend what he saw as weakness in his son.

The night terrors and bouts of panic were deeply unsettling, even for the strongest individuals. However, these challenges had taken a toll on the once-strong bond between Aaron and his father. Aaron's mental illness posed a life-altering challenge for which he had no solution. Following an episode, he sometimes recalled his actions and words, but at other times, he could not. The VA doctors made persistent efforts to identify the right balance of medications. Still, the side effects were occasionally unbearable for him.

His mother remained a rock, and her love for him was unfailing. She defended him like a lioness protecting her cub. But Aaron needed to be on his own; after all, he was nearly thirty years old. One day, his mother ran into Billy, his high school friend. He recently went through a divorce, was single, living in an apartment, and working at an Amazon fulfillment center in the city. He mentioned that they were looking for a few workers. Within a short time, Aaron was employed as a stocking clerk at the beginning wage of fifteen dollars per hour. In 2011, the two acquired a two-bedroom apartment; their beginning rent was $1,086.

Initially, Aaron had a stable living and working environment. However, Billy started enjoying his newfound freedom and began frequenting bars and their flies. Despite being advised by his doctors to avoid alcohol, Aaron began drinking as a way to escape from his difficult life. However, mixing medication with alcohol had serious consequences for him. Meanwhile, Billy was secretly addicted to opioids and managed to access the illegal drugs late at night behind his local convenience store. Worse still, he introduced Aaron to them.

Of course, at first, Aaron thought he could control the liquor and drugs. Still, his life's journey led him to a day and evening of binge drinking and drugs, culminating in his veering into a drug-induced mental delusion. The effects of drinking and drugs seemed to put him back into Afghanistan, where he was under attack, and his buddies' bloody body parts lay strewn on the floor. The haunting images of death and carnage, along with the faces of innocent children ravaged by war, tortured him relentlessly. To Aaron, the episode was very real; he could taste the dusty surroundings and smell the dusty canvas that made up his tent and hear the sounds of children's cries and the loud blasts, and see the bullets as they passed him by.

But, of course, it wasn't real. During the episode, Aaron broke Billy's arm, cracked some of his ribs, and badly bruised and tore his face. This episode led Billy to leave the apartment and quit his job. Aaron was on his own and alone for the first time in his life. The episode also resulted in neighbors filing complaints with their landlord, and a police record was filed against him.

For Aaron, the timing of this episode couldn't have been worse. His landlord had sold the property, and the new owners took this opportunity to evict him swiftly. Their goal was to convert the building into luxury condos. To accomplish this, they needed to find an excuse to evict all tenants, including the long-time residents.

When Aaron walked out of the police station, he discovered that he had nowhere to go. The entire episode was a blur, and he struggled to decipher the real from the imagined. He hadn't taken his medication for some time now. Weeks later, he woke up in the VA hospital with his mother by his side. Once again, he found himself caught between the realms of fantasy and reality. Still, with the doctors' help, he gradually reoriented himself. One morning, as he awoke and glanced at his mother, he jokingly remarked, "You look terrible; what's up with you?" Her smile revealed her relief at having her son back, if only temporarily.

After several weeks, Aaron's doctors decided it was time for him to move out and live independently. Reluctantly, he moved back into his childhood bedroom, facing resistance from his father, who criticized him for being weak. The doctors had advised his mother that Aaron needed to live independently as soon as possible and also find a support group for help. It took a couple of months, but with his mother's assistance, Aaron located a support group that helped him cope with the challenges in his life.

In 2012, he secured a job as a stocking clerk at another large retail store and began searching for his own apartment. The dynamics of the housing industry were undergoing significant changes at the time. With his mother's assistance and a support group, he discovered an older apartment building tailored to veterans like himself. The monthly rent for the apartment was $1,069, but the rental process had become more complex. It involved numerous fees, and the rental contract spanned forty pages. Due to his prior eviction, the landlord insisted that his mother guarantee the rental agreement and make substantial deposits. Additionally, the apartment building was located nearly twenty-five miles from his workplace. Once again, his devoted mother came to his aid, arranging for him to receive a public bus and light rail pass.

Aaron faithfully attended his support group, forming a genuine connection with his mental health provider. Initially, his mother visited often, but after a few months, her visits became less frequent. However, Aaron's older brother helped him regain his driver's license, and he was actively saving to purchase his first pickup truck. He had previously found the dating process to be too challenging, but he found companionship by adopting a golden retriever puppy named Betsy. The two of them settled into a comfortable routine.

In October of 2012, he and the other tenants in the building were informed that the building had been sold yet again and that a new property manager had been introduced. Over the next two months, he received several notices from the new management company outlining forthcoming changes. However, in November, he received a notice informing him that his rent would increase by $158, or 14.78%. Moreover, there would be additional fees and charges for pets. The actual increase in rent would result in his housing consuming over half of his wages. The new management also required increased security deposits, which would deplete all the savings for his pickup. Furthermore, they demanded that his mother continue to guarantee the rental contract.

Aaron found himself slipping back into the memories of war, plagued by intense night terrors. He then sought help from his mental health provider, and his medication dosage was increased. During a support group session, he discovered that many others were also struggling with the rising cost of living, causing significant mental strain. Financial uncertainty made it increasingly difficult for them to envision a brighter future.

In December, the family had made plans for Aaron and a couple of his siblings who lived out of town to spend Christmas at their parents' house. The other two families lived nearby, making it convenient for their holiday gatherings. However, Aaron was preoccupied with the notices from the management company, particularly the one that required his mother's signature. His mother had signed the contract without his father's knowledge, making it their "little secret."

At the family home, the holiday bustle included all the children and grandchildren. Aaron struggled to find a moment alone with his mom until several family members left the day after Christmas. Seizing the opportunity, he observed that his mother was unwell, claiming it was just the flu and assuring him not to worry. Despite her illness, she expressed her pride in his progress and urged him to keep moving forward. When he finally confided in her, she sat up straight, surprising him, and said, "Okay." And that was the end of it—a devoted parent, all too "able and willing" to help their child in need.

However, 2013 was a financially challenging year for him. Not only did his rent increase to $1,227, but his utility bill also rose nearly double. The added pet fees and other charges also ate deeply into his budget. Worse still for him, the support group he had come to depend on, like family, was dwindling. Many had already moved away to cheaper housing. The apartment building he was living in no longer catered to veterans. Instead, younger minority families were moving in, and the noise from the children playing outside his windows became very difficult for him to process mentally. Some of the neighboring families had complained about him to the management company. Then, his mental health provider left the area without any notice to him.

In November, he was notified that his rent would increase by $495 to $1,722 per month, representing a 40.34% increase. Additionally, there would be increased fees and charges, and his mother would need to sign the contract again. With this increase, his rent would consume more than his entire gross pay. Although he was a hardworking young man who had faithfully served his country to protect it from weapons of mass destruction, he had become part of the "priced out by design" population. He turned off the lights and lay on the floor with Betsy curled beside him. The distant sound of bombs grew louder as they approached his location. Questions swirled in his mind—where was his platoon, and what were his orders?

When he awoke in the VA hospital bed, it was summer 2015. He had no memory of the past year, not a clue. Betsy was nowhere to be found. He was under heavy sedation. A few days later, his sister came to visit him. She had the unfortunate task of letting him know that his mother had passed away from breast cancer a few months ago. They had tried desperately to find him, but it took months.

Upon hearing the news of his mother's passing, Aaron curled into the fetal position and began to sob. No, no, no, he kept repeating in between his sobs. His mother had been his rock, his center of gravity. His sister continued speaking, tears streaming down her face as she delivered the speech she had prepared. Bombs were exploding all around him, and he began to scream for help. He saw blood and carnage everywhere. His sister last stated that he wasn't allowed to go home. Not after his dad received the notice that his mother owed over $18,000 for his back rent, early termination fees, eviction fees, and many other fees. His father had banished him. The bombs and gunfire got louder and louder. Then, the screaming became unbearable.

The Rental Housing Pricing Cartel, its shared pricing platform, and, for lower-income tenants, the Ten Steps to Homelessness.

Today, one unintended side effect of the Platform's success in the rental housing industry is that the technology has designed a ten-step process to homelessness. These tenants are intentionally priced out. This is how the homeless crisis unfolds:

Step 1: The Cartels' Massive Data-gathering Campaign

Step 1 begins with their massive data-gathering campaign, a genuinely Orwellian process reminiscent of George Orwell's novel 1984. To hold this data, they created the seven databases. However, to obtain, move, manipulate, and utilize this information, they developed the Property Management System (DOP), which is further supported by its two-sided Platform arrangement with Experian. Without this data, the Platform could not manipulate the market. But this sharing of data, technologies, and pricing strategies sits at the heart of the homeless crisis today.

Step 2: The Cartel's Pricing Strategy Manipulates the Housing Supply and Restricts the Number of Applicants in the Renter Pool

In Step 2, powerful corporate landlords and their cartel members use deceitful practices to maximize profits. It begins with balancing demand by limiting the number of tenants allowed in the qualified rental pool at any given time, which leads to the beginning of the homeless crisis. They further exacerbate the imbalance by keeping rental units off the market, thereby increasing the number of homeless individuals. On any given day, hundreds of thousands of rental units remain intentionally vacant.

Step 3: The Cartel Members Charge Junk Fees, Increasing Rent by up to 35%

Step 3 of the pricing process begins once the tenant has a signed lease. It's designed to increase the landlord's profits by up to 35% while their wages increase by mere pennies. Our example of the Johnson Family in Chapters 8 and 9 provides an excellent example of how the process works. In this case, the landlord advertises a rate of $2,400 per month, then adds $490 in various junk fees, bringing the effective rent to $2,890. That's a 20% increase over the advertised rate.

The increase in actual rental costs over and above the advertised rate now places the family in a category referred to as severe rent burdening, with 50% of their total income directed to housing, and, therefore, can only cover 90% of their household expenses. The result leaves two-thirds of all American working-class families struggling to maintain a standard of living. In this typical scenario, the new working-class family is being pushed into becoming the new vulnerable population. Just one hospital bill away from the streets.

Step 4: The Cartel uses Algorithmic Price Fixing to price out over 15% of all Applicants.

Then, once the market is in balance—supply and demand—they push rental rates so high that they intentionally price another 15% of all tenants out of housing; this creates massive homelessness. For example, in Metro Seattle, between 2013 and 2014, the Platform pushed rates as high as possible, increasing by over 40%, and pricing more than 35,000 people out of housing, forcing over 4,200 people onto the streets.

Today, their price-fixing programs have destroyed the affordable housing market. The results of their programs leave only 29 affordable and available rental units for every 100 very-low-income households.[5] In other words, for every 100 very low-income families seeking housing, only 29 units are available. Thus, the other 71 families fall under the "15% tenant elimination rule," a term used to describe the situation in which 15% of tenants cannot find housing and end their housing search by moving their families onto the streets.

Step Five—The tenant falls behind on the rent.

Unfortunately, for the 66% of working-class tenants who struggle to make their rent payments, the unrestrained rent increases of the cartels' leasing program have had a negative impact on their lives. For example, many working tenants often struggle to pay their rent in full and on time. The ever-increasing rents result in tenants needing to juggle the timing of paying their bills, including rent. However, in most situations, the tenant pays the rent, just not in a timely manner. However, in the end, the ever-increasing rents cause 15% of the tenants to run out of money and fall behind on their rent. At every step, the landlords intentionally harm people with low incomes and the financially vulnerable, pushing them into a state of crisis.

Step Six: The Cartel Members' use of Fee Stacking—that is, Fees on top of Fees—and their use of overly high early termination fees

Once the tenant falls behind with the rent, property managers often pile on additional fees and late charges, doubling the tenant's debt. The practice of "stacking late fees" by charging additional penalties on top of late fees, even when rent is current, is illegal, but it still happens. Fee Stacking occurs when a tenant incurs multiple fees, such as late monthly rent fees. However, when the tenant makes their next monthly rent payment, even if it's on time and in full, the manager first applies it to the unpaid fees from the previous month. Then, they charge more fees because, in their eyes, the new rent payment is now short, and the fees continue to compound. The result is that the tenant remains delinquent despite having paid the rent.

Conversely, once the tenant realizes they no longer have the resources to pay their high rent, they begin to search for more affordable housing elsewhere. However, AI revenue management technology has been trained to alert landlords to tenants' internet activity. The landlords won't let them leave because they have locked them into that contract with the early termination fees. Late payments trigger early termination fees, which financially cripple the tenant. For example, if the Johnson family couldn't afford their rent and had to move, the early termination fee would be nearly $7,000, pushing their effective rent increase from 20% to almost 35% above the advertised rate. At this point in the process, the tenants begin to drown in the massive fee machine that is revenue management.

Step Seven—The Cartel Members' Eviction Process

In the Seventh Step, we turn to a 2017 Seattle eviction report that sheds light on how the eviction process works. The report discovered that evictions are one of the primary causes of homelessness, including forced relocation due to significant rent increases. Nearly half of the eviction proceedings were four days or less for delinquency. In other words, once the tenant has become delinquent, even within four days, the property manager can now call the rest of the supposedly delinquent tenant's contract due and payable.

In America today, the process is stacked against tenants. Many believe the courts would step in and correct the many eviction injustices. However, that isn't the case, as legal counsel represents more than 90% of landlords. Still, fewer than 10% of tenants have representation. The cozy relationship between landlords and judges, primarily facilitated through re-election campaign donations, has eroded tenant protections. In short, by applying the principles of the new Management Standard, the industry has leveraged its relationship with the Legal System to significantly boost its profits. In other words, taxpayers cover a significant portion of the landlords' collection costs.

Just how toxic has the eviction process gotten? A study from Chicago, titled "No Time for Justice: A Study of Chicago's Eviction Court," sheds light on the deplorable relationship between the courts and landlords. The report concluded that a typical fast-food restaurant can serve a meal in three minutes and nine seconds. Not to be outdone by the fast-food chains, the average time of a trial in Chicago's eviction courts is one minute and forty-four seconds.

However, the study found that judges failed to examine the notice of termination in 35% of the cases. In other words, eviction court judges do not require powerful corporate landlords to prove the elements of their case. Worse still, despite the importance of testimony in eviction proceedings, parties were only sworn to tell the truth less than 10% of the time.[6] Meaning landlords don't have to tell the truth. The court system has developed a "don't ask, don't tell" approach to evictions. If a landlord seeks to evict a tenant, the courts have increasingly become complicit in their eviction practices. According to the study's authors, the most striking aspect of their observations was the lack of dignity shown to tenants in the administration of the eviction process.

Step Eight—The Pricing Cartel and Its Debt Collection Process

Property management firms have also decided to leverage this renter application data to enhance their debt collection process by granting debt collectors access to the same databases. One of the more troubling findings is its Debt Collection Program. The program is an incentive-based plan developed to encourage staff to take all necessary steps to collect the debt before referring it to a collection agency.

The term "incentive basis" refers to a compensation system where employees are paid based on the amount of debt collected; the collection is then divided between the debt collector and the company claiming to be owed the obligation. However, the debt collector gets to pocket all the gains beyond the debt collection terms. Therefore, the incentive to break the law is enormous in a risk-versus-reward scenario. The Consumer Financial Protection Bureau (CFPB) found the collection process to be aggressive and abusive, and that debt collectors routinely violated collection laws.

Now, with the legal and court systems stacked against those who have been priced out, the Platform, its participating landlords, and their legion of corrupt lawyers engage in abusive practices to maximize profits. However, the extent of this abuse cannot be overstated. The mistreatment by landlords' attorneys toward their low-income tenants rivals the gang violence associated with drug cartels in Mexico or South American countries that are often discussed today.

As discussed earlier, this industry has gained the ability to remain unregulated—no regulatory agencies are watching, and no one is listening. Today, our legal system has devolved into a state of self-serving rot, catering only to the whims of the wealthiest individuals, who have become a law unto themselves, empowered by their ever-growing economic power and wealth. The courts have embraced the powerful corporate landlords, becoming part of the corrupted practice of forcing people with low incomes into the streets until they pay their landlords in full and without due process. Today, Americans receive justice based on what they can afford rather than on the justice guaranteed by our Constitution.

Step Nine—Experian and the Pricing Cartel Form an Embargo on Housing Improving Debt Collections

Managers connected to the Platform support each other's debt collection efforts by preventing tenants from moving without the "group's" consent. Landlords working with Experian have formed a debt-collection-driven embargo against the tenants who owe them money. It works like this: They hold those tenants in the streets. This pricing algorithm prohibits other landlords from renting to any applicant who owes money to them until their former landlords have been paid in full, without due process.

It's a stark reality that property management firms operating under RealPage have seen a 61% decrease in skips and evictions while collecting over half a billion in debt annually and creating billions in property valuation. Yet, the cost for the tenants is staggering. Those who find themselves homeless are the ones locked out of housing indefinitely as a result of these unjust property management practices.

The Story of Angie and Jamal, Two American Kids Born on the Wrong Side of the Wall

Meet Angie (Angelina), a twenty-five-year-old Black woman born in Boise, Idaho. She was raised in the Idaho foster care system, never knowing her parents or anything about her family history. However, once she heard that her father played basketball for Boise State University. She possessed a quiet demeanor and was kind by nature. While in the system, she was shuffled from one home to another, never establishing lasting familial ties. She understood what it meant to feel lonely and to be alone.

At the age of twelve, she was diagnosed with a treatable mental health disorder that required her to remain on medication. By the time she turned fourteen, she found herself pregnant with her first child and was subsequently expelled from the public school system. She was then placed in an adult school, which she never actually attended. When the foster care system offered no alternatives but to proceed with the pregnancy, her foster parents attempted to coerce her into giving up the child for adoption. Faced with this unbearable situation, she chose to escape with her child from the foster care system and eventually found refuge on the streets of Tacoma, Washington.

She met Jamal when she was fifteen years old. He was a young Black man, and the two formed a close relationship, a family bond. She moved in with him. He, too, was raised in the foster care system in Montana, but ran away to the streets at thirteen, having only a sixth-grade education. Although they never married, they welcomed two more children together.

More than anything, they wanted to be part of a family—to belong. He worked as a clerk in a convenience store, and she worked as a caregiver in a nursing home. They both earned minimum wage, and their combined annual earnings were less than $35,000. She worked during the day while he watched the children, and then when she returned from work, he worked the night shift. They were able to acquire subsidized housing. Subsidized housing is taxpayer-funded housing in which the renter pays 30% of their income toward rent. Their family of five was very close.

In 2013, the tenants started getting letters from the new property owner. The new owner had increased fees, charges, and rent, similar to what happened to Aaron Carter. The abuse is a common occurrence in many states, where property owners exploit the lack of affordable housing and the vulnerability of low-income families. They planned to renovate the property and evict all tenants through a legal process known as a no-cause eviction.

However, there were no subsidized housing units available in Tacoma. As a result, most tenants, including Angie and Jamal, along with their three young children, ended up on the streets. From 2004 to 2017, almost half a million Washington residents, like those in many other states, faced similar no-cause eviction notices; the process has become epidemic.

In the winter months of 2014, compounded by the lack of affordable housing, the youngest child fell gravely ill and passed away in the hospital. This episode was devastating for Angie and Jamal. Angie internalized her pain and, without adequate medical care, started to suffer from profound depression and mental illness. Jamal did his best but was unable to secure any housing, whether subsidized or not, for his young family.

Drug use was not new to them, but they had made a strong effort to avoid it, especially after starting a family. Angie's situation worsened when she was caught stealing jewelry at the nursing home and lost her job, which contributed to her decline in mental health. Jamal, wanting to help Angie, learned about a new type of drug called opioids. To afford the drug, he started selling illegal opioid drugs late at night behind the convenience store where he worked until he was caught by the police and arrested for drug trafficking.

However, the abuse of AI-powered revenue management algorithms, such as those used by RealPage, is pushing our nation toward a future of two separate and unequal societies. Consider Brazil, where on one side of a wall you find the very wealthy; on the other, the impoverished in "favelas," makeshift urban settlements reminiscent of Depression-era Hoovervilles, characterized by shanties and a lack of infrastructure. In the United States today, the contrast in quality of life between the rich and the poor is stark. People experiencing poverty find themselves in a society reminiscent of Upton Sinclair's 1905 novel The Jungle.

On one side, we have the wealthy Sackler family (Chapter 4), the 21st-century drug lords who manufacture OxyContin. On the other hand, we have the poor, like Angie and Jamal, who are driven to crime by their circumstances. However, the wealthy Sackler family faces no consequences for their role in the crime, the mass murder of half a million of our citizens. In America today, there is a lack of accountability for the wealthy investor-billionaire class. The rich inhabit a world of their own, funded by taxpayers while paying minimal taxes in return. The rich live in multiple mansions around the globe, travel on taxpayer-funded jets from their private airports, and vacation at their exclusive resorts.

They have access to a private medical system and ensure their children enjoy limitless opportunities, including enrollment in prestigious private schools. Moreover, their children will never need to work. Still, they will secure the highest-paying jobs, contributing little to the workforce or society. Conversely, the working class sacrifices their personal lives to enrich their billionaire employers even further. All the while, they struggle to afford their rent.

In fact, when historians reflect on history, the years from approximately 2012 to 2025 will be seen as the Second Gilded Age, a period with striking parallels to the 1920s. This era, rather than being propelled by the Industrial Revolution, was driven by the Technological Revolution. Consider the actions of President Trump in 2025. On one hand, he has plans to tear down the East Wing of the White House and spend over $300 million to build a grandiose ballroom for his wealthy oligarchs. That same week, they cut food subsidies for over forty million Americans struggling to cover their living expenses and feed their little children.

However, the consequences are severe for Jamal, who represents those living in poverty. In stark contrast to the wealthy Sackler family, he will be held accountable and sentenced to serve fifteen years to life in a for-profit prison system owned by investors, effectively making him a modern enslaved person for his role in the crime. He will be forced to work without pay, contributing cheap labor to benefit yet another billionaire investor. This fate will likely separate him from his family forever. Erased from civilized society.

When he is released, if he survives the brutal prison system, he will have no life to return to, forced to scavenge from garbage cans while the rich Sackler family feasts in the most exclusive restaurants. He will be homeless while the rich live like royalty. These stark disparities, where one is condemned to a life of poverty while the rich revel in luxury, are entirely based on chance—the side of the wall on which one is born. This social injustice should raise serious concerns about the direction of our society.

However, Angie's fate is similar to that of Jamal. Yet, the silver lining to this terrible storm, if one could find it, was that Angie became involved with the Tacoma Urban League. This community organization offered her limited financial aid but provided significant emotional support, as well as a way to reunite with her two young children. This pathway included her breaking free from drug use, attending a support group, acquiring her GED, maintaining a job, and securing suitable housing. However, one of the most beneficial aspects of the program was that she received mental health support and access to her much-needed medication, highlighting the crucial role of community support in addressing social injustices.

Above all, Angie loved her children and wanted to provide them with a caring home. She adored them. Her children loved her, and more than anything, they wanted to live with their mother. She battled her drug addiction and regularly attended her support group. She earned her GED and found a stable job paying minimum wage.

The final hurdle to regaining custody of her children was securing suitable housing. However, acquiring housing became a formidable hurdle. The reason? The same property managers who oversee private investor-owned housing also manage public, government-subsidized housing (Figure 10.3). It's worth noting that Angie and Jamal owed a small balance to their previous landlord before the entire building was evicted. However, due to compounding fees and added interest, that amount ballooned to over $2,500. Angie's minimum wage earnings do not provide a feasible way to pay off that balance.

Figure 10.3: Property Managers Control All Housing Types

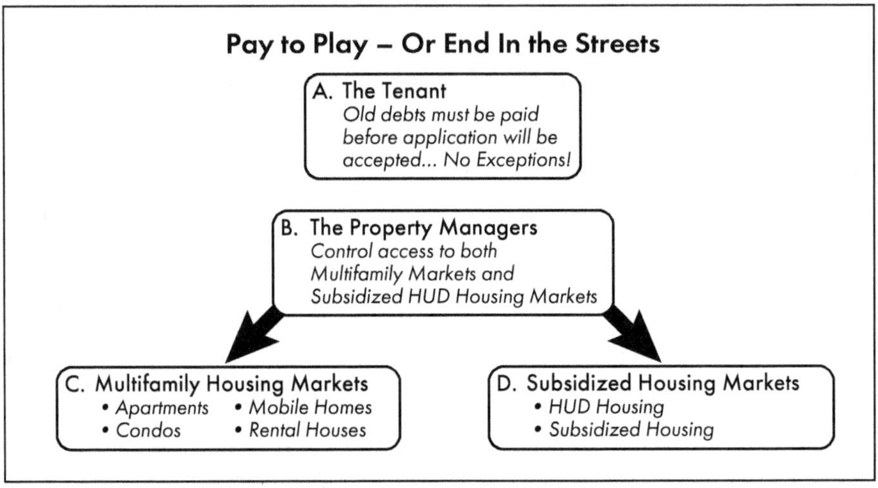

In short, the property manager's blockade of housing is a glaring injustice. It prevented Angie from obtaining subsidized housing because the same managers refused to rent to her or anyone else with an outstanding balance to a prior landlord until that balance was paid off in full. To put it simply, she cannot secure housing without paying that balance.

Worse still, once Experian found out she had secured a job—and its AI-powered algorithms always do so—they prepared paperwork for her previous landlord to garnish her minimal wages—effectively trapping her and locking her on the streets forever, making it impossible for her to leave.

In fact, the cartel has forced evicted tenants into a form of indentured servitude, offering no legal means to obtain housing. For example, filing for bankruptcy is not a viable financial option, as the cartel refuses to rent to anyone in or emerging from bankruptcy, which constitutes a clear violation of the law. In summary, the previous landlord must be paid; otherwise, there will be no housing. It's all part of the corporate landlord's process of being priced out by design.

It's heart-wrenching to witness her children enduring the hardships and loneliness of the foster care system. Meanwhile, their homeless mother struggles with the daily challenges of life on the streets and just barely getting by. Angie's life is not merely a statistic but a profound human tragedy. In America today, hundreds of thousands of evicted tenants find themselves in this exact scenario, where they can never leave the streets because they have no means to secure housing.

Homeless American citizens seen along roadsides or camping on public lands are permanently barred from accessing housing. The process where powerful corporate landlords use their algorithms to forever lock their low-income tenants out onto the streets is reminiscent of the classic 1976 Grammy-winning song by the Eagles, "Hotel California," where the lyrics read: "Relax, said the night man, We are programmed to receive. You can check out any time you like, but you can never leave."

Step Ten—The Cartel Members' Pricing Strategy is designed to force their low-income Tenants into homelessness

At the end of that long eviction journey, the tenant realizes they do not have the funds to cover the excessive fees at their current location and are not permitted to move into another apartment complex. Their options are limited to friends or family as they navigate this entire "eviction" situation. Ultimately, far too many tenants have no choice but to end up on the streets. Since 2015, well over 12,000 citizens have become permanently homeless in Metro Seattle. Worse yet, nearly half of them are living unsheltered on the streets.

The homelessness crisis is not a localized issue but a widespread problem. The declaration of states of emergency in ten major metropolitan cities across the western U.S. underscores the urgent need for action. The total homeless population has reached alarming levels, with over 80,000 in Los Angeles and nearly 100,000 in New York City. In 2017, approximately 1.3 million American schoolchildren were found to be homeless. The stark reality is that children are twice as likely to be homeless as adults, which adds urgency to this issue, emphasizing the dire situation our children are facing.

It is evident that property managers play a significant role in the homelessness crisis. The decision by property managers in the ten metropolitan cities to evict the bottom 15% of tenants, known as the "priced-out," is driven by income inequality.

Opioid addictions, drug use, and alcoholism have become commonplace among once-productive tenants who have fallen on hard times—some of the many who are only one hospital bill away from the streets. However, drug use isn't the only cause of suffering. Unhoused individuals face horrifying scenes of death and violence. For instance, in Metro Seattle in 2012, the annual number of homeless individuals who died was 78; however, by 2018, the number of fatalities had dramatically increased to nearly 200 annually. These statistics are comparable to those in all metro areas across the US.

These deaths and horrifying scenes are not caused by illegal immigrant gangs or transgender citizens, but rather by the most deadly cartel to ever infest the United States: the Rental Housing Pricing Cartel. Its members include some of the wealthiest American landlords, their investors, and their political operatives.

Conclusion,

The pricing algorithm's base programming lies at the heart of the homeless crisis. The foundational coding in the algorithm necessitated the elimination of the "priced-out"—the bottom 15% of income earners—to allow investors to maximize profits over people. This algorithm, used by property managers to fulfill management contracts and increase the bottom line, is a key factor in the systemic issues that lead to homelessness.

The pricing algorithm isn't just a tool, but a weapon of mass destruction in the hands of the pricing cartel members who prioritize profit over people. Truth be told, the weapons of mass destruction that President Bush enlisted Aaron Carter and his comrades to seek and destroy were not found in Afghanistan or Iraq. Instead, it was a pricing algorithm concealed in a black box, hidden in plain sight right here in America, which has pushed nearly a million-and-a-half citizens onto the streets and another fifty-one million Americans into a state of crisis—it's truly a weapon of mass destruction.

Homelessness isn't just happening. It's being done to people—property managers and their gang members are waging a vicious war, similarly described in the 1934 Pecora Report—that famously stated: "Men of might—not because of principle, but because of economic power and wealth.[7]" In 1932, during the great and terrible Depression, Democrats coined the phrase: "Human rights before property rights." This statement cries out ever louder today.

The study concludes that homelessness is a man-made catastrophe caused by greed and fueled by moral hazard. The cartel's part in the crisis was both foreseeable and avoidable. The providers of Property Management Systems understood their actions and the potential outcomes. But the potential for massive profits was simply too tempting to ignore.

However, the amount of money needed to resolve the homeless crisis is massive, and it will take decades for legislators or the courts to unify a response at the scale required to address such an enormous man-made catastrophe. Homelessness in America today has reached epidemic proportions; it has truly climaxed into a national state of emergency, underscoring the urgent need for systemic change.

CHAPTER 11

The Fair Housing Paradox

Then said Jesus unto his disciples, I say unto you, It is easier for a camel to go through the eye of a needle, than for a rich man to enter into the kingdom of God. (Matthew 19:16-24)

Key Concepts:

What is Institutionalism?

Institutionalism is the process by which a set of activities, laws, beliefs, or principles becomes entrenched in a formal societal structure. Over time and spanning generations, it becomes accepted or normalized in everyday life. However, this does not mean it's based on truth or reality; instead, it is simply accepted as fact and becomes a part of life as we know it. The most common forms of institutionalism occur in religion and political party affiliations. However, it also encompasses perspectives on wealth creation, poverty, race, and LGBTQ matters.

Nonprofits and Their Beginnings in America

Nonprofit or tax-exempt organizations began in 1867, following the Civil War. The first nonprofit was the Peabody Education Fund, which aimed to unite poor White and formerly enslaved children in the South into a single educational system. However, by 1976, the Nixon and Ford administrations had significantly expanded the concept of nonprofits to encompass charities and, more specifically, religious organizations.

Today, it has evolved into an industry that annually receives nearly $1.5 trillion in tax-exempt donations, with the vast majority of funds directed toward a select few religions and political parties. Today, the two largest business organizations in the world are not businesses like Microsoft or Apple, but rather nonprofit religions. But how do they wield this economic power and wealth in the face of the largest humanitarian crisis since the Great Depression?

Introduction

Imagine, if you will, waking up one day to find yourself possessing immense, magical-like power over your life and the lives of those around you. Pecora referred to it as "economic power and wealth." But the question remains: What would you do with that power? Would you be inclined to utilize this power to enhance the lives of those around you, or would you be tempted to enrich yourself excessively?

Nevertheless, the use of economic power and wealth is the ultimate measure of who we really are—it's life's ultimate test. And we cannot hide from it. Our individual choices not only shape who we are but also the society we live in, whether we cede to our darkest animal instincts or choose to rise above them. It's a responsibility we all share. However, unjustly usurping economic power and wealth over another, is the ultimate crime against a civilized society.

The Constitution, for instance, allows property ownership but doesn't define it, much as our current laws lack a clear definition of "reasonable." This lack of specificity was similarly exploited by large, rich landowners in the past when they abused their economic power and wealth to distort and manipulate the definition of the word "property" to include enslaved people. It took a war to end slavery and their demented definition of property.

Gaining freedom marked a significant milestone for formerly enslaved people. Still, it was only the beginning of their journey toward equality. To compete in the American labor force, they needed an education equivalent to that of their former owners and opportunities to compete for higher-paying jobs. Unfortunately, this has yet to materialize. As a result, those earning below the area median income (AMI) are disproportionately people of color and minorities.

Today, in 2024, the U.S. housing market is a $62 trillion industry, and controlling it means controlling who reaps the benefits of wealth creation. For the billionaire class, no price is too high in their pursuit of creating it. Nevertheless, as Chapter 4 underscores, the laws of economics are unequivocal: The creation of wealth necessitates a balance between a wealthy population and a much larger impoverished one, which today disproportionately consists of people of color. The larger the wealth divide, the greater the impoverished population becomes. In his novel Animal Farm, George Orwell best sums up our current controversy regarding wealth creation: "All animals are equal, but some animals are more equal than others. A proclamation by the pigs who control the government."

At its core, the wealthy class aims to create a cheap labor force to maintain its opulent lifestyle. But how does this unfold? What does that process look like? In America, wealth creation begins with homeownership. The equity in our homes, which accounts for over 40% of the net worth of all households, represents the single largest asset. Therefore, if the goal were to create a cheap labor force, the strategy would be simple: Strip the less fortunate of the opportunity to find and acquire a decent home and a safe living environment. The oppressive wealth-creation strategy underscores the pressing need for fair housing policies that ensure equal opportunities.

The Fair Housing Laws

The Fair Housing Act, also known as Title VIII of the Civil Rights Act of 1968, is a pivotal piece of legislation. It effectively bars discrimination in the sale, rental, or financing of dwellings and other housing-related activities. This act, overseen by the U.S. Department of Housing and Urban Development (HUD), is a powerful tool in combating discrimination.

The Fair Housing Paradox

In 1932, President Franklin Delano Roosevelt rebranded the Democratic Party as the party of change, the new party of Lincoln, where all were welcome and equally protected under the law. To him, adequate and affordable housing was not just a need but a right. President Roosevelt and the New Dealers believed that in return for taxpayers providing unlimited financial guarantees to the housing industry, they should receive a constitutionally guaranteed right to a safe and decent home and be free from discrimination.

Conversely, investors believe they have a constitutional right to unfettered access to profits in the housing industry, without regulation or oversight. However, according to the Constitution, neither definition can survive while the other exists. And therein lies the heart of the Fair Housing Paradox: The right to a decent home and safe living environment, free from discrimination, versus the right to unfettered access to profits.

The 1967 Kerner Commission

Continuing from Chapter 4, let's revisit the 1950s and 1960s when peaceful marches and protests emerged during the Civil Rights Movement. As time passed and conditions worsened, for instance, the press published news articles detailing that a larger number of poor Black boys from the slums were forced to serve and die in the Vietnam War when compared to their White peers. The disproportionate number of deaths, combined with the lack of educational and job opportunities and the fact that people of color were largely excluded from Roosevelt's New Deal in Republican controlled states, including access to decent and safe housing, resulted in more urgent protests against these unjust conditions.

The fierce debates on Capitol Hill threatened to send America back into a civil war. President Lyndon Johnson took a significant step in response to the civil unrest among people of color and to better explain the causes of this unrest to the American people. He established the Kerner Commission in July 1967, a pivotal move that aimed to investigate the root causes of the riots and provide a comprehensive understanding to White Americans.

The Kerner Commission's report was a stark wake-up call, declaring that America was "moving toward two societies, one black, one white—separate and unequal." It identified institutionalized segregation as a primary cause of racial tensions. It boldly stated, "White society is deeply implicated in the ghetto. White institutions created it, White institutions maintain it, and White society condones it."

The Housing Industry and Its Participants

Who were the White institutions responsible for creating and maintaining the underlying causes of that unrest, and what did they aim to accomplish? Additionally, is there a correlation between political unrest and the drive of wealthy institutions to create an impoverished class to fulfill their cheap labor requirements?

This chapter focuses on the groups that drive the housing industry and how they accomplish and institutionalize their wealth-creation goals. It's primarily made up of four groups. The first group is the investors, as detailed in Chapter 4, who purchase the land, construct, and own the properties. They control the narrative and serve as the driving force behind this industry and its participants. The investors determine when and where the property will be developed for housing.

The second group is the National Association of Realtors, which includes those who market or sell properties. They play a crucial role in shaping the narrative and influencing who can buy homes and where they are permitted to purchase them. The third group is the American Bankers Association, which finances properties, thus determining who qualifies to purchase homes and where they can buy them.

The U.S. Chamber of Commerce, a powerful lobbying group, is the fourth key player in the housing industry. In the rental housing industry, political power is acquired and exercised to influence the government's decisions and actions on housing policy. The Chamber's influence is used to shape and control the behavior of others by leading and guiding them toward the desired outcome. Their influence on housing policy primarily serves the interests of wealthy investors, further entrenching housing discrimination.

Our analysis will shed light on the housing industry's discriminatory practices across two periods: before and after the development of revenue management, specifically during the Industrial Age versus the Technological Age. We will outline the programs, processes, and methods the coalition implements to limit certain classes of people from equal access to housing. These practices prevent certain groups of people from accessing decent housing, forcing them to live in unsafe neighborhoods and thereby significantly impacting housing accessibility and wealth creation.

Today, America stands at a crossroads. Do we allow the richer, more influential investors to drive the wealth-creation process without regulation and oversight? Or do we, as a society, recognize the urgency and importance of providing oversight and regulation to ensure that everyone has an equal chance at the American Dream?

The History of Housing Discrimination During the Industrial Age

This period was marked by overt discrimination. Overt practices or behaviors refer to observable and measurable actions or verbal expressions that are readily apparent. Discrimination can take overt forms, involving direct, intentional actions. Overt discrimination is the most common type. For instance, when someone refuses to sell or rent a housing unit to another person based on their race, religion, or sexual orientation, this is a clear example.

Let's refocus and examine the four groups more closely to understand the housing coalition participants, the coalitions' broad reach, and how they collaborated to create wealth while restricting it for some, with the goal of establishing a cheap labor force. Notably, these participants seem to advocate for their communities at the local level. However, on a national scale, they primarily align with the wealthiest investors and often oppose the best interests of the local level.

The Investors' coalition to build wealth

Chapter 4 examines the strategies investors use to build wealth by leveraging a low-cost labor force composed predominantly of vulnerable minority groups. They leveraged their influence with the other three groups to achieve their objectives. In other words, the investors and their three selected groups not only worked together to openly discriminate against minorities and people of color but also did so with great efficiency.

From the beginning, this coalition established a framework for defining with whom they would or would not do business, setting the stage for potential discrimination. Together, they determined who could own a home, engage in wealth creation, or reside in rental properties or on the streets. To accomplish this vision, this group pushed three underlying assumptions of homeownership onto White society in America: (1) people could be divided by race; (2) only

White communities held property values; and therefore, (3) segregation by race was necessary to protect White property values.

This process is similar to how property management system providers generate "qualified leads" from the broader pool of rental applicants, deciding whom they will or won't do business with, as discussed in Chapter 7.

National Association of Realtors (NAR)

NAR is America's largest trade association, boasting 1.5 million members. Founded in 1908, NAR standardized real estate practices and oversees numerous Multiple Listing Services (MLSs) that serve as nationwide information exchanges for real estate transactions. In 1969, at the request of the investor class, the NAR established the National Association of Realtors Congressional Fund, a super PAC, to advocate for the interests of investors. Between 2004 and 2018, NAR devoted significant resources to lobbying efforts, spending nearly half a billion dollars. In 2018, the organization's lobbying expenditures ranked second only to those of the U.S. Chamber of Commerce, and *Fortune* Magazine has consistently recognized NAR as a powerful lobbying force.

Origins of Discrimination: Historically, NAR opposed fair housing legislation on a national level and implemented exclusionary practices that prevented non-White men from joining their organizations. For example, countless local REALTOR® associations would block anyone who wasn't a White male from becoming a member and gaining access to MLS listings and other essential resources, which was a typical approach to doing business. Frequently, their bylaws clearly stated that Black people, women, Jews, and other groups were not allowed to join.

In 1947, NAR established the National Association of Real Estate Brokers, a counterpart for non-whites, whose members were known as REALTISTS. However, it wasn't until the 1970s that NAR finally made a weak attempt to abolish its discriminatory policies, which had prevented Black and other minority real estate professionals from joining their local boards. Even after enacting the Fair Housing Act, many local boards continued to discourage or deter Black real estate brokers from membership. But worse still, like their banking counterparts, they employed the practices of redlining and steering to keep non-Whites from their neighborhoods. We discuss these practices in more detail below.

American Bankers Association (ABA)

The ABA is a trade association that represents the U.S. banking industry, based in Washington, D.C. Founded in 1875, it lobbies Congress on behalf of banking interests, including efforts to deregulate, such as those related to Fair Housing. In 1943, at the behest of investors, it established the Political Action Committee, a Super-PAC, to advocate for those investors. Until 2010, the financial industry contributed equally to both political parties. However, after that year, it began to heavily favor the Republican Party. For example, the industry contributed over half a billion dollars in 2014, with 70% of contributions going to the GOP.

Origins of Discrimination: Lenders and realtors engaged in redlining, a practice of denying housing loans to creditworthy applicants in specific neighborhoods, even when they met all other eligibility criteria. This practice involves drawing red lines on a map to indicate areas where they would not lend or sell properties, typically in lower-income neighborhoods and regions with a high concentration of minorities.

They also employed racial steering, a tool used to divert non-White creditworthy applicants from White neighborhoods to areas predominantly inhabited by non-Whites. For instance, even if you met the criteria for a mortgage, it did not guarantee approval for your desired home. Furthermore, they incorporated restrictive covenants into loan and mortgage documents, effectively prohibiting people of color and other minorities from owning properties.

U.S. Chamber of Commerce

The U.S. Chamber of Commerce, founded in 1912, claims to represent the interests of over three million businesses of all sizes, sectors, and regions. However, the interests of large corporations dominate its agenda. The Chamber was established to advocate for the interests of large businesses as workers' rights, consumer protections, and environmental concerns became national priorities. The Chamber's influence in the U.S. should not be underestimated.

In 2015, its lobbying expenditures exceeded those of all other organizations, including the American Medical Association. It's crucial to understand that the Chamber's funding does not come solely from its core business members. A *New York Times* report from October 2010 revealed that over half of its contributions—around $140 million in 2008—originated from a small group of forty-five donors, raising questions about the transparency of its operations.

The Chamber, which evokes images of Main Street, Little League teams, and significant financial resources devoted to lobbying efforts, has maintained a longstanding and powerful presence on Capitol Hill. However, its shift in attitude can be traced back to Tom Donohue, a former CEO of the American Trucking Association, who became Chamber president in 1997—the same time frame during which the rental industry was being framed. Donohue said he wanted "to build the biggest gorilla in this town—the most aggressive and vigorous business advocate our nation has ever seen."[1]

The Coalition Leverages the Republican Party

In the 1968 presidential election, Richard Nixon opposed the recently enacted Fair Housing Act. He ran on a platform of "law and order," which many believed was coded language for repressing

Black Americans. Despite this, the 1968 election was very close. Nixon's supporters urged him to choose George Romney, his former presidential rival, who had run an effective campaign against him. Romney was the former chairman and president of American Motors Corporation and the former Governor of Michigan. Nixon encouraged Romney to exit the presidential race and serve as his Secretary of Housing and Urban Development (HUD).

However, unbeknown to Nixon, Romney advanced racial and economic integration by proposing an "Open Communities" program that would condition HUD financial assistance on a community's acceptance of subsidized housing. Subsidized housing refers to units designated for the impoverished and owned by the federal government. Secretary Romney "strove to move Blacks from ghettos into suburbs." He and other "HUD officials had construed the Fair Housing Act very broadly, as a mandate for integration."

In the end, the influential Nixon supporters in the Southern and Northern suburbs took their grievances directly to him. On February 2, 1972, he froze Secretary Romney's lending programs, stating, "I am absolutely opposed to this. Knock it in the head now."[2] This resulted in the dismissal of Secretary Romney. Following this, Nixon and the investors would execute their plan—the Housing and Community Development Act of 1974. However, this block grant program included Secretary Romney's Fair Housing rules. We will finalize the discussion on the Act in Chapter 13.

The Results of Discrimination

The coalition of investors actively enforced their discriminatory practices with the support of their three selected groups—the realtors, the bankers, and the Chamber—and their extensive, well-established networks spanning the entire country. Their unified efforts effectively excluded people of color from their White neighborhoods, intentionally restricting their ability to accumulate wealth.

When President Ronald Reagan nominated Robert Bork, the antitrust scholar and one of the chief architects of Reaganomics (introduced in Chapter 4), to the U.S. Supreme Court in 1987, he had spent five years as a federal appeals court judge. He amassed an extensive paper trail of controversial legal writings in both his judicial and academic roles. For example, in 1964, he published an article in *The New Republic* arguing that any law requiring businesses to serve people of all races would be "subversive of free institutions by self-righteously imposing upon a minority—that is, upon racist White businessmen—the morals of the majority."

Additionally, he was quoted as saying, "The Civil Rights Act was based on a principle of unsurpassed ugliness." Further explaining, "That might lead to an even more nightmarish future for businesses, requiring not merely fair hiring of Negros in subordinate positions, but the choices of partners or associates...without regard to race."[3]

We will now focus on the effects of Nixon's housing policies. In a 2015 report titled "Living Apart: How the Government Betrayed a Landmark Civil Rights Law," Nikole Hannah-Jones discussed Romney's HUD program. She noted that since 1974, the grants to needy communities have delivered $137 billion through Nixon's public-private partnerships (P3s). To qualify for the funds, however, communities must identify obstacles to fair housing, document their findings to address them, and certify that they do not engage in discriminatory practices.

Hannah-Jones could find only two instances since Romney's time in which the department withheld money from communities for violating the Fair Housing Act. In many cases, records show that HUD has sent grants to communities even after courts found that it had promoted segregated housing or been sued by the DOJ for ongoing Fair Housing violations.[4]

These were the overt methods this group employed to discriminate against people of color and other minorities. The sole purpose was to create a cheap labor force to enrich themselves by abusing their economic power and wealth. These practices had significant implications for housing accessibility and contributed to the perpetuation of housing inequality.

The History of Housing Discrimination During the Technological Age

Imagine, if you will, it's the late 1990s. You are seated in a boardroom in California's Silicon Valley, attentively listening to a presentation about one of the most significant discoveries of our time—a groundbreaking technology known as revenue management, enhanced by artificial intelligence. Its potential knows no bounds and will create immense wealth for those few who harness its power. This wealth creation is almost immediate, happening overnight—almost like magic. Consider the wealth generated by the owners of Facebook, Twitter, Google, Microsoft, Apple, Amazon, and other prominent companies.

Our previous discussions detailed how investors leveraged this immense power, including AI's role in artificially doubling our housing costs through revenue management technology. However, does AI serve any other purposes? How can wealthy investors effectively utilize this significant power, particularly in their pursuit of wealth? Unfortunately, the implications for the minority members of the working class are severe. This technology could potentially lead to the creation of a cheaper labor force by unfairly discriminating against certain groups of people. But what would this scenario look like today, and how is it different from their overt methods in the past?

Today, overt or open discrimination is no longer accepted in modern society; instead, it has been replaced by a more subtle expression of hate, such as disparate impact. Disparate impact, which is a legal concept, refers to policies or practices that may seem fair on the surface but actually harm specific groups, including people of color and other minority groups. This form of discrimination is not overt but rather concealed. In simpler terms, it's like a rule that appears fair to everyone, but upon closer examination, you realize it actually hurts some people more than others.

Ultimately, investors active in the rental housing industry devised a plan to use AI to discriminate against certain classes of people. As discussed earlier, creating a cheap labor force merely requires interfering with one's ability to acquire a decent home and a safe living environment. Consider the story of Juan Carlos in Chapter 7.

Today, it's no secret that systemic racism is a significant issue in America. However, what may surprise some is that modern AI revenue management technology is being used to reinforce racism within our current housing system. When individuals seek to rent a home or apartment, the most critical screening process is the tenant background check that occurs behind the scenes, which can result in the difference between securing a home and facing homelessness.

The investor class, relying upon the principles of the new Management Standard, would leverage its relationship with HUD to create a cheap labor force. In 2019, the Trump administration appointed Ben Carson to lead HUD, aiming to implement his agenda while giving the appearance of fairness. HUD Secretary Carson would betray his oath of office by announcing his intention to modify the 2013 Disparate Impact Rule, which focuses on equal access to housing as established by President Obama.

Carson refers to his plan as "Open Communities," which ironically mocks Romney's Open Communities Plan. In 2020, Carson approved this rule change, overturning President Obama's fairness-based rule and replacing it with a system devoid of regulation, allowing participants to discriminate using a third-party algorithm.

Following HUD Secretary Carson's rule change, investors, realtors, and lenders now have qualified immunity, a highly prejudicial judicial doctrine underpinned by racist disparate practices, developed by the Supreme Court that protects certain classes of people from liability for misconduct, even when they have violated the law. In this case, it safeguards them from the repercussions of algorithms provided by third parties, such as RealPage. Essentially, this means it is very challenging to take legal action against a landlord for discrimination if the landlord claims that a third-party algorithm guides their actions. Nonetheless, this rule change raises serious concerns about potential discriminatory practices in the housing industry.

For example, the 2019 screening algorithm that RealPage acquired, as discussed in Chapter 6, was intended to serve as a tool for fair evaluation. However, it was discovered that it had been trained to discriminate against certain groups based on race, skin color, or other demographics. Several companies, including RealPage, Yardi, and AppFolio, have been repeatedly found to use deceptive practices, such as adding criminal records or other false information to their applicants' final credit reports. These practices are meant to exclude certain classes of people from their apartment communities.

So, what is really happening here, and how widespread is this practice? In 2019, there were nearly 30,000 registered complaints of housing discrimination, all of which went unanswered by Republican Ben Carson. Shockingly, over 90% of all reported acts of housing discrimination occurred during the rental pre-screening process, significantly affecting housing affordability—this happens before the applicant even signs an application, leaving no paper trail. This result occurs when the technology pre-qualifies an applicant using the vast databases of information available to it, and all its processes remain hidden within the black box.

Let's revisit Chapter 7 to examine how the algorithm trained to discriminate is used to select tenants. Using a real-life example, we return to Juan Carlos and his family. The property owner at 17 Cherry Tree Lane implemented revenue management technology that evaluates an applicant's financial capability and willingness to accept rate increases. Unfortunately, this technology was also designed to discriminate against people of color with small children, like Juan Carlos and his family. Reports indicate that a false felony record was added to Juan's credit report and subsequently used to deny his rental application.

In a broader example from 2017, a complaint was filed in Washington, D.C., against property managers for a policy that barred renters with certain criminal records, including misdemeanors—consider the "stop and frisk" policy—from obtaining housing. This policy violates the Fair Housing Act and disproportionately affects African Americans and Latinos. These aren't just statistics; they are lives being impacted.

In Conclusion,

For Renters

To outline their current methods of discriminatory practices, we consulted a case study conducted in Seattle, WA. In 2015, the Seattle Office of Civil Rights (SOCR) filed complaints of illegal discrimination with the Washington State Human Rights Commission against the owners of thirteen apartment properties. Our Seattle Concentration Study (Chapter 5) found that all thirteen property managers accused of discrimination were members of the RealPage Platform. Not only were they members, but they also ranked among the top twenty-five largest managers, all of whom have strong ties to Harlan Crow.

The SOCR conducted 124 tests to investigate housing discrimination. The report found evidence of discrimination in more than half of the tests, highlighting the widespread nature of the issue. For example, African-American testers were shown fewer units, quoted higher prices, and were more frequently informed about criminal background and credit history checks than White testers, which constitutes a clear violation of their rights.

In a typical case, the SOCR states that an agent informed an African-American tester that a one-bedroom unit would cost $2,300 per month and would be available in one week. However, within ninety minutes, the same agent told a White tester that the unit would cost $2,000 and would be available immediately. These tests weren't isolated incidents; they revealed pervasive discriminatory practices.

Furthermore, the complaint states that three months later, an agent from the same apartment complex quoted $1,825 to an African-American tester and $1,700 to a White tester for the same unit. "These test results are not isolated incidents. They demonstrate patterns of behavior that have profound impacts on people's lives," SOCR Director Patricia Lally emphasized.[5] The Platform is actively involved in discriminatory practices, as evidenced by the illegal discrimination complaints filed against its many, many cartel members.

For Homeowners

The coalition's discriminatory practices have significantly affected the net worth of Black and minority American households. By 1995, the median White family had more than eight times the net worth of the median Black family, starkly illustrating the economic inequality perpetuated by these practices. The disparity is even more pronounced for Latinos, with the median White household having more than twelve times the wealth of the median Latino family.[6]

It is essential to recognize that owning a home is integral to achieving the American Dream, as it provides stability and a sense of self-worth. Equity in homes is a significant asset, accounting for over 40% of the net worth of all households. Today's considerable income inequality is primarily due to investors' discriminatory practices, which have prevented certain individuals from realizing equal access to wealth creation.

The significant difference in net worth for minorities arises not only from the value of the homes they purchased, but also from substantial disparities in the value and net worth of the homes they wanted to buy and were qualified to purchase; but were ultimately denied solely due to the discriminatory practices of the investors' coalition. As Richard Rothstein, a Distinguished Fellow of the Economic Policy Institute, asserts in his acclaimed book Segregation by Design, "This enormous difference in wealth is almost entirely attributable to federal housing policy implemented throughout the 20th century."[7] This underscores the systemic nature of the problem. These are the methods investors currently use to create a cheap labor force by employing AI technology to discriminate through disparate impact.

Discrimination in the Workplace

It's important to acknowledge that the same cartel coalition that discriminates in housing also engages in discriminatory practices in the workforce. They infringe upon the civil rights of people of color by denying them opportunities in management roles. This practice reflects Robert Bork's 1964 article, which warned that laws requiring businesses to serve all races could lead to a more harmful future for businesses.

In 2020, *Biznow*, a prominent news outlet covering the housing industry, reported a disheartening truth in its article: "These Developers Have Built Up America." Their Executives Are 93% White. According to their research, the most influential development firms in the U.S., including Trammell Crow, Hines, Tishman Speyer, CIM Group, and Greystar, are still predominantly led by White males. Their analysis of twenty-four of the nation's largest private commercial and multifamily development companies revealed a stark reality: Only 31 of the 435 top-level executives were people of color, representing a mere 7%.

Results of Discriminatory Practices

This chapter aims to expose the wealthy investors' abuse of economic power and wealth in their methods of wealth creation, which is underpinned by discriminating against certain classes of people, primarily people of color and other minorities. Their entire wealth creation program is centered on creating a cheap labor force through discrimination and preventing certain classes of people from obtaining decent homes and safe living environments.

Since the adoption of the New Deal, the wealthy, including those investors who own apartment properties, have exerted a profound and often detrimental influence on our laws. They relentlessly manipulate and distort these laws to serve their own interests, crushing anyone who dares to oppose their path to wealth creation.

Initially, the investor coalition, which included realtors, lenders, and the Chamber's lobbying efforts, along with their extensive and well-connected networks that spanned the entire country, employed overt methods to promote their discriminatory actions, which were readily apparent to everyone. However, they have now turned to the concept of disparate impact, hiding their true motives from the public to maintain the working class's support. Over the years, historians have often underestimated the size, scale, and influence of this coalition, as well as its impact on the housing industry and politics in general.

Yet, perhaps the greatest tragedy faced by the impoverished today arises from the actions—or more likely, the inactions—of nonprofit organizations. For instance, by the end of 2018, the investor's wealth-creation methods had sparked a crisis in affordable housing, which disproportionately impacted people of color. According to Chapter 10, nearly fifty-one million Americans—43% of households in the U.S., constituting two-thirds of the labor force—found themselves unable to afford housing within their monthly budgets. Even worse, nearly a million-and-a-half citizens have been forced to live permanently on the streets. It's the greatest humanitarian crisis since the Great Depression.

However, just as the judicial system detailed in Chapter 10 has failed the impoverished, these nonprofits have also fallen very, very short of expectations. One might expect nonprofits to step in and provide humanitarian aid, but unfortunately, that's not the case. Instead, the wealthy investor caste has exploited its relationship with these nonprofits. Regrettably, only a tiny fraction of the enormous $1.5 trillion in nonprofit tax-exempt donations is directed toward helping those in poverty. Instead, this vast stockpile of cash is used to further their own agendas and support the wealth-creation goals of the richest.

However, what is more troubling is that these investors and their nonprofit organizations, instead of providing funds to help those in need, promote the idea that homelessness is a moral failing of individuals and, therefore, they don't deserve assistance. They contend that the use of AI-driven revenue management strategies by the investor class and their operatives to exclude specific groups from housing is often dismissed as mere "woke" nonsense. Worse still, they work harmoniously to hide their insidious history of racism and bigotry.

Instead of providing food and shelter for those in need, their disparate-impact methods involve hiring external nonprofit firms to discriminate on investors' behalf. An example is Harlan Crow, who hired Supreme Court Justice Clarence Thomas's wife, Ginni Thomas, to do just that. In 2009, it was discovered that she had created numerous organizations, including Liberty Central and Groundswell. By 2011, she had received more than $1.5 million in tax-exempt donations from anonymous sources. *Politico*, a respected news agency, would eventually discover that the initial $500,000 of funding came from Harlan Crow. With those funds, she—a U.S. Supreme Court Justice's wife—has built an empire of hate where she openly and with great hostility crusades against minorities and pushes extreme hate campaigns against the LGBTQ community.[8]

Despite spanning over 150 years of Fair Housing and other credit-related violations, the investors' coalition remains self-regulating. Worse still, they haven't adopted the Fair Housing Act. Today, it's clear that the divide of the Fair Housing Paradox has never been wider. The investor class has gained significant freedom from oversight and regulation from the corrupt MAGA U.S. Supreme Court, which continues to bestow additional economic power and wealth upon them. Meanwhile, people of color and minorities lack access to decent homes and safe living environments, as well as freedom from the burden of discrimination.

The consequences of discrimination by this massive coalition, as reported in the *Stanford News*, is a society that is deeply divided along racial and economic lines. In fact, the U.S. ranks at the bottom among all industrialized countries in terms of residential segregation. Today, in America, nearly half of all Black Americans and Latinos live in neighborhoods without a White presence. The average White person resides in a community that is almost 80% White.[9]

CHAPTER 12

The Bottom Line on Revenue Management

Key Concepts:

What is the legal definition of "Wealth Transfer"?

Wealth transfer is a legal concept in which dominant monopolies with exclusive market control and power artificially inflate prices, diverting income from consumers to the company's owners. This occurs because a monopoly can set prices above those in a competitive market. Such practices constitute a form of wealth transfer, as the monopolist effectively exerts unjust enrichment by extracting resources from consumers with no alternative options for the good or service. This behavior is generally considered illegal.

Introduction

In April of 2021, Supreme Court Justice Clarence Thomas issued a concurrence over Trump's Twitter account. He suggested that social media companies be regulated like a common carrier, like a telephone company. "A person always could choose to avoid the toll bridge or train and instead swim the Charles River or hike the Oregon Trail," Thomas wrote. "But in assessing whether a company exercises substantial market power, what matters is whether the alternatives are comparable. For many of today's digital platforms, nothing is."[1]

These digital platforms include the RealPage common pricing platform and its use of revenue management. It manages and prices up to 95% of the market, leaving no reasonable means of housing without its use. Today, applicants and tenants consistently encounter the same powerful corporate landlords and home builders (Chapter 13) who maximize profits by employing unregulated revenue management technologies across all areas of housing, from design and construction to property management. Regardless of the housing type—single-family or multifamily—investors and their shared technologies dominate the market. There isn't a corner of investment where they do not exist. They now occupy every corner and aspect of the housing industry, to the extent that they own and control the "housing river."

Today, no river remains for the price-out; they can't afford the toll. For them, housing has been shut down, leaving no trails to hike. The Platform guards nearly every door and holds almost every key. They are forcing the bottom 15% of income earners out onto the streets and making the working-class taxpayers foot the bill. Today, there is no competition in the housing industry—no rivers left to ford—forcing nearly a million-and-a-half people onto the streets and fifty-one million hardworking Americans into a state of crisis.

This practice parallels Justice Thomas's assessment of former President Trump's Twitter account, specifically the lack of competition with Big Tech companies, their exercise of economic power and wealth, and the lack of alternatives. However, here we are talking about the most basic human need—housing—rather than tweeting.

AI-Powered Revenue Management sits at the Heart of the Affordable Housing Crisis.

Chapter 2 prompts the reader to consider how prices for commodities like eggs and gasoline are determined. The answer is that various economic sectors use AI-powered revenue management technology to set industry-wide prices. This practice contrasts with that of individual business owners, who set their own prices based on a free-market system in which providers of goods and services compete for consumers' business. Therefore, it isn't inflation causing the chaotic pricing swings, but rather the industry's use of revenue management technology. Chapter 14 examines the impact of President Trump's tariffs on the economy and price inflation, particularly in relation to revenue management technology.

In the rental housing sector, this technology serves as the cornerstone for setting rent prices. The process begins with Step 1, in which all data on applicants, tenants, and properties is accessed and shared in real time. The data set used to determine rental rates includes information from not only individual landlords but also their shared thirty-three million units, as well as data from third-party providers and data brokers.

However, obtaining all that data was only half the task. The landlords needed a place to store it. So, they started building data centers, and lots of them. Data centers are central to algorithmic price-fixing; they depend on each other—the pricing technology and the sources and storage of large amounts of data. Without storage capabilities, algorithmic price-fixing could not happen.

The second step in the pricing process involves the industry-wide practice of selling technology through white labeling. This practice further complicates the claim of independence. It ensures that truly independent operators cannot exist because the landlords, their data, and their shared technologies and pricing strategies all reside in a controlled vacuum of shared data encompassing information from the thirty-three million units. Consequently, their pricing algorithms and technologies operate identically, yielding the same recommended rental rates.

The third step of the pricing process is further complicated by the fact that landlords use the same Economic Occupancy Pricing Strategy as their competitors, including the practice of holding rental units off the market. In the fourth step of the pricing process, their common pricing algorithms recommend rental rates. However, over 90% of the industry accepts those recommendations. Therefore, technology—not individual landlords—sets industry-wide prices.

However, that's not all; they also work harmoniously to price out the bottom 15% of tenants and participate in a debt-collection-driven embargo against those who owe them money, keeping those tenants on the streets until they are paid in full. They also boost profits by discriminating against minorities and people of color in a coordinated manner.

In summary, it appears that the rental housing industry is involved in tacit collusion. This term refers to landlords in a market coordinating their actions without explicit communication. Instead, technology serves as the intermediary, conveying information to potential competitors on their behalf. Although these landlords do not openly share their pricing strategies with competing landlords, property management system providers have access to this information and use it to establish industry-wide prices. This practice enables them to exert market power and artificially inflate rents, significantly affecting the rental housing market.

The rental housing industry's use of tacit collusion restrains trade. It has created a pricing cartel with monopoly power, affecting up to 95% of all rental units. Moreover, users of revenue management technology have already faced prosecution for such conduct in Europe. Their behavior involves an agreement to reconfigure automated pricing software to avoid undercutting each other. Another court case revealed that they also agreed to implement an algorithm for allocating customers and territories among themselves.[2] Worse still for global consumers, this same AI-powered revenue management technology is used throughout the U.S., as well as across Canada, Asia, Britain, Europe, Australia, and Saudi Arabia.

This cartel behavior limits competition, enabling algorithmic price-fixing to manipulate rental prices. However, the pressing question is: Why? Why would an entire industry collude and place its independence into question? The answer is simple: Occam's razor—it's the massive profits that can only be generated by working together through their pricing cartel. This action concludes that the industry has violated the Sherman Antitrust Act, specifically by reducing output (by holding rental units off the market) and creating market power that allows it to artificially raise prices.

Conclusion: The Wealth Transfer

However, the nature of those profits is now in question. The pricing technology wasn't designed to create a better product or service; it was built to transfer wealth from renters to landlords and their investors. It artificially inflates revenue by withholding rental units, manipulating the market, and charging excessive junk fees, thereby generating significant unearned income (unjust enrichment). Nevertheless, this technology's main drawback is its primary goal of maximizing profits, regardless of the resulting side effects. It's the calamity of our age. This technology is used solely to price-gouge rather than to improve the lives of everyone. It's a win-win for investors but a lose-lose scenario for tenants, the consumers.

Seattle serves as a compelling case study. The Platform significantly inflated rents by over 40% between 2013 and 2014, from $1,227 to $1,719, or $5,904 per year per rental unit. In total, this resulted in staggering $2.3 billion in artificially inflated rents that Seattle residents pay to their landlords each year. Their practice is not just a local issue but a national one. The fact is that metro Seattle is only the 15th-largest in the country. Therefore, on a national scale, tenants pay tens upon tens of billions of dollars each year for artificially inflated housing costs.

As we conclude our examination of the impact of AI-powered revenue management technology on consumers, it's essential to acknowledge its role in contributing to the affordable housing crisis. Property owners, powerful corporate landlords, and the management companies they hire have achieved significant financial success; however, this success has come at a steep price for their consumers. In short, their artificially generated profits represent a wealth transfer, which is an illegal practice. This shift primarily benefits property owners and their investors, who are far wealthier than the average renter. For instance, in the Metro Seattle area, there has been an annual wealth transfer of $2.3 billion—that's $23 billion between 2014 and 2024. That amounts to nearly $60,000 per renter household.

This wealth transfer from renters to property owners is directly a result of using revenue management technology to establish industry-wide pricing. This significant wealth transfer contributes significantly to the affordable housing crisis it has created. The economic impact of this crisis is profound. Today, in America, two-thirds of our workforce—over fifty-one million people, or 43% of all Americans—are unable to afford housing within their family budgets. Currently, we face the greatest homeless crisis in our country's history. If left unaddressed, this trend is unsustainable for metropolitan areas, hindering any effort to grow or sustain a city's economy.

What could be worse for American consumers? The entire economy is saturated and drowning in revenue management technology. The oil-and-gas industry is raking in record-high, multi-billion-dollar profits. The grocery and retail industry is also reaping record-high multibillion-dollar profits. The insurance industry is also seeing record-high multibillion-dollar profits. Yet, conversely, our pay increases by mere pennies. Today, in America, the steep price increases that consumers face are not driven by inflation. Instead, they are a well-orchestrated criminal enterprise fueled by unregulated algorithmic price-fixing, which is made possible by these shared revenue management technologies.

What could possibly be worse? Today, our healthcare system is undergoing significant changes due to the adoption of AI-powered technologies, which are leading to the formation of pricing cartels. The pressing question is: Will these developments exclude the bottom 15-23% of Americans from accessing healthcare, all in the name of maximizing profits for the most wealthy? Consider the 119th Republican-controlled Congress (2025–2026), which aims to remove 43 million lower-income earners from Affordable Care Act insurance programs, primarily to benefit their billionaire donors.

The question is: Are we really willing to abandon a quarter of our citizens, leaving them not only homeless and on the streets but also at risk of dying on the streets? Are we willing to remain complicit and accept the investors' wealth-creation strategies, in which no price is too high for their wealth? What kind of society have we, as Americans, become? How many more millions of our children will be forced to find refuge on the streets before we as a society become concerned? At what point will the investor's price ever become too high?

What's more, since Robert Bork's 1978 (Reaganomics) shift in antitrust legislation, the number of billionaires this technology has created has also skyrocketed, along with their profits. For instance, between 2006 and 2018, the number of billionaires almost tripled from 793 to around 2,200. According to a *Forbes* study, billionaires collectively grow $2.5 billion wealthier every day, amounting to more than a trillion dollars annually.[3]

The process of wealth creation continues to accelerate rapidly. A December 2025 study by *The Wall Street Journal* indicates that the number of billionaires has increased to 2,900 since the 2020 pandemic. Their collective wealth has grown by 62% amid these turbulent times.

Revenue management technology is the vehicle for transferring that wealth, like an hourglass, transferring $2.5 billion every day from the working class to the very wealthiest. This wealth transfer must be condemned as the most egregious act of class warfare in our nation's history.

In Chapter 4, it was detailed that the ultimate goal of Reaganomics was to transform our economy back to the 1920s when unregulated monopolies dominated the landscape. The key tool at the heart of this transformation is revenue management technology. However, as Robert Bork, the chief architect of Reaganomics, pointed out to Congress, this policy could only be implemented as long as the financial benefits to the wealthy investor class do not outweigh the harm to consumers. In other words, do the ends—operational efficiencies and massive profitability—justify the means—skyrocketing rental rates leading to massive gentrification and homelessness?

It's clear that the financial benefits of revenue management technology for wealthy investors do not outweigh the tremendous economic and societal damage inflicted on consumers. The use of revenue management has caused crushing damage to the working-class economy overall.

As we begin to understand the challenges of revenue management technology, the dilemma we face as a society is that the immense wealth it creates isn't a dream. At the boardroom meeting in Silicon Valley during the late 1990s, when the upcoming release of AI-powered revenue management technology was discussed (Chapter 11), it was not just a hypothetical scenario; the meeting actually happened. The pages of this book outline how investors decided to implement this newly developed and immensely powerful technology. Now, we as a society must confront the consequences of their corrupt methods of implementing that technology. After all, it's the abusive methodologies incorporated into the technology that have become the problem, not the technology itself.

Today, America stands at a crossroads. The urgent, escalating affordable housing crisis, primarily driven by unregulated and unfair AI revenue management technology, demands immediate, decisive attention. The suggestion to deactivate this technology to address the root problems raises critical questions about why this action hasn't been pursued more vigorously. The question remains whether the response would change if the roles of the landlords and their tenants were reversed.

At the end of the day, it comes down to this fundamental question: How do we balance the need for technology and its requirement for massive amounts of personal and private data against the rights of naive consumers and their willingness to trade their safety and privacy for convenience?

At the heart of the problem is that revenue management technology cannot be adequately regulated; doing so contradicts its very design. Since its inception, this immensely powerful technology has been created to manipulate the fundamental principles of supply and demand and, in turn, the market. It was also designed to circumvent the laws of the land (Database 7). This technology was developed for one purpose and one purpose only—its prime directive—to maximize profits for property owners and their investors, by any means necessary. It has become the incurable cancer at the core of the struggle between affordable housing and homelessness. Therefore, regulating revenue management technology isn't an option—it truly serves as a weapon of mass destruction.

The Fix—The Final Solution:

As previously mentioned, this work underpins the Department of Justice's 2024 lawsuit against RealPage and its pricing algorithm, as well as the lawsuit against the member landlords accused of participating in algorithmic price-fixing. However, Donald Trump's election has jeopardized this legal action, as his administration has expressed its intention to settle the case on very favorable terms to the industry. In February and March 2025, Trump issued several Executive Orders aimed at removing key DOJ management personnel and attorneys he viewed as disloyal, as part of his effort to fully deregulate and privatize the economy.

Of course, would it surprise the reader to learn that Trump has a massive conflict of interest in this case? He was one of the original users of the Rainmaker Revolution price-fixing technology (Chapter 7). In 2006, The Rainmaker Group issued a press release that Trump Entertainment Resorts had implemented Rainmaker's Revolution in all three of its gaming resorts, with 2,900 rooms.[4] Therefore, the settlement will not put an end to their price-fixing schemes. Without implementing new laws and institutions to regulate the industry, nothing will truly change.

The basis of this claim rests on the DOJ's prior experience with antitrust cases. For example, in 2018, the airline industry accepted a $45 million fine but admitted no misconduct in connection with its algorithmic price-fixing case. Our investigation found that they probably did not alter their practices. For instance, have your airline ticket prices dropped significantly since 2018? The answer is: Not likely. According to industry reports, the average ticket price has increased by 22%.

In this book, we examine Greystar, the largest property management company, overseeing nearly a million rental units. They agreed to stop using certain data-sharing practices and are scheduled to pay a $50 million fine in this legal case. However, as discussed, despite the hefty fines, they are relatively small compared to Greystar's scale—about $50 per rental unit. Meanwhile, this chapter reveals that, over the past decade, tenants in cities like Seattle have been overcharged by approximately $60,000 per rental unit, totaling around $32 billion across the market. The fine represents a minuscule percentage of Greystar's profits. In other words, the fines rarely deter the practice—just the cost of doing business in the digital age.

Thus, although renters in Seattle have each been overcharged by $60,000, the renters will be lucky to receive five to ten dollars in compensation. Therefore, to truly bring about change in the rental housing industry and the economy as a whole, the punishment of disgorgement must be imposed in cases involving algorithmic price-fixing. Disgorgement is a legal term where 100% of all ill-gotten profits must be returned to the victims. In this case, each renter household in the Seattle market must receive $60,000.

Step 1:

We must design laws to adequately regulate AI-powered pricing technologies as detailed in Chapters 6 - 9.

The core issue is that pricing cartels with monopoly power can only endure by exploiting unlimited and substantial amounts of consumer data, which they access and share without restriction or oversight. To make matters worse, as discussed in Chapter 6, the data center industry is projected to grow by $7 trillion by 2030. This indicates that American businesses have no intention of voluntarily discontinuing the use of pricing technology to maximize profits through algorithmic price fixing.

Therefore, to foster trust and responsibility, strong laws must be enacted to safeguard personal data and privacy rights. Ensuring that these technologies are adequately regulated. Pricing Cartels must be abolished. Our democracy depends on these protections. Democracies cannot survive in a scenario where citizens lack control over their personal data and their privacy rights are disregarded. Even more concerning is a scenario where large, unregulated companies have unfettered access to detailed private information and exploit it for malicious purposes. Consequently, regulations should be carefully crafted to effectively oversee AI-powered pricing technologies, including the Truth in Rental Housing Act, as detailed in Chapter 9.

Step 2:

We must separate the data gatherers from the data users as detailed in Chapter 6.

Step 3:

Establish new institutions dedicated to overseeing AI-powered pricing technologies.

As detailed in Chapter 9, new institutions are needed to ensure effective regulation and enforcement. These agencies will be essential for maintaining oversight and protecting consumer rights in this evolving landscape.

- A new institution responsible for regulating consumer data collection and preventing its sharing. For instance, the Consumer Financial Protection Bureau could add a division focused on technology and consumer data-gathering protections.
- An independent agency responsible for regulating AI-powered technologies, similar to the Federal Reserve, free from political influence and corruption. Truly independent agencies will ensure unbiased oversight and protect public interests.
- An institution to regulate the rental housing industry, as outlined in Chapter 9.

The time has come for America to make a choice. Will we have the courage to follow the example set by our ancestors after the financial crash of 1929 by instituting new laws and institutions to regulate this technology, and in cases where it cannot be controlled, discontinue and prohibit its use? The necessity for action is clear, and it's time for us as a society to respond. Or will we, as a society, choose to play the role of Nero, the Emperor of Rome, and fiddle while "home" burns?

CHAPTER 13
A Place to Call Home

It's almost always about the money. Therefore, to better understand history, follow the money trail.

Introduction

The housing program introduced during the New Deal, as discussed in Chapter 1, serves as a testament to the potential of big government to greatly improve the lives of the working class. A primary benefit of the program was establishing a benchmark for housing costs relative to wages, with policymakers suggesting that housing expenses be limited to 20% of a family's budget. This approach enables individuals to save money for retirement or other household expenses, such as their children's college education. The program's success was so remarkable that by 1939, purchasing a home became less expensive than renting an apartment. This result had never happened before in the industrialized world.

Furthermore, the Housing Act of 1949 solidified the New Deal housing program, which states that **every American deserves a decent home and a safe living environment.** By 2005, homeownership in the United States reached an all-time high of 70%. Homeownership and the American Dream had become synonymous terms.

In stark contrast, by 2022, housing had become unaffordable for most Americans, especially those living in metropolitan cities, where the working class now pays half or more of their wages on housing. According to Chapter 7, affordable homes are priced under $300,000 or $400,000 in metropolitan cities, based on a 30% debt-to-income ratio. But how can essential services such as housing transition from a significant benefit to a massive detriment for the working class?

Who Is Responsible for the Affordable Housing Crisis?

To better understand the affordable housing crisis, it is essential to identify who is responsible for it. To find the answer, we need to look back in time. In 1972, a tenant, in a display of remarkable courage and determination, stood up to their powerful landlord. The conflict began in 1969, when the Portland, Oregon, Bureau of Buildings declared a home unfit for human habitation and issued a 30-day notice to vacate. The tenants had refused to pay rent until certain violations of a local housing code were addressed. This action prompted the landlord to threaten eviction for nonpayment of rent. In response, the tenants filed a class-action lawsuit in federal court.

The U.S. Supreme Court's decision in Lindsey v. Normet (405 U.S. 56, 1972) was a watershed moment that significantly influenced housing law, marking a turning point in tenants' rights. It also established that housing is a matter for legislative bodies, with the power to enact change resting with cities, counties, and states rather than the judicial system. However, Congress has the ultimate power to effect meaningful change in this matter.

The Single-Family and Multifamily Construction Industries Today

We seek to answer the question: What has caused the skyrocketing housing costs that now consume more than half of the working class's income? Are the causes of these price surges a shortage of housing units, or is something more sinister afoot within the housing industry?

To better understand the high cost of housing, in 2017, the National Low-Income Housing Coalition, an organization established to monitor national affordable housing issues, conducted a nationwide study of housing availability. Their report revealed a staggering shortage of more than seven million affordable housing units. In short, the report suggested that the probable cause of the skyrocketing housing costs was a shortage in the housing supply.

In response to this urgent crisis, the private sector (big business) has invested trillions of taxpayer dollars by 2022, constructing 8.7 million units and creating a new housing construction boom. Nearly 2 million apartment units have been completed. In the Single-Family Residential (SFR) industry, some 6.7 million new homes were built.

Figure 13.1: Sales Price of Existing Single-Family Homes

Year	Total U.S.	Northeast	Midwest	South	West
2020	$ 300,200	$ 341,700	$ 235,400	$ 265,100	$ 451,500
2021	$ 357,100	$ 394,100	$ 236,300	$ 317,500	$ 558,800
2022	$ 392,800	$ 426,000	$ 281,900	$ 359,500	$ 617,100

Source: NATIONAL ASSOCIATION OF REALTORS® https://cdn.nar.realtor/sites/default/files/documents/ehs-03-2023-single-family-only-2023-04-20.pdf

However, unlike in the past, when housing construction focused on providing homes for the working class, which was subject to the 30% income rule. Instead, the new construction mainly occurred at the high end of the market's price point. For instance, in 2019, 52% of newly constructed homes were priced under $300,000. However, by 2022, that figure had plummeted to only 13%. Additionally, construction mainly occurred in the twenty largest metro areas, predominantly in the South, with exceptions including New York City and Seattle. This shift in focus toward higher-priced homes has significant implications for housing affordability, particularly for low- and middle-income families, who are bearing the brunt of this crisis.

Affordable housing advocates pressured their lawmakers for answers to the escalating housing costs. In a 2022 legislative hearing, the housing industry quickly pointed out that they couldn't build housing priced under $300,000 because the cost of building materials was too high.

So, the question we aim to answer is: Are the steep rises in housing prices the result of uncontrollable costs for building materials, or are they the consequence of market manipulation? It's a crucial question, especially when we compare and contrast the claims made to Congress with the financial reports of residential building giants, such as D.R. Horton, the nation's largest single-family home builder, which reported a $7.6 billion profit in 2022. The second-largest builder, Lennar Corporation, reported a net profit of $4.6 billion. The third-largest builder, PulteGroup, reported net profit of $2.6 billion. Yet, they assert they cannot afford to build a home for under $300,000.

Seattle, WA. A Case Study on Housing Costs

The sharp increase in housing costs can be better understood by examining what is actually happening in the marketplace rather than the industry's false narrative. To accomplish this, we will continue with our discussion with the city of Seattle as a case study. During this period, most newly constructed apartment units, similar to the rest of the country, were built using various HUD financing programs discussed in Chapter 9. For instance, Seattle turned to the Multifamily Tax Exemption Program (MFTE) to address their housing shortages.

Initially, the HUD lending program, MFTE, was designed to provide tax incentives for nonprofit homebuilders who are personally connected to their communities, with the goal of improving affordable housing for consumers. However, according to a 2019 Washington State Legislative Report, the program has become dominated by for-profit Wall Street conglomerates that build rental units in neighborhoods where they didn't need incentives to produce housing. These conglomerates have shamelessly gorged themselves on taxpayer-funded subsidies meant to provide housing for those who have been priced out and are in need.

By 2021, Seattle had an excess of over 9,000 rental units for those earning over $80,000, while facing a shortage of nearly 30,000 affordable rental units for those earning under $50,000. Adding to the issue, over 6,000 affordable units renting for under $800 were demolished to make way for new, more expensive units renting at over $2,000, worsening the affordable housing shortage. This practice resulted in more than 35,000 workers with jobs paying less than $50,000 per year now living more than twenty-five miles from their workplace—a commute that takes up to two hours each way.[1] Today, driving until you qualify for affordable housing has become the new norm.

The Chapter's Objectives

Still, with construction at all-time highs and affordable housing inventory at all-time lows, will more unregulated home building solve the crisis? After all, as taxpayers, we guarantee these loans, which now total well over $7 trillion—an all-time high. Can we rely on this industry to build affordable housing?

Previous chapters focused on the rental industry, where soaring rental rates were attributed to the use of AI revenue management technology. The first part of this chapter will focus on the single-family residential (SFR) housing and multifamily construction industries, exploring the likely causes of today's skyrocketing housing costs and emphasizing the SFR industry. The second part of the chapter will focus on changes to the New Deal housing program that shifted benefits away from the working class toward the investor class. We will also explore who is responsible for the crisis and what we, as citizens, can do to address it.

This crisis has placed America at a crossroads. Does every American have the right to a decent home and a safe living environment, or is this right currently reserved for only some Americans, such as the wealthy, as in George Orwell's novel Animal Farm, where some are more equal than others? But if we are truly equal, how will we create affordable housing for those who need it? Do we rely on the current housing construction industry, or are there other options to choose from?

It is imperative to understand that without housing investments for lower-income communities with vulnerable populations, we will witness a continued surge in homelessness, illness, mortality, and a general decrease in the quality of life for both the less advantaged and the working class. Metro areas like Seattle already spend over a quarter of a billion dollars annually on emergency funding to care for unhoused people (these funds do not include funds to provide permanent housing). This figure escalates to tens of billions nationally. These numbers are unsustainable for taxpayers, underscoring the urgent need to reform the current housing system.

Let's meet Alex and Karen Kim and follow their journey as they purchase their first home.

Alex and Karen first met in Seattle, WA, in 2015 while they were both attending college. Following Alex's graduation in 2016, they relocated to Spokane, WA. There, Alex secured a position as a private banker with a base salary of $70,000 plus commissions. Karen also completed her studies and found a job as a middle school science teacher. In 2017, Karen gave birth to their first child, but health complications required that she leave her job. They lived in a one-bedroom apartment, paying $1,700 monthly, and diligently saved to buy their first home.

Alex grew up in Spokane (Western Washington), where his family owned a popular restaurant chain. At a young age, he and several cousins began working at the restaurant. They didn't receive a steady paycheck but were promised that, in return for their help, they would each receive financial assistance for college and, eventually, help with the down payment for a home.

In 2018, Karen discovered she was expecting their second child. With their growing family in mind, Alex and Karen sought a new home in their hometown of Spokane. Thanks to a $50,000 down payment commitment from their family business and a $250,000 prequalification letter from United Wholesale Mortgage, the largest nonbank or shadow bank lender in the country, they were able to start their house-hunting journey after engaging a realtor.

After a challenging month of searching, they eventually discovered a home that seemed like the perfect match. Despite making a full-price offer, they were disappointed to learn a week later that their bid had been surpassed. Undeterred, they continued their search, determined to find their ideal three-bedroom, two-bathroom home. Once again, they made a full-price offer, only to receive the same disheartening news.

After a frustrating house-hunting experience, they sought advice from their family and other more experienced realtors. They learned that the main obstacle was that they were competing against professional buyers who were purchasing homes as rentals. These buyers made full-price offers with all-cash and quick escrow closings, making it difficult for regular buyers who rely on financing.

The family business was thriving, but rising rents led them to take out small-business loans to buy two properties for their restaurants. The purchases left them temporarily short on cash and unable to provide the $300,000 needed to compete with all-cash buyers.

They needed home financing to complete their purchase, and despite making offers over the asking price, subject to funding, they were repeatedly outbid while searching for a home.

In late 2019, Karen gave birth to twins. Surprise! With their family growing to five, the need to find a larger home became overwhelming. However, by the fall of 2020, the young Kim family had placed bids on seven homes and was outbid by all-cash buyers each time. Making matters worse, the sales prices of affordable houses had climbed from $300,000 to $425,000.

At that point, the Kim family had moved into a two-bedroom, one-bathroom rental unit that cost a staggering $2,800 per month, almost half their income. By the end of 2021, they had attempted to buy nine different homes but were outbid each time. To make matters worse, home prices had shot up to $450,000 by the end of 2022. Even though United Wholesale had approved their pre-qualified mortgage at $400,000, the monthly payment would take up over half of their take-home pay. The stress and uncertainty of their housing situation took a toll on their mental and emotional well-being, a heart-wrenching reality for many families affected by the affordable housing crisis.

Their new realtor tried to reassure them that the market dynamics had shifted, with higher interest rates and property values deterring many cash buyers. The realtor and the lender encouraged them to continue their home search. However, for Alex and Karen, the question remained: Should they continue their pursuit of a home that had initially cost $300,000 but now demanded $450,000? All the while, their income had not increased.

The Primary Causes and Consequences of the Affordable Housing Shortage of 2017

This analysis will focus on today's housing industry to provide Alex and Karen with a well-informed perspective on their decision to invest in an overpriced home. We will commence by examining the role this industry plays in the high cost of housing, determining whether the high prices are caused by out-of-control building costs or market manipulation. Secondly, we will discuss the current U.S. taxation policies and how they have profoundly impacted the affordability crisis. Thirdly, we will include the phenomenon of affordable housing disappearance. Since the 2008 Great Recession, over 20% of all affordable homes have been removed from the homeownership market by a new industry: The rise of single-family residential absentee owner-investors. We will explore how this new industry sits at the heart of the housing crisis.

The Role of Revenue Management Technology in the Residential Construction Industry

When examining the underlying causes of the unrestrained increases in housing costs in the construction industry, we consulted a 2018 study published by Johns Hopkins University, (Cosman and Quintero) titled "Market Concentration in Homebuilding." The study revealed that, between 2013 and 2017, new-construction home prices increased artificially by 50% due to limited competition among builders. By 2016, two or fewer builders were responsible for up to 70% of all new construction in most markets. The downside of consolidations for consumers is that the study suggests an additional 150,000 homes could have been built annually if the industry had not consolidated, potentially helping to meet housing demand.

Historically, housing demand drove supply. The demand side, i.e., consumers, was subject to economic constraints, such as the 30% income-to-housing cost rule, which determined the location and type of housing required in the market. However, this marketing principle no longer dictates where housing is constructed. According to a HUD study published in July 2019, "Multifamily Supply and

Demand Varies by Metropolitan Areas," developer profits now drive the construction industry.

In other words, consolidations have led to market power being concentrated in fewer and fewer hands. Like the rental industry, these Wall Street-funded conglomerates wield disproportionate influence over prices by deploying AI-powered revenue management platforms. One of the primary digital operating platforms (DOP) in the single-family residential construction industry is Procore, which operates similarly to RealPage in the rental sector. Conversely, RealPage and Yardi provide the DOP pricing platform for most new multifamily construction. These unregulated platforms have gained access to massive amounts of real-time data on their customers and properties.

In conclusion, much like the rental industry, it appears they use shared data and technology to manipulate the market and set the highest possible prices. In short, the construction industry, similar to the rental industry, is likely experiencing the consequences of algorithmic price-fixing.

Unfavorable U.S. tax policies favor investors over homebuyers.

The affordable housing crisis is deeply rooted in the current tax code, which unfairly favors investors over homebuyers. At the core of this issue is the fact that owning a rental property can generate substantial income. However, unfair tax codes shield much of that income from taxes, creating an uneven playing field—basically, tax-free income streams for investors.

For instance, mortgage interest on a loan used to acquire a rental property is fully tax-deductible. However, the most substantial advantage lies in the ability to leverage depreciation (and appreciation)-type deductions, which are exclusive to investment properties. For example, for a $300,000 property, investors can deduct a minimum of $10,000, plus all property improvements, annually from their rental income, thereby significantly reducing or even eliminating taxable income on rental profits. As a result, investors can drive up prices on affordable homes because they have the financial capacity to spend significantly more on a property, utilizing tax codes to avoid income taxes. In contrast, homeowners are not afforded the same opportunity to deduct costs from their income.

For homeowners, the situation is even more dire. In the U.S., many property investors can avoid paying taxes on the increased value of their properties when they sell them by utilizing a legal tax avoidance program known as the (ten thirty-one) 1031 Exchange. This program enables them to defer tax payments by reinvesting proceeds from the sale of one investment property into a similar one. One advantage of this structure is that the investor can withdraw significant cash from the sale and use it to acquire additional residential properties.

Unfortunately, many investors exploit this system by failing to report these transactions to the IRS, as the IRS cannot monitor all such exchanges. Consequently, many investors never pay taxes on their gains, severely impacting affordable housing.

Affordable housing disappearance: properties removed from the market by investors

We will now transition from discussing the use of AI revenue management for the rental and construction industries to its application in renting and managing single-family homes. The advent of this technology has given rise to a new industry sector: single-family residential absentee owner-investors.

The Propertyware technology program, founded in 2001, offers a property management system (PMS) or Digital Operating Platform to the Single-Family Residential Rental Industry, including companies such as Vrbo and Airbnb. In 2009, RealPage acquired them, significantly enhanced its technology and data capabilities, and then began pricing SFR rentals on its common pricing Platform. Before this, large-scale investments in the single-family market did not exist. The Platform changed all that, transforming affordable housing into a highly lucrative, investor-driven industry.

Urban areas face a profound and urgent challenge today. Now, with the ability to efficiently and profitably manage these SFR properties, institutional and local investors have been systematically withdrawing millions of affordable housing units from the marketplace. Unfortunately, they have targeted affordable homes valued at under $300,000. Once again, unregulated AI-powered revenue management technology that uses algorithmic price-fixing sits at the heart of the housing crisis. We will now turn to the various investment instruments implemented to legally remove affordable housing from the market.

- **Single-Family Rentals**

The scale of converting single-family homes into rentals is a staggering trend. For instance, a 2018 study published by *Curbed*, a reliable news agency, revealed that approximately 200,000 single-family homes are owned by large corporate investors, such as Invitation Homes. However, non-institutional investors also pose a significant threat to the housing market. For example, between 2006 and 2016, approximately 3.9 million affordable homes were converted to rental properties.

The new normal, beginning in 2020, is that over a quarter of all affordable homes listed for sale are being acquired for rentals. This significant shift in the housing market, driven by investor acquisitions, is a cause for concern. Investors are drawn to this type of housing as an investment because they can charge up to 30% higher rates than comparable housing alternatives, such as apartments.[2] Therefore, they can afford to raise the prices of affordable housing as their higher income allows for the increased purchase cost.

Worse still for homebuyers, the market has been flooded with investor cash through 2022, making home purchases more difficult.

According to Redfin, over a third of U.S. home purchases since 2021 have been all-cash, with 74% of investors now paying cash. The primary obstacle that all-cash buyers pose to those seeking affordable housing is that sellers no longer consider non-cash buyers relevant.

- **The Vacation Rental Industry**

The unregulated short-term rental industry, often referred to as the Vacation Rental Industry, is exacerbating the housing crisis by converting over a million affordable housing units into vacation properties during this period. These units, which could have been available for home ownership or long-term rentals, are now being used for short-term stays, further reducing the available housing stock. However, the biggest downside for homeowners is that the occupancy rate is below 25%, leaving over 800,000 housing units idle at any given time.

This situation also adversely affects renters by reducing the availability of affordable housing options, leading to higher prices. For instance, in 2018, a study by the Joint Center for Housing Studies at Harvard University revealed that Airbnb alone led to higher rents in New York City, costing renters approximately $178 million annually.

- **The Emergence of Build-For-Rent Communities (BFR)**

According to industry insiders, a new trend is emerging in the home construction industry. BFR, or Build-for-Rent communities, refers to entire subdivisions of newly constructed single-family homes that are sold to investors for rental purposes. Billions of taxpayer-guaranteed investment dollars have already been committed to finance this emerging market.

This trend has profound implications for the housing market. In the past, investors could only purchase individual residential properties; however, they can now acquire entire subdivisions (entire communities) of newly constructed units for their rental portfolios. In

2019, BFR construction accounted for only 6% of all new residential construction, but by 2022, this had increased to nearly half. This rapid increase in BFR construction could significantly decrease the number of homes available for purchase, further exacerbating the affordable housing crisis.

Additionally, BFR properties have the potential to significantly impact the industry's overall financial health. This investment strategy is considered extremely risky by banking regulators. In short, they are building significant inventories of vacant homes, which is likely to have a similar impact to overproduction, as seen leading up to the 2008 Great Recession. In short, these homes are viewed as overpriced and financially out of reach for most working-class consumers.

- **The Platform holds rental units off-market to improve profits**

Chapter 8 states: On any given day, the Platform holds hundreds of thousands of rental units off the market, up to half a million rentals. This practice means that these units, which could have been available for rent, are not accessible to potential tenants, contributing to the affordable housing shortage.

The summary of the primary causes and consequences of the affordable housing shortage from 2017 to the present day

In 2017, the National Low Income Housing Coalition (NLIHC) reported a shortage of over seven million affordable housing units. In response, between 2017 and 2022, the housing industry built 8.7 million housing units to solve the shortage. However, in 2024, that same NLIHC "coalition" reported that a shortage of over seven million affordable housing units still exists. Yet, conversely, despite efforts to build affordable housing, taxpayers now hold more government-backed housing debt than ever, rising to well over $7 trillion.

Today, the severe shortage of affordable housing has placed America at a crossroads. Can we rely on this industry to build affordable housing? Or is America caught in a perpetual time loop of funding massive profits for this industry? Meanwhile, an increasing number of our citizens find themselves unhoused due to the lack of affordable housing options.

The construction industry perpetuates the narrative that it can't build affordable housing due to high construction costs. However, upon closer examination of the industry, although building materials may be overpriced and, as some suggest, the permitting process may be excessively burdensome, neither of these scenarios has directly led to the shortage of construction numbers. Ultimately, they built 8.7 million units rapidly, marking our second-largest housing construction boom in history. So again, we ask: What is the real reason for skyrocketing housing costs, and why can't they build affordable housing?

To address this question, we will focus on the Fair Housing Paradox discussed in Chapter 11, where investors believe they have a right to unfettered access to profits. Contrary to the industry narrative, the primary driver of the high cost of housing is not the cost of building materials or delays in the construction timeline due to permitting, but rather the use of AI-powered revenue management technology. In conclusion, the industry is facing the consequences of algorithmic price-fixing.

The housing crisis is further exacerbated by investors who exploit tax loopholes to purchase affordable housing, severely disrupting the market. These investors purchase affordable homes in the millions by leveraging tax loopholes, artificially inflating housing prices, and enabling them to offer more for properties. These inflated prices are further supported by artificially high rental rates, which have increased by more than 30% over similar types of housing. The consequences significantly hinder millions of Americans from achieving their dream of owning a home. This exploitation not only disrupts the market but also perpetuates inequality, leaving millions of hard-working Americans without a place to call home.

In the third part, since 2006, over 20% of all affordable housing has disappeared from the homeownership industry, millions and millions of units. The results of the study lead us to consider: Do we genuinely face a shortage of seven million housing units, or is our larger issue rooted in unfair tax policies favoring investors over homebuyers? This question prompts us to examine the root causes of the housing crisis more closely.

At the end of the day, American taxpayers must ask: According to the principles of the Fair Housing Paradox, do the taxpayers have a right to a decent home and safe living environment, free from discrimination? Or do the constitutional rights of investors take precedence over the rights of the homebuyers? It's not just a philosophical question but a practical one. On the one hand, the investors have substantially more wealth. On the other hand, they do not pay more taxes. Instead of paying their fair share, they have hired a multitude of lobbyists to influence legislation in their favor, such as lobbying to eliminate their taxes.

Additionally, the rights of investors appear to violate the fundamental principles of the Housing Acts of 1949, which continue to influence our housing policy today. These principles affirm that every American deserves a decent home and a safe living environment. However, the rental housing industry, instead of promoting homeownership, seems to prioritize investors over homeowners. Thus, we conclude that they shouldn't have more say just because they are richer and can use that wealth to bribe politicians.

The Primary Causes and Consequences of the Changes Made to the New Deal Housing Program: A Brief History

Since the adoption of the New Deal in the 1930s, a significant conflict has arisen regarding how the housing market should function. The rental housing sector currently represents a $12 trillion industry.

When combined with the single-family housing sector, valued at $50 trillion, the total value of the housing industry in 2024 is estimated at $62 trillion. Controlling this vast industry determines who holds the key to wealth creation, whether it be the investor class or the working class.

But who can provide housing more affordably and reliably to the American people—"big business" or "big government"? And who should benefit most from the housing programs: the people or big business? By 1939, the program had paved the way for the largest middle class in our history; however, today, housing has become unaffordable for most Americans.

In this second part of the chapter, we will focus on the changes to the New Deal housing program that shifted benefits from the working class to the investor class. To accomplish this, we will focus on the industry's history, specifically at three critical inflection points. The inflection points begin with the housing shortages after World War II, and the 1960s, and thirdly, the Attacks on American Soil—September 11, 2001. Then, we will compare and contrast our findings with the current housing shortage of 2017. We will also complete the discussion on who is responsible for the crisis and what we, as citizens, must do to tackle the affordable housing crisis.

Inflection Point 1: The Housing Shortages After World War II

After World War II, the return of soldiers led to a severe housing shortage. In response, Congress enacted the Housing Act of 1949, a significant policy measure designed to address the housing shortage. The Act expanded various lending programs, including Veterans Administration housing loans and other types of loans for veterans. However, the housing programs benefited the working class. The act solidified the Housing Acts of 1933–1937. It issued its mission statement: "That every American deserves a decent home and a safe living environment."

Inflection Point 2: The Housing Shortages of the 1960s

Another affordable housing shortage emerged in the early 1960s, following President Eisenhower's Highway Act, which constructed more than 41,000 miles of interstate highways, thereby opening up a new network of potential suburbs.

However, the tragic assassinations of President John F. Kennedy in Dallas, Texas, and later his brother Robert, would sharply shift the American political landscape away from the principles of the New Deal and its housing programs toward the investor class and their chosen representatives—the Republican Party.

To solve the shortage, after years of discussions, the Democratic-controlled Congress passed the Housing and Urban Development Act of 1968, which authorized over $50 billion to construct or rehabilitate twenty-six million housing units, six million of which were intended for low- and moderate-income families. This initiative was the largest government-assisted housing program ever attempted in the world's history, with construction scheduled to be completed over a ten-year period. So, what happened? In November 1968, Republican Richard Nixon, who opposed the Fair Housing Laws and whose campaign incited significant prejudice and fearmongering, was elected president. The Act was effective; however, after nearly a million units were constructed, President Nixon ended the program in 1972.

White resistance to racial integration and hostility to "big government" and its housing efforts, especially in northern cities, was intense. The investors, as discussed in Chapter 11, with the backing of their three chosen groups—the realtors, the bankers, and the Chamber—in combination with their extensive and well-connected networks that spanned the entire country, had stirred up racism. Consequently, President Nixon declared a moratorium on the entire federal housing effort in 1972, and the housing policy that started during the New Deal in the 1930s ended abruptly. In effect, the Nixon administration set the housing industry on the path of privatization.

Under the HOLC program, the government worked directly with communities to ensure affordable housing construction, providing funding and technical assistance. However, the Nixon Administration changed the rules, shifting away from government support and direct involvement (big government) back to the failed Public-Private Partnerships (P3s) of former President Hoover (big business). In this instance, HUD transfers much of the housing process and programs (the utility) to private companies, primarily nonbanks or large management companies, like the Crow Empire, which is located in Dallas, Texas, the same city where Kennedy was assassinated.

At the heart of the matter, the home builders and their Wall Street investors have adopted the New Deal housing program. However, these private companies operate outside the reach of federal oversight agencies. The industry remains self-regulated; yet, win-lose-or-draw, taxpayers guarantee their risky bets while getting very little, yet very expensive, housing in return. This shift in policy resulted in a significant decline in the construction of affordable housing units.

Nevertheless, during the Nixon administration, private capital, or big business, initiated the largest volume of housing construction in American history for any decade. Between 1969 and 1979, nearly twenty million housing units were built. Yet, only a few of the six million affordable housing units were built. Eventually, the lack of oversight led to skyrocketing housing costs. Since the Nixon era of privatization, for example, nationwide income has only grown by 29%. In comparison, home prices have risen by over 300%-400% in the West.

By the 1980s, uncontrolled housing costs had led to unchecked inflation. Thus, in 1982, the Republican-controlled Congress passed the Garn-St. Germain Depository Institutions Act, which was the first step in deregulating the financial industry. The deregulation led to the Savings and Loan Industry being open to manipulation by the investor class, which it was, causing its eventual collapse. The taxpayers were called on to bail them out at a cost of $124 billion. This bailout burdened taxpayers and had long-term implications for the housing industry, leading to skyrocketing housing costs.

Inflection Point 3: The Attacks on American Soil—September 11, 2001

In 1998, the residential construction industry, led by the Crow Empire (one of the country's largest contractors), lobbied then-Texas Governor and U.S. presidential candidate George W. Bush for a government-assisted large-scale residential construction program similar to the one in the 1970s. The housing industry was recently recovering from its financial crash and massive losses in the 1990s and was eager to test-drive its newly developed AI-powered revenue management platforms, such as Procore.

Then, on September 11, 2001, a terrorist attack plunged the stock market into chaos, causing a $1.4 trillion loss in market value. Over 600,000 people lost their jobs, and over 18,000 small businesses closed their doors. The Bush Administration called on Crow and the housing industry to use HUD financing programs to rebuild the "frozen economy."

To accomplish his goal of stimulating the economy, in 2001, President Bush pushed the Federal Reserve to significantly lower home mortgage interest rates, a move that marked a pivotal policy decision. They lowered the target for the federal funds rate eleven times in 2001, reducing it from 6.5% at the end of 2000 to 1.75% by December 2001.

Then, as a means to stimulate the economy, Bush urged HUD to introduce subprime loans. A subprime mortgage is a loan granted to borrowers with a higher risk of default, typically those with lower credit scores, limited credit history, or high debt-to-income ratios.

Bush then introduced the adjustable-rate mortgages (ARMs), which start with very low "teaser" rates for three-, five-, and seven-year periods. These ARMs, with their initial low rates, led more than a quarter of all homes to be refinanced into these high-risk mortgages. However, at the end of the initial period, the rates would increase dramatically by an average of 300-500%, for example, from a low 3% to as high as 12%—significantly raising the risk for borrowers and lenders alike.

Then, in June 2002, the Bush administration pledged to construct 5.5 million homes, dubbed "To Improve Black and Minority-Owned Home Ownership." The Act pushed for $1.1 trillion in spending. To make this program work, Congress severely weakened applicant qualifications, similar to the refinance industry, for instance, by increasing the debt-to-income ratio from 30 to 50%. Then, Congress provided many low-income applicants with cash down payments and further eased the debt-to-income requirement by extending payment terms from thirty to forty years. Bush had to, in his words, "use the mighty muscle of the federal government" to meet his housing goals.[3]

In other words, all the concessions for home-buying qualifications occurred on the consumer (demand) side of the equation. The industry failed to conduct even the simplest research to determine whether the refinancer or buyer could afford those homes. Ten million of whom couldn't afford the new cost of housing.

Worse still, Congress paid no attention to the moral hazard on the supply side—Reaganomics. What were the consequences? Using their newly acquired AI revenue management technology and devoid of any regulatory oversight, the construction industry began artificially inflating housing prices through algorithmic price-fixing, resulting in a profit surge for the builders, reminiscent of the current situation between 2022 and 2024. Between 2005 and 2006, the cost of affordable housing had doubled in most metropolitan areas; for example, it rose by 241% in Miami, Florida; 249% in Los Angeles; and 200% in Washington, DC, Las Vegas, and San Diego.

In 2006, housing became unaffordable in just one year, as the number of households facing housing cost burdens surged by 2.3 million, reaching a record thirty-eight million citizens. The steep rise in housing costs mirrors the situation in 2018, where housing unaffordability has now increased to over fifty-one million citizens.

Then, as those new and refinanced ARM mortgages began to mature, the banking industry faced a crisis similar to that of the Great Depression, with thousands of banks collapsing and leaving no institutions capable of refinancing the ARM loans. The result led to the collapse of the U.S. economy.

The fundamental flaw in the Nixonian housing privatization programs is that investors, without proper oversight and regulation, can make massive, high-risk bets, and the risks ultimately fall on the government and, eventually, taxpayers. In 2008, investors' bets on the housing industry triggered a financial crisis that ultimately brought down our entire economy. On average, home values dropped by 25%. However, some regional areas experienced a decline in home prices of as much as 40%. In other words, a $400,000 home dropped to $300,000. However, the mortgages remained unchanged, leaving nearly half of homeowners underwater in their mortgage-to-value ratios.

The aftermath of the housing crash was devastating. Between 2006 and 2014, over ten million Americans lost their homes to foreclosure; that's approximately 3.7 million houses. Taxpayers were left to foot a staggering bill of over $4.5 trillion to cover the losses due to the moral hazard and greed of the residential housing industry. In summary, this disaster was largely a result of the privatization of the housing industry.

The Federal Reserve's decision to give BlackRock, a Wall Street behemoth, no-bid contracts to manage the toxic housing bonds, which, without further governmental oversight, have now ballooned to $8.5 trillion (as of 2019).[4] It serves as a stark reminder of the necessity for accountability and regulation in the housing industry to prevent such crises in the future. Unfortunately for the taxpayers, those defaulted housing bonds now sit in your 401 (k) retirement plans.

To make matters even worse, the builders and investors (the Crow empire) who caused the financial meltdown, instead of being held accountable, were given contracts by the Republican-appointed chair, Sheila Blair, the head of the Federal Deposit Insurance Corp (FDIC) at the time, to sell those 3.7 million homes. This unwise assignment was in contrast to having a disinterested third party, such as the National Association of Realtors, sell those homes. Unfortunately for the taxpayers, the FDIC ultimately had to cancel its contract with the Crow empire due to blatant fraud and mismanagement. They were found to have been paying their salespeople commissions of up to 30% as well as massive amounts of junk fees. In contrast, the National Association of Realtors usually employs a 6% rate.

This practice loops us back to the rise of single-family absentee owner-investors. In the end, almost all of the affordable housing inventory created by the 2002 Bush housing program and the 2017–2022 housing construction boom has ended up in investors' portfolios. Despite the working class contributing trillions of dollars in funding and bailouts, tens of millions of Americans do not have a place to call home.

Conclusion on the Affordable Housing Crisis: Housing Benefits Have Shifted to Investors and the Massive Corruption Machine that is the Affordable Housing Industry.

The failure of the privatized 2002 Bush housing program, tied to the Attacks on American Soil—September 11, 2001, and the 2017–2022 housing construction boom to produce affordable housing, raises serious questions about the industry's reliability in building affordable housing today. But of course, we already knew this. One of the chief architects of the New Deal housing program has already answered the question. As detailed in the first Washington Conference on Public Housing in January 1934, Frederic C. Howe would close his speech by reminding the attendees that "private capital, whose primary interest is in turning a profit, will not supply enough homes for persons of small means."[5] Apparently, he was right.

According to the preamble of the Housing Act of 1949, the consequences of the privatization initiatives raise the same questions Howe posed nearly a century ago: Does every child born into this country have an equal opportunity under the law with every other child? Does every one of our children have access to that decent home and a safe living environment? Yet the taxpayers remain on the hook for trillions upon trillions of dollars targeted for affordable housing, which this industry has yet to build.

To conclude, despite the industry's more than $7 trillion in taxpayer-guaranteed debt, the industry has failed to produce affordable housing. There is currently a shortage of seven million affordable housing units, and this number is expected to grow.

The reader should consider the consequences of removing the Kennedys from political power. In this alternative scenario, the housing programs might not have been privatized. Instead, if the Kennedys had stayed in control of the government, the housing industry, including the massive $50 billion spending bill—the twenty-six million homes—would have been regulated and overseen by big government, ensuring the benefits of the housing sector stayed with the working class and that everyone had an affordable place to call home. Instead, the Nixon administration created a scenario where a very small group of investors and their contractors became immensely wealthy,—multi-billionaires—all the while, fifty-one million Americans can no longer afford their housing.

Just how much wealth has been transferred due to privatization? Recent studies, such as those reported in Gregory S. Burges' book, "Do Tenants Capture the Benefits from the Low-Income Housing Tax Credit Program (LIHTC)?" Suggest that about two-thirds of the actual benefits in taxpayer-funded housing programs now go to investors. LIHTC is a HUD-sponsored affordable housing construction program similar to MFTE. The LIHTC and MFTE are the two primary HUD-supported building programs, both of which are underpinned by tax credits (tax-shifting).

Worse still, recent HUD studies show that the affordable housing construction lending programs are plagued by fraud and abuse. In other words, the Nixon administration's privatization has led to two-thirds of the benefits of the housing market going to investors and Wall Street rather than the working class, trillions upon trillions of dollars in benefits transferred to the wealthiest. In conclusion, privatization has more than tripled the cost of housing, while our wages have increased by mere pennies. This scenario presents a cautionary tale against privatizing essential services.

Final recommendation for Alex and Karen Kim

Let's refocus on Alex and Karen Kim. They are currently contemplating the purchase of their dream home, which was initially priced at $300,000, and plan to make a payment of 30% of their wages. However, due to market manipulation, the cost has now escalated to $450,000, accounting for over half of their wages and placing them in a category of severe cost-burdening. In this situation, more than 50% of a household's income is spent on housing. This situation leads to the question of whether they should proceed with the purchase or continue renting.

Based on historical market trends following Nixon's housing privatization, a market correction is likely to occur, potentially causing the home's value to decrease by 25-40% or stabilize at around

$300,000 again. Understanding these trends is crucial. If they have already bought the house, they could face a scenario similar to that of home buyers in 2008, where they would lose their $50,000 hard-earned investment and be left with a $400,000 debt on a property now valued at $300,000. It's a double financial whammy: the loss of their $50,000 down payment and owing $100,000 more than the property is worth. Surprise!

The reason affordable housing hasn't been built is due to privatization.

A significant issue plaguing affordable housing is that privatizing the entire housing program has led the private sector to repeatedly ignore the affordable housing crisis. First, during the housing construction boom of the 1970s, the Nixon-era housing program was circumvented by failing to construct the six million affordable housing units it was intended to fund.

Secondly, on 9/11, we lost 3,000 citizens to a terrorist attack. President George Bush warned the American people of the dangers of weapons of mass destruction. He promised the American people that we would catch the perpetrator—"Justice will be served." That promise ultimately cost American taxpayers over $2.3 trillion—enough money to construct approximately eight million affordable homes.

The result of Bush's housing program? Despite his promise to the American people, he did not build the five-and-a-half million affordable homes meant to improve homeownership among Black and minority communities. As a result, since 2008, homeownership rates among Black Americans have dropped to an all-time low, the lowest level since the Fair Housing Act of the 1960s. This decline has led to a scarcity of decent homes and safe living environments for these communities.

Thirdly, the 2017–2022 housing construction boom has not provided affordable housing. Instead, builders have invested their resources in constructing more expensive housing, much of which now sits empty, with vacancy rates exceeding 10%. Additionally, most of the new construction is being acquired by investors rather than homeowners.

The author concludes that we cannot depend on this industry to construct affordable housing. Today, the housing industry has become like a self-licking ice cream cone, a closed loop, a self-perpetuating system with no purpose other than to sustain its own massive profit centers; it's totally self-serving. The fact is, they have never built affordable housing in sufficient numbers; they aren't building it now, and history concludes they never will. Any attempt to rely on them to build affordable housing using these unregulated AI revenue management platforms will be as doomed as Frankenstein and his monster.

Congress and the court systems have failed to provide affordable housing. Corruption exists among the Housing Industry Investors, Congress, and the Legal Systems.

At the beginning of the chapter, it was discussed that Congress is ultimately responsible for housing affordability. In stark contrast, today, in 2022, our legislative branch, which is legally responsible for housing, no longer represents the people's interests. In large numbers, elected politicians now embrace the housing industry, big business, taking $billions in payola or bribes from them. These billionaire investors have pushed states like Tennessee, Florida, and Texas to make homelessness a felony. Worse still, these states actively and knowingly participate in the landlords' pricing schemes.

What could possibly be worse than that? Today, the MAGA Supreme Court, which is legally tasked with overseeing congressional legislation and unjust laws, no longer represents the interests of the people. Instead, it, too, has become entangled in corruption, taking in tens of millions of dollars in bribes from this industry. And as a result of those bribes, in June 2024, the MAGA Supreme Court issued a decree that homeless people are not really people because they lack the resources to defend themselves against economic power and wealth; therefore, they have no rights as U.S. citizens.

This ruling is reminiscent of an equally horrific Supreme Court ruling issued in 1857, where that court ruled that people of color are not people but beasts of burden whose only reason for existence is to serve their rich masters because they, too, lacked the resources to protect themselves from the abuse of economic power and wealth.

Today's MAGA Supreme Court exhibits a pro-business, anti-labor stance reminiscent of the Lochner-era Court of the 1920s and the 1857 Court, which held discriminatory views toward people of color and minorities. Its level of corruption surpasses that of all previous courts. In simpler terms, the courts have ruled that for people experiencing poverty, let them eat cake.

So, with housing programs privatized and two-thirds of the benefits from the $62 trillion housing industry shifting into private hands, and with Congress and the courts bribed into supporting that wealth transfer, where do we, as citizens, find affordable housing—a place to call home? It's complicated, but Chapter 14 will answer this question.

CHAPTER 14

The End of Roosevelt's New Deal Era—And, Where Do We Go from Here?

In a mortal world, everything has a beginning, and everything has an end, as it is written in the book of life.

Key Concepts

How the New Deal transformed the lives of the working class

As we grow and develop, we become increasingly aware of the world surrounding us. The common misconception, however, is that we assume the world we are born into has always existed in that way. But that isn't the case. Before the New Deal, the working caste hadn't had a seat at the governing table for thousands of years, if ever. Before this, the governing table had been reserved for the wealthiest.

Truth be told, over the years, the wealthy class has been remarkably successful in undermining the federal government and the New Deal programs, leaving most Americans largely unaware of the initiatives designed to benefit the working class. Today, many consumers' perspectives have been influenced by institutionalism. For instance, many believe that historically, big business, not big government, has largely improved their lives.

An excellent example of this is the conveniences we enjoy in our daily lives. Consider what it's like to wake up in the morning and reflect on the conveniences we often take for granted, from warm showers and indoor restrooms to electric lights and a fully modern kitchen where meals are prepared with electricity and natural gas. But these conveniences extend beyond that. Additionally, consider the benefits of education, medical services, healthy food options, clean water, and a maximum forty-hour workweek. Before the New Deal in the 1930s, these conveniences were reserved for the wealthiest 10% of the population—and only them.

In stark contrast, everyday life was vastly different for the working caste. They lacked access to clean water, indoor plumbing, electricity, and refrigeration. Work hours started and ended according to management's direction; if a job required sixty hours, the worker stayed on the job until it was completed without overtime pay. If a worker is injured, the employee is responsible, as the employer accepts no responsibility.

The New Deal changed all of that for the working class. For the first time in history, the working class had an equal seat at the governing table. For the first time in our history, the government would serve the interests of the working class, not just the whims of the wealthiest. The massive benefits of Roosevelt's New Deal were the gift our ancestors bestowed upon us.

What is Big Government?

Unfortunately, today, big business, through institutionalization, has convinced most Americans that the term "Big Government" has come to mean a large, intrusive, and excessively bloated entity that is corrupt and serves only its own interests. In reality, however, it's quite the opposite. Big Government occurs when a group of citizens decides that big business is not adequately addressing a need or providing a service. On a national scale, the New Deal, for instance, represents the most extensive big-government intervention in our economy ever.

However, it can also include state and local issues. For instance, many citizens are unaware that when Roosevelt began his presidential term in 1933, fewer than 10% of the population had access to indoor plumbing or electricity. The wealthy investor caste had refused to undertake this initiative under the pretense that it was too costly and wouldn't provide a sizable enough return on their investment. However, by the time of his untimely death in 1945, over 90% of the population had these conveniences, all because of big government.

Thus, the term Big Government encompasses any citizen-driven initiative that big businesses have not adequately provided, whether at the national level, such as Social Security, or at the state level, such as a utility company. Unfortunately, many citizens often confuse big government with government programs or services that have been "taken over" by special-interest groups or big business, such as privatized prisons, schools, or Medicare.

Introduction

Every 4th of July, America celebrates its independence from a distant ruling class that imposed high taxes and seized vast amounts of wealth without providing anything in return to the working caste. This day is commemorated because, since 1776, America has represented freedom and opportunity. Those who are willing to work hard and make sacrifices have found chances to achieve the American Dream.

However, the Hoover coalition, established in 1934, set us on a path to dismantle the New Deal and redirect those benefits, not to a distant ruling class, but to a ruling class in waiting, right here in America—the billionaire class. Those benefit programs the billionaire class has been waiting to pillage include Medicare, Social Security, 401 (k) and related retirement funds, the postal services, education, public safety, and housing. The process functions similarly to how the investor class achieved the privatization of our housing programs. In short, their methods involve taking over or dismantling programs established by big government and manipulating the rules to redirect much of the benefits to themselves rather than the working class.

In addition to housing, another prime example of program dismantling was the Social Security Amendments of 1983, launched by President Ronald Reagan. This Act would raise the retirement age and begin taxing Social Security benefits. Before this, Social Security benefits were not taxed. However, the $2.7 trillion in tax revenues generated by the Act was never used for its intended purpose—replenishing the fund—because the tax was a ruse. Instead, these funds were diverted to other governmental expenditures. In short, the money was used to fund wars, provide tax cuts for the wealthy, and support other programs. It redirected $2.7 trillion away from the working class, who contributed to the fund, placing it on a path to bankruptcy.

Another example was in 2003 when investors pressured President George W. Bush and the Republican Party to pass the Medicare Modernization Act. This act allowed "big pharma" to emerge. The act made it illegal to compel them to compete on drug prices. In short, the industry operates and generates massive profits because it is allowed to function as a legal monopoly. Meanwhile, Americans, in comparison to the rest of the industrialized world, spend hundreds of billions of dollars each year on overpriced medications that primarily benefit the wealthiest among us.

Another example is America's spending on the military-industrial complex. Although the country hasn't been at war for eighty years, the military has been. For decades now, over half of all tax dollars have gone to the military. Unfortunately, most of these funds end up in the hands of private military contractors, diverting trillions of dollars more to the most wealthy.

For instance, Bush's war over the events of 9/11 cost the American taxpayers over $2.3 trillion. The disregard for taxpayer funds and the prevalence of fraud, waste, and abuse lie at the core of the current affordability crisis. That $2.3 trillion in taxpayers' investment has been lost without providing any benefits to the working-class taxpayers who funded that war.

Again, instead of providing housing or other services to benefit taxpayers, a few private military contractors, like what happened with the 1960s $50 billion housing bond, became extremely rich. For example, Erik Prince, owner of Blackwater and brother of Betsy DeVos—Trump's 2016 Secretary of Education—became a multi-billionaire.[1] His wealth came primarily from the war—his work as a private military contractor. All the while, our soldiers, according to Chapter 9, live in squalor while privatized military contractors earn as much as ten times the amount our soldiers earn for doing the same work.

Another example is federal farm subsidies and bailouts to large-scale agriculture. In 2020, taxpayers provided over $55 billion; in 2021, nearly $30 billion; and by 2025, the amount had surpassed $15 billion. Meanwhile, the working class receives no benefits from these tax dollars, even as Americans pay higher food prices than most industrialized countries.

In 2017, Trump signed the Tax Cuts and Jobs Act into law, which was created to transfer nearly $2 trillion from the working class to the wealthiest. Most of those funds ultimately ended up in the stock market, artificially inflating its value. Like Reagan, he raised taxes on the working class to achieve this tax cut.

The 2024 Trump tariffs will exacerbate the ever-rising cost of living by raising the underlying prices of goods. The overall effect of increasing those costs on foreign-produced goods will significantly benefit the billionaire class. Tariffs are designed to create market fluctuations, also known as supply chain disruptions, and revenue management technology is intended to maximize profits during these fluctuations. For instance, the technology uses the principles of price surging discussed in Chapter 9. Therefore, the cost of living will continue to skyrocket, and tariffs will exacerbate these soaring prices.

Worse still, every Republican presidential candidate since the New Deal has been highly divisive to the working class, relying on unfounded, baseless fearmongering and consistently attacking the most vulnerable populations of the time. Even more appalling are those who would stand and bear false witness on their behalf. In return, each Republican president would transfer trillions of dollars from the working class to the wealthiest individuals.

In short, the greatest deception ever perpetrated against the American people is the claim that the Republican Party is the party of the working class. Instead, it is truly the party that favors the wealthy. After all, the trickle-down economic theory sits at the heart of the Republican Party's platform. The entire principle of the theory is to transfer taxpayer funds to the wealthiest. Essentially, it's a wealth tax funded by the working class, just like our ancestors endured before the Boston Tea Party. Since 1934, the Republican Party has shifted trillions of dollars to the wealthiest.

However, it's not just that they transfer wealth to the rich; it's their methods that raise the most concern. For instance, the Republican Party was responsible for the 1929 financial crash, which led to the Great Depression and ultimately contributed to the outbreak of World War II. Reaganomics created the financial crisis of the 1990s, leading to the downfall of the Savings and Loan Industry, which had initially been responsible for financing our housing programs and ultimately cost taxpayers hundreds of billions of dollars in bailouts.

Then, it was the George W. Bush administration whose policies bankrupted the economy in 2008, costing taxpayers tens of trillions of dollars in losses and pushing ten million Americans out of their homes and onto the streets. In fact, every Republican president since

1920 who served more than one term has bankrupted their economy as a means to transfer massive amounts of wealth from the working class to the most wealthy. Unfortunately, for the American taxpayer, these market corrections are becoming exponentially worse than its predecessor.

The more sinister side effect of the chaos they create is that the wealthiest accumulate immense wealth during times of significant upheaval. Consider the wealthy war profiteers of World War I and World War II. More recently, think about the COVID-19 pandemic. According to *Forbes*, U.S. billionaires experienced a 62% increase in wealth during this time of chaos. For instance, Elon Musk's wealth grew by 612%, Zuckerberg's by 136%, and Jeff Bezos's by 66%. As of the end of 2024, billionaires are holding a cash reserve of $17 trillion in anticipation of the next economic downturn. A downturn that the investors are creating.

The American Dream for the Working Class is Under Siege

Today, the American Dream for the working class is under siege. The introduction of unregulated revenue management technology, driven by profit maximization above all else, poses a significant threat to the working class. The American Dream, a cornerstone of our national identity, is no longer a product of hard work and potential but a result of a pricing algorithm.

In the rental housing industry, the influence of the RealPage pricing algorithm is not only significant but also profound. This technology, which can transfer trillions of dollars from the working class to the wealthiest, is a fight the rich feel they must win. For them, no price is too high to claim this enormous wealth transfer.

However, to claim this wealth transfer, the wealthy elites and investors want the working class to believe in their propaganda that the high cost of housing and living isn't due to their use of powerful technology that cheats the people. Instead, they claim that illegal immigrants and transgender individuals cause it. They are spending billions of dollars to divert people's attention from the truth and reality. Worse still, the Trump administration plans to allocate over a trillion dollars of taxpayer funds to a bloody and gruesome mass deportation campaign. All the while, two-thirds of our working class can no longer afford the cost of housing in their family budgets. Again, taxpayer funds are wasted, providing no benefit to taxpayers.

The Republican Party's narrative that the investor class will always serve the public better than big government is gaining traction. In this chapter, we will examine the validity of their claims. After all, big government's intervention in our housing markets has made housing a political issue. Yet, in a land devoid of truth, where truth has become a matter of perspective, what is truth?

Understanding the Benefits of Big Government vs. Big Business: A Historical Case Study

Two thousand years ago, in Rome, the fire department was a private enterprise. It was owned and operated by Crassus, the richest of the Romans. When a fire broke out, Crassus rushed to the fire with his workers to extinguish it, but nothing was done until the homeowner appeared. Then, there was bargaining over how much the owner would pay to have the fire put out.

Ferrero, the Italian historian, talks about how it was done. At first, the price was reasonable. As time went on, however, Crassus charged what the market would bear. In the end, the price for extinguishing the fire was fixed at such a high point that the homeowner accepted a small sum and turned over the property to the fire department.

Crassus also contacted neighboring homeowners whose properties were in danger. They, too, were asked to pay to see that their property was not destroyed. They, too, paid all that the traffic would bear. The net result of this process was that Crassus became the largest landlord and homeowner in the city of Rome. He took ownership of a great part of the city. The historian hints that the workers of Crassus started fires so that their master might put them out. In any event, in a short time, he became rich and powerful enough to be Rome's greatest moneylender and formed their first alliance of men holding great political power.

Frederic C. Howe shared this story at the beginning of the first Washington Conference on Public Housing in January 1934. Their task was an assignment from the New Deal to establish a housing program for the people. This story serves as a cautionary tale, illustrating the potential consequences of privatization and the dangers of allowing essential services to be controlled by big, unregulated businesses and profit-driven enterprises.

The Great Pie Dilemma

Since the New Deal era, a significant conflict has been brewing in America. It's a battle over who can serve the American people more affordably and reliably—"big business" or "big government?" This conflict, which I've dubbed "the Great Pie Dilemma," is a metaphor for the struggle between these two entities to control the "pie" of resources and benefits.

However, the question remains: Which method is better for the consumer—big government or big business? To answer this, let's consider my favorite food holiday, Thanksgiving. During this holiday, many people look forward to enjoying turkey, dressing, and mashed potatoes. But, for me, it's all about the pie—whether it's fruit pies, cream pies, pumpkin pie, or even an occasional turkey pot pie after the holidays. Sweet or savory, I simply love pie.

However, America's love of apple pie isn't what we should focus on. Instead, let's consider the pie chart. It helps us visualize how a whole pie or benefit is distributed. In this instance, the entire pie represents the total sum of a particular benefit or product. Simply put, each method consumes a portion of the pie to provide a specific benefit (see Figure 14.1). For instance, big government uses a smaller portion of the pie for production costs compared to big business, allowing more benefits and resources to be available to the people. However, one drawback of big government is its potential inefficiency. Over time, it can become bloated, resulting in the wasteful use of resources.

Figure 14.1: The pie chart

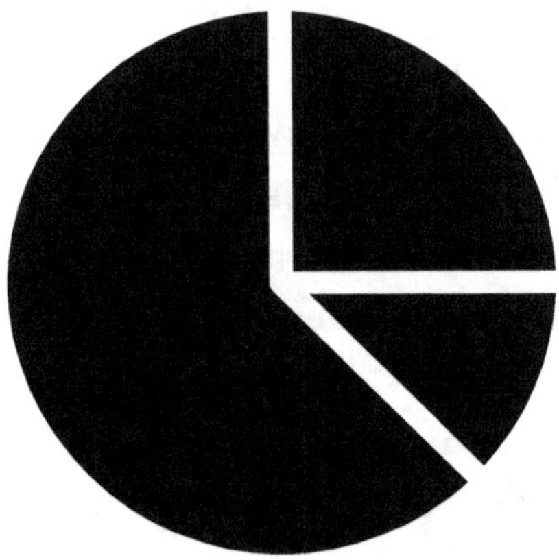

Conversely, the primary objective of big business is to claim as much of the pie as possible, leaving minimal pie or benefit for others. Yet, with vigilant oversight and robust regulations, big business can be restrained from taking more than its fair share of the pie. However, when big businesses are allowed to evade regulation, they will, to some extent, consume the whole damn pie, leaving no benefits for the people whom the benefits are meant to serve, which underscores the crucial need for regulation to protect public interests.

Big Business versus Big Government: A Summary

Let's revisit Howe's account of the Roman Crassus and examine its implications for today. Initially, Crassus's price for firefighting was reasonable. However, as time passed, he became very greedy. He began charging what the market would bear until the price for his services became so high that, in the end, the price for his services was the house itself. With striking parallels to our housing industry today, which utilizes revenue management technology, the New Deal initially suggested that a reasonable price for housing should be 20% of income. However, as time passed, investors likewise pushed housing prices to what the market would bear. Then, HUD deemed it acceptable to charge 30% of income, but after 2005, it considered it fair to charge well over 50%.

The results show that after the 2008 Great Recession, ten million Americans found the cost of their housing services to be so high that for them, the price of housing became equivalent to forfeiting the house itself. Likewise, today, the price of rental housing is equally so high that for over 15% of our population, the cost of housing also translates into forfeiting the house itself. And worse, over fifty-one million Americans now face the peril of being priced out of their housing.

Today, the rental housing cartel has grown rich and powerful. Similar to Crassus in Rome, it is now the largest homeowner and landlord in the country, reaping significant financial rewards and holding substantial political power. Today, their economic power and wealth extend to their influence over Congress and the judiciary.

In conclusion, big monopolistic businesses, when compared to big government, will always consume the largest portion of the pie when left to act solely in their own interests. As companies grow larger, regulation becomes increasingly problematic. On the other hand, although big government can sometimes become bloated and inefficient, it consistently delivers more benefits to the working class.

Yet when big government and big business work harmoniously, they can together provide the best and most affordable pie for consumers. However, therein lies the challenge for the taxpayer: Appropriately regulating big government and public-private partnerships (big business). As history has shown us, when it comes to partnerships, management, or government—one person acting alone can lead to corruption; two will often divide their followers, but three partners create stability. In this instance, the third party should be an independent, robust regulator. To ensure that the interests of all parties are equally protected.

The End of the New Deal Era and the End of Big Government

For ninety years, the Hoover coalition—a powerful faction within the Republican Party—has consistently opposed big government, seeking to restore the wealthy elite to power over our government and legal system. Then, with victory in sight on January 6, 2021, former President Trump, backed by his corrupt army of lawyers, judges, false prophets, and Supreme Court justices, executed one final coup d'état against big government and our democracy.

For the next four years, supported by his tech bros—a term used to describe wealthy and influential individuals in the tech industry who controlled social media networks—and public broadcasters like Fox News, an organization known to be foreign-controlled, orchestrated a multi-billion-dollar campaign to convince the American people of the false narrative that the 2020 presidential election had been stolen from Donald Trump. But it was more devious than that; they also aimed to destroy the Democratic Party, claiming it was they who were the criminal enterprise.

The Republican Party, led by its far-right faction MAGA, with its anti-government rhetoric and pro-business stance, effectively persuaded Americans that it was big government, not big business, that was truly responsible for our financial woes. Then, on November 5, 2024, a significant political shift occurred. The American public came to the consensus that the New Deal programs, created in response to the financial crash of 1929 and intended to address the moral hazards associated with the investor class, had become obsolete. Instead, America has once again chosen to be ruled by the billionaire caste.

The result of the 2024 presidential election emboldened the wealthy caste. The confluence of Trump's broligarchy—led by Elon Musk and his Department of Government Efficiency (DOGE), or as it is pronounced, the Dodgy Department, Jeff Bezos, and Mark Zuckerberg, and his like-minded billionaire caste of cabinet members, aims to dismantle the remnants of Roosevelt's New Deal, transferring billions of taxpayer dollars to their pocketbooks.

Since Trump's reelection in November 2024, his administration's coalition of corrupt special interest groups and cabinet members, which includes convicted criminals, White nationalist extremists, and Communist Russian operatives, has been looting the Treasury, siphoning off or destroying trillions of taxpayer dollars intended for essential services. Never before in our history has there been such a gathering of self-serving psychopaths, each with their own extreme agenda. Yet staunchly united in their primary goal, this criminal enterprise aims to burn the "government" to the ground, and it's happening right before our very eyes. Worse still, it owns and controls the fire department.

After nearly ninety years, the New Deal programs that transformed our financial systems and established a framework of regulations and policies to prevent future economic disasters are now being abruptly dismantled, a decision that will have profound and far-reaching effects on the future of our society.

Meanwhile, the New Deal programs, intended to benefit the working class, such as education, health care, and retirement, are being privatized to serve the wealthiest. For instance, Chapter 13 discusses how the investor class has reaped over two-thirds of all the benefits from housing programs. Likewise, we can reasonably anticipate comparable outcomes for the other former New Deal programs, including Social Security, Medicare, education, retirement savings programs, and more. The oligarchs will continue to take an increasingly larger share of the economic pie through the privatization process.

The coordinated assault on the principles of our Constitutional Republic by the Republican MAGA coalition has effectively ended the New Deal as we knew it. But perhaps, in the scope of American history, future generations will remember the New Deal and its powerful support for the working class, yet unlikely to be witnessed again by the working caste for another millennium.

The billionaire caste is trying to put the working class "genie" back into the bottle, as it were, and pull the working caste back out. Sometimes in life, the greatest gifts are lost forever—whether intentionally or unintentionally—and are never seen again. I suppose this could be the fate of the New Deal, but I hope that isn't the case.

Understanding the Trump MAGA Relationship

Nevertheless, to truly understand Trump's MAGA following, it's essential to understand him and this relationship. Consider Carlo Collodi's classic 1882 novel, The Adventures of Pinocchio. This classic can also be viewed in Disney films, preferably the 1940s version. This story features the main character, Pinocchio, a wooden puppet who aspires to become a "real boy." However, in one of his first adventures, he meets the character, "Honest John" (think of Trump), who becomes one of his earliest antagonists. Honest John befriends the naïve Pinocchio and promises him immense wealth and fame. He talks a big game, but his true intent is to sell Pinocchio to the highest bidder, keeping all the profits—or, as it were, the pie—for himself. Unfortunately, naïve Pinocchio is repeatedly fooled by Honest John.

But how did the political character of Honest John emerge? Was the Tea Party a movement of the working class, or did the wealthy elite hijack it and become its real authors? In 2010, the Supreme Court delivered the Citizens United ruling. In essence, Citizens

United served as the ultimate weapon of choice for the wealthy elite to dismantle the New Deal and its principles.

It enables them to control the narrative of what constitutes truth through a disinformation campaign across various news and social media platforms, including the influencer space. It allows them to spend unlimited amounts of tax-exempt money to influence elections. Worse still, they not only invest unlimited sums, but they also do so anonymously, through secrecy and under the cover of darkness. The ultimate goal of Citizens United has always been to guide voters toward an "Honest John" political candidate who would fulfill their wishes of world domination. It is the polar opposite of Franklin Delano Roosevelt and his New Deal, where the interests of the working class were at the heart of his policies.

However, the more sinister side of this transformation is that Honest John and his big business grifters will absorb big government. This assimilation, if allowed to reach its conclusion, will evolve into an authoritarian dictatorship, similar to Communist Russia, where a single dictator, Vladimir Putin, controls both big government and big business with the full force and effect of the legal system and military. In other words, the ultimate concentration of economic power and wealth—a king with a massive nuclear arsenal at its disposal.

The time has come for Americans to recognize that the Republican Party has turned into the cult of Donald Trump and his billionaire caste. By all means, maintain your association with them, but you do so at your own peril, as the book of life will judge them accordingly. The Party, fueled by its extreme MAGA coalition and bearing a striking resemblance to the Nazi regime of 1930s Germany, is a movement that we as democracy-loving Americans can no longer ignore. Trump's entire administration operates behind a veil of darkness and secrecy.

However, even more disturbing are the religious leaders who support him. Today in America, these large nonprofit organizations, rather than feeding and caring for the poor and their children, spend hundreds of millions of dollars every year bearing false witness on behalf of Honest John. In return, he is granting them significant control over our personal lives. These false prophets seek to take away our divine right of free agency—the right to choose for ourselves.

The End of the New Deal Era—When the "Economic Bough" Breaks and the Cradle Falls—the End of the Social Safety Nets

Of course, it goes without saying that attempting to predict the future is a tricky business. There are numerous uncertainties at play. For example, the working class might unite overwhelmingly to elect a government that genuinely champions its interests. However, such a scenario appears to be quite unlikely.

Nevertheless, history is full of cause-and-effect examples that provide powerful insights into likely outcomes as history repeats itself. For instance, during the early 1930s, President Hoover deported millions upon millions of immigrants. Then, to further enrich his "billionaire caste," at the expense of the working caste, he entered into a program of excessive tariffs. The final round of tariffs imposed a 40% rate hike on over 900 products.

However, Hoover's tariff program backfired when the world retaliated with its own tariffs. The net effect would reduce overall world trade by more than 40%. Rural America, which included half of our citizens, was hit especially hard by the retaliatory tariffs and would see its income drop by two-thirds. The agriculture industry and rural America sat in ruins until Roosevelt's New Deal.

According to a survey released by the Department of Labor, the urban working class was also hit especially hard as their cost of living increased by 15% due to tariffs. To worsen their financial strain, over 25% of all households had no income; for those maintaining their jobs, their income dropped by more than 40%. The effects sent

America and the world into a deep economic depression. This devastating downturn lasted for more than twenty-five years. The Hoover coalition has always been underpinned by corruption and deception.

Nevertheless, the issue of how to respond appropriately to corruption is not limited to Democrats or Republicans; it affects everyone. This government is our circus, and its members are our monkeys. The ultimate question is: Will we as American citizens and taxpayers work together before the next economic crash to secure a future for our children and grandchildren? Or will we, like our predecessors in 1928, fall into the trap of believing in the propaganda that "Honest John" will always have our best interests at heart?

As a reminder, during the five years leading up to the 1929 stock market crash, the market surged by approximately 400%. Similarly, today, Wall Street has seen substantial growth over the past ten years, increasing by nearly 500%, from 17,000 in 2015 to 50,000 in January 2026; however, it has similarly increased by over 400% in the past five years. However, over the last decade, similar to the late 1920s, the government has injected trillions of dollars into the stock market, artificially inflating that growth.

For instance, Trump's 2017 Tax Cuts and Jobs Act lowered the tax liability of the largest corporations by about $2 trillion. However, the trickle-down economic theory did not, as Trump promised, deliver higher wages to the working class; instead, most of those funds were used for stock buybacks and dividends, which significantly benefited the wealthiest. However, the net effect of the tax cuts was to dramatically inflate the stock market. Worse still, Trump's 2025 "big, beautiful bill" will extend those tax cuts and continue to artificially inflate the stock market.

Truth be told, since the creation of the Securities and Exchange Commission (SEC) and the laws protecting consumers from unscrupulous stockbrokers and fund managers, the investor class has, over the years, been remarkably successful in removing nearly all of the laws and regulations established by our ancestors. Today, the stock market has become little more than legalized gambling, mirroring the scenario that occurred during the 1920s.

However, the biggest misconception among the working class about the stock market is that it accurately reflects the overall health of the American economy. But that simply isn't true. For example, when comparing the stock market's growth to the total increase in nationwide debt (including government, business, and individual debt), the growth in debt has far outpaced the growth in the stock market.

The stock market reflects the asset side of our nation's balance sheet. However, it's rarely—if ever—the asset side of the equation that causes an economic or financial collapse. That would be the liability side of the equation. And that's where the problem lies—it's always about the debts. Due to the increased adoption of revenue management technology, living expenses for the working class are skyrocketing. As a result, more consumers are compelled to finance an increasing share of their family expenses. This has led the working class to rely heavily on consumer debt, such as credit cards, auto loans, student loans, and mortgages, to make ends meet.

For example, household debt has more than doubled from $10 trillion in 2008 to $20 trillion by the end of 2024. The corporate and business sectors (excluding banks) also saw their debts more than double during this period, from just over $35 trillion to $80 trillion. Total U.S. government debt grew by 370%, from $10 trillion to $37 trillion, in the same time frame.[2] Sadly, our national debt will more likely than not exceed $40 trillion by the end of the Trump administration in 2028.

Except for 1928, neither the U.S. nor the world has ever experienced such a large stockpile of debt. Similar to 1928, America and the world are drowning in debt, and no appreciation in the stock market can offset this huge drag on our economy. The more troubling side effect of this debt buildup is that it wasn't caused by investing in infrastructure, which could help generate new wealth. Instead, it's an accumulation of debt spent on wars, financial losses, and injecting cash into the stock market through government bailouts.

Meaning that the economy isn't creating wealth for the working class; instead, as Chapter 12 explains, there has been a significant transfer of wealth—a massive consolidation—to the wealthiest individuals who control a large portion of the stock market. Therefore, for this wealthy group—the top 10% of wealth holders—the stock market serves as a good indicator of the health of "their" economy.

This wealth transfer also occurred during the 1920s. By 1930, the concentration of wealth and power had led to 130 companies controlling over 80% of the nation's wealth. In comparison, today, the top 1% of individuals hold nearly half of the nation's wealth—that's 1% consuming over half of the pie. The top 10% consume over 70% of the pie, leaving only 30% of the pie for the remaining 90% of the population.

What's even more troubling is that the 90% possessing only 30% of the wealth are compelled to support the government through increased taxes. The working class bears the greatest burden of government expenses because the wealthy, who hold 70% of the wealth, do not pay their equitable share of taxes.

It appears that the only real competition remaining in America now exists within the 90% of the population—including the entire working class—that competes for the 30% of the country's resources, wealth, and opportunities. In this economy, life becomes more of a struggle for survival rather than the pursuit of the American Dream. Today, the American Dream is out of reach for the working class; it has become too expensive and unattainable, and the odds are not in our favor. As Chapter 10 states, the ultra-wealthy have built a world that favors them.

Worse still, once again today, just like in the 1920s, there are massive conflicts of interest between government officials and Wall Street titans, including U.S. presidents, Supreme Court justices, judges, governors, and members of Congress. This malfeasance between government officials and Wall Street titans now looms on the edge of a massive financial cliff similar to that of 1929.

Today, the widespread conflicts of interest within the housing industry have enabled investors to assume massive amounts of risk. For investors, exerting control through vertical integration of the entire $62 trillion housing market and its processes is the ideal scenario to guarantee substantial profits.

However, from a regulator's point of view, the risk associated with their real estate loans is deeply troubling. Today, 43% of Americans—two-thirds of our labor force—can no longer afford to pay their rent because they are forced to spend more than half of their income on housing costs—that's over fifty-one million Americans.

In the starkest of ironies, these investors depend on the very individuals they are pricing out of the market to pay their housing costs, which provides the investors with the funds necessary to meet their own loan payments. Yet when this investor-driven, tight payment-processing system falters, its house of cards will collapse. In short, investors employ a highly volatile investment strategy that involves holding trillions of dollars in housing debt. However, they have very little of their own capital or cash invested in the transaction (also referred to as "skin in the game"); instead, they depend on highly leveraged loans from regulated commercial banks or unregulated investment companies to finance those loans.

Therefore, when even a small percentage of renters are unable to pay their rent, or homeowners are unable to pay their mortgages, the investor portfolio collapses due to a lack of cash to cover their loan payments. Historically, when these construction loans or housing bond funds fail to make their payments, the fund collapses, and the government and, eventually, taxpayers are forced to bail out their defaulted investments. Today, taxpayers, not investors, are the ones who personally guarantee these loans. Worse still, the investors are entirely unregulated.

Consequently, the source of repayment for their loans is considered highly questionable. The lack of funds to make their payments was precisely what occurred in 2008, when thirty-eight million Americans couldn't afford their housing costs, and ten million Americans lost their homes to foreclosure. They also couldn't make their housing payments, which caused the investors' house of cards to collapse.

Essentially, the GSEs' (government-backed loans) lax standards regarding their overly leveraged and high-risk real estate loans could result in losses amounting to tens of trillions of dollars for American taxpayers if the investors' gamble does not pay off. In conclusion, the industry is potentially setting the stage for another massive economic meltdown at the taxpayers' expense. And worse, their investments are now twice the size and risk of those in 2008.

As a reminder, in 1929, following the unrestrained growth of the stock market and the rapid consolidation of corporate wealth and power between September and November, the market crashed, losing over 90% of its value. The crash shook the very foundations of the world, which contained two billion people, leading to the loss of nearly one hundred million lives during the ensuing chaos.

The process of collapse begins with erratic swings in the stock market, but one day the bottom falls out, and the market fails to recover, marking the start of the collapse. During each of these significant downturns in the economic cycle, investors operate under the delusion that they can control the chaos. However, their beliefs always prove to be fallacious. And the working-class taxpayers always end up with the bill.

Today, as we examine the economic landscape, another financial crisis appears to be imminent. The investors' coalition of false prophets and corrupt oligarchs is rapidly ushering in a financial apocalypse of our own making. However, today, the world has over eight billion people. For them, the market collapse will likely be swift, like a thief in the night, as history repeats itself.

Institutionalism has led many to believe that our essential services will always be provided and accessible. Unfortunately, that assumption is unfounded. Consider the toilet paper shortage and crisis during the COVID-19 pandemic. Or since then, the shortage of eggs, the shortage of beef, the shortage of coffee, and the shortages of critical medicines, to name a few. Our infrastructure, once robust and plentiful, will likely be unable to withstand a collapse, as it was unable to in 1929. Trump's administration is literally setting our essential resources—such as health care, clean water, and food production—ablaze.

Consider Chapter 5 and the narrative surrounding infant formula. Nowadays, these consolidations and concentrations of commodities have occurred in nearly all areas of production, from egg and gasoline production to the production of essential medicines. For instance, in the fresh egg market, four companies hold nearly 90% of the market share. These critical supply chains for food and medicine, which take decades to build, are collapsing under the strain of the Republican Party's chaotic administration.

Wealthy investors can destroy our essential services because only the working class relies on them. As discussed in Chapter 10, the wealthy inhabit a world of their own—one completely disconnected from the working class. The result will likely lead America into an age of political, educational, and spiritual darkness that could last for decades or even centuries. This practice is precisely what Putin did to Communist Russia, and it mirrors the path Xi Jinping is currently taking in Communist China, as well as what Viktor Orbán is doing to Hungary.

As previously mentioned, predicting the future is a tricky business. However, when consumers pull back the curtain, so to speak, the reality of our concentrated and monopolized markets is clear. The result is that America and the world will likely descend into the second Great Depression. In the resulting chaos, countless millions, perhaps even billions of people, are likely to lose their lives. Of course, the scale of the suffering depends on which side of the wall you were born on. The wealthy will likely feel little pain, insulated from the chaos they engineered, having created their own world with their own sources of essential services.

However, the sad truth of the matter is that it doesn't have to be this way. Because "We the People" have a choice. We always have a choice until we don't. When we allow corrupt billionaires unfettered access to consumer data and then let them use that data with their algorithms to divide us—by race, wealth, color, religious beliefs, political ideology, or sexual orientation—and then let these divisions deepen so much that we, as the working class, lose the ability to govern ourselves, we leave ourselves vulnerable to losing our rights as working-class citizens.

When we allow false prophets and nonprofit organizations to enter our schools, teach history with no basis in reality, and then present it as if it were true, we undermine the integrity of our educational system. When our children fail to learn from history and our past mistakes because some consider it to be "woke," our children become more susceptible to propaganda. Instead of learning from past errors, they may perpetuate the cycle and repeat those mistakes because the line between fantasy and reality has become blurred. However, perhaps the most significant damage has been inflicted upon our children. In an era driven by technology, a highly educated workforce is essential, yet our children remain painfully unprepared for this new age.

And worse, when we allow false prophets to bear false witness against the less advantaged—accusing them of their own moral failings—instead of focusing on the corrupt programs of oligarchs and their wealth-creation goals, we lose our humanity.

When we allow oligarchs to further divide us through their "billionaire games" and persuade us that entertainment and sports are more valuable than essential services such as food production, healthcare, decent and safe housing, news, or education, we erode our society's ability to reason.

When we allow our law enforcement to divide us between the haves and have-nots by their thin blue line, and we further allow corrupt politicians to lie and use propaganda to promote false patriotism and to divide us further, we allow them to weaken our nation and surrender our government over to the most corrupt among us.

When we allow social media platform algorithms that intentionally drive misinformation and further allow misleading news analysts, reporters, and journalists to manipulate our history, whitewash it through institutionalism, and push alternative facts, hide, and distort the truth. When we allow them to tear truth from our hearts and minds, and rip it from our very eyes and our very lips, the American Dream dies. And when our dreams die, hope dies with them. And when hope dies, democracy dies because democracies are, after all, built on hope. And when democracy dies, the truth is lost and becomes a weapon in the hands of the most powerful. Once again, it doesn't have to be this way.

Yet, as we ponder America's future, let us not forget that in the Gospel of Matthew 19:23-24 (see Chapter 11, the camel through the eye of the needle), the Lord conveys the message that there will be very few rich people in heaven. This scriptural passage prompts us to question why, despite this divine judgment, our society's "rich men" are treated as more equal than others. Today, just like in the 1920s, the working class views these rich men as exemplary role models for their children, rather than the banksters they really are, and have always been.

Truth be told, until the working class acknowledges the harsh reality that we have more in common with those experiencing homelessness than with the ultra-wealthy, social equality will never take hold in America. And America will never again be the home of the brave but of the broken, with its citizens left to aimlessly wander in a world devoid of truth. However, one must consider whether Honest John's promotion of the "Make America Great Again" doctrine is truly meant for all Americans or just the wealthiest? Making America Great like 1928.

The Day the Democrats and Roosevelt Made America Great Again—A Historical Perspective

By 1932, a dark shadow of despair had engulfed the nation, and most Americans had lost all hope. There was no one left to fight for the once proud Union. After all, what was left worth fighting for? Over two-thirds of the population was impoverished, and more than half couldn't afford a roof over their heads. Then, the greedy banksters came to collect their mortgages and debts, backed by the courts, prioritizing property rights over human rights.

Hoover and the Republican Party urged Americans to be "very fearful," a sentiment reminiscent of the 2024 presidential campaign. America was at its most vulnerable and began to tear itself apart. Deporting or imprisoning millions of people of color, including nearly a million American citizens, under the false pretense that they were illegal, all in the name of wisdom. Worse still, Jim Crow and his laws lynched thousands out of pure hatred.

The wealthy elites and their false prophets pushed their dogma. They urged Americans to return to the ideals of the past. And then they pushed the narrative that the Pecora Report was woke news. After all, wasn't it all the drinking and whoring around by the working caste that got us into this chaos in the first place?

What reason was left to fight? Poverty? The one idea the North and South would finally agree upon was, "What was the point?" American democracy has only ever worked for about a quarter of the population. So, our ancestors asked the question once again, "What's the point?" And so, the story goes...

On that, our darkest day, the day Americans lost all hope, a great nation was reborn from the ashes: E Pluribus Unum, "from many, one." On that day, a voice echoed on the radio. That voice belonged to Franklin Delano Roosevelt. He was no Honest John, but he reminded the country, "The only thing we have to fear is fear itself." After so many years of darkness, a ray of hope emerged—hope that had long since been forgotten.

Through FDR's New Deal, America invested billions of dollars—equivalent to trillions today—in the construction of vital infrastructure, including roads, bridges, housing, schools, railways, dams, irrigated farmland, and electrical power plants and sewer systems. This robust infrastructure ensured a reliable water, food, and power supply, vaulting the country's status as the world's largest and most powerful economy for future generations to come. And all of this was accomplished during the worst economic calamity in our history.

Furthermore, our ancestors purchased those war bonds and allowed the government to tax their wages to repay these debts. Their financial contributions and sacrifices were significant investments, driven by their hard work, perseverance, and, in many instances, their very lives.

What did President Roosevelt do for America? He extended a helping hand when it was most needed. America reached up and grasped Roosevelt's hand while the rest of the world was falling into utter chaos and darkness; it was a hand-up, not a handout.

Ultimately, America recognized that achieving greatness required embracing everyone, all of our citizens. Diversity enriches our collective knowledge, and each person brings something unique to the table. Together, as one, we stood, and we stood tall. The day we united as "one" was the day that America truly became great again.

America's true strength lies in our unity—stronger together, "<u>We</u>, the People." Our ancestors united and marched into battle arm in arm, saving a dying world. Together, our ancestors transformed the world for future generations, serving as a guiding light of democracy and hope for everyone to see. This was the gift our ancestors bestowed upon us through Roosevelt's New Deal.

So, Where Do We Go from Here?

Today, we find ourselves in a situation reminiscent of that faced by our ancestors in 1928. Back then, as now, the wealthy elite employed the age-old tactic of bait-and-switch. However, just as our ancestors learned the hard way, cake is not pie. Ultimately, unregulated economic power and wealth will never resolve the financial issues of the working class.

The question remains: How will we rebuild our society after the impending economic collapse and as America descends into chaos once again? This book sheds light on the choices our ancestors made, offering a unique opportunity to examine what they said and did. The magnitude of their challenges led some to propose plans that literally saved the world. In contrast, others pursued misguided strategies and became the villains of wars. We must learn from past choices and use those experiences to create a path forward.

At the end of the day, only "We the working-class People" can address our financial challenges. We must elect educated individuals from the ranks of the working class, not based on their looks, wealth, or celebrity, but, more importantly, on their understanding of how economics, mathematics, and the principles of science and the economy work. On that day, America will need to find another hero—a leader like Roosevelt—who is free from the influence of big business and truly believes in the American Dream, not just for themselves or the wealthiest, but for all citizens—a uniter, not a divider of people.

Ultimately, America will need a "New Deal" similar to the one Roosevelt proposed. Affordable housing—access to that decent home and a safe living environment—must be at the core of our new transformation. As our ancestors learned—and we are just beginning to understand—housing and other essential services are a right, not a privilege reserved for the wealthy. Our united government—not big business—must provide these essential services.

However, the severe shortage of affordable housing and the rising rates of homelessness are expected to worsen. Today, we already have an emergency in the lack of affordable housing, directly leading to exploding homelessness. This situation is truly a federal crisis, and therein lies the solution. In 1932, the American people faced an economic crisis triggered by the actions of our financial institutions and their investors. Today, we face a similar emergency, and a state of emergency declaration is the only way to address it.

As outlined in Chapter 1, Roosevelt sought emergency powers from Congress to act swiftly and decisively. Legal experts advised him to utilize the Emergency War Powers Act, which provided broad authority to issue executive orders. While fully aware of the risks involved, FDR used this act to implement his New Deal initiatives. He declared a State of Emergency to address the financial crisis, aiming to ensure that everyone eventually received their fair share.

With the same determination as our ancestors in the 1930s, the most reasonable solution to address our crisis is for the President of the United States, one who is not beholden to the wealthy investor class, to officially classify the affordable housing crisis and the related homelessness crisis as what it truly is—a federal disaster. The

President must declare a state of emergency, return our housing program to the foundational fires from which it was forged, and reimagine the New Deal program for application with AI-powered systems that can thrive in the digital age, shifting the benefits of the $62 trillion housing industry back to the consumers and taxpayers.

This seemingly simple move would ensure that every child born in America has an equal opportunity under the law with every other child. Every child would have equal access to a decent home, a safe living environment, and freedom from the wealthy's oppressive economic power and wealth.

It's time for big government to rise from the ashes like a phoenix, be reborn, and build affordable housing and provide other essential services for its people so that we all have a place to call home—a home that offers peace and equal opportunity in the pursuit of happiness—and an equal shot at our own American Dream.

For 250 years, our ancestors fought and died to protect our constitutional republic and democracy. The ultimate question remains: Will we rise to join the fight for justice and democracy, or will we yield and surrender our very souls to the darkest elements of our society? What gifts will we bestow upon our descendants?

Today, our democracy is at a crossroads. It stands on the edge of the Red Horseman's blade. Will we turn the tide and follow our ancestors' path and fight for democracy and the American Dream? Or will we choose another path? The choice for the American people is clear; the time for reckoning has arrived, and the hour is late—it's 11:59.

A Call to Action

In April 2023, a meeting was held with attorneys involved in lawsuits against RealPage for algorithmic price fixing. During this meeting, the law firms Scott + Scott and Hausfeld, LLP were selected as co-lead counsel for the litigation. Additionally, the author took on the task of raising public awareness of the significant risks associated with algorithmic price fixing.

The publication of this book, "PRICED OUT BY DESIGN. How AI, Big Data, and Corporate Landlords crashed our housing market, and how to fix it," marks a significant step toward addressing the pressing housing crisis. It aims to hold property managers accountable for contributing to skyrocketing housing costs and engaging in anti-competitive practices. These actions generate substantial profits for property owners while exacerbating housing insecurity for tens of millions of hardworking Americans.

This work supports the Department of Justice's 2024 lawsuit against RealPage and its pricing algorithm, as well as the member landlords accused of participating in algorithmic price-fixing. However, Donald Trump's election has jeopardized this legal action, as his administration has expressed its intention to resolve the case on very favorable terms to the industry.

What You Can Do to Get This Message Out?

Today, the Fourth Estate, commonly known as freedom of the press, is under siege by the Trump Administration. Today, his tech bros control our news. Their algorithms determine who gets a voice and who is silenced.

I invite you to join me in the conversation—share your thoughts on this important book! Reach out to colleagues, peers, and others who may find this discussion meaningful. Use your own social media platforms to share this important message. The housing crisis requires urgent action, and it's clear that the Trump Administration is not prioritizing solutions. And the fact is, the affordable housing crisis won't fix itself. Therefore, each of us must advocate for affordable housing for everyone. Making this issue a top priority and getting involved can truly create meaningful change.

If not us, who? If not now, when?

Run, Don't Walk! Take an active stand today!

About the Author

James M. Nelson is a highly experienced professional with over forty years in the U.S. banking industry and as a real estate broker. He authored the 2020 book "Stealing Home: How Artificial Intelligence Is Hijacking the American Dream" and the 2026 book "PRICED OUT BY DESIGN. How AI, Big Data, and Corporate Landlords crashed our housing market, and how to fix it.

He holds a degree in economics from Brigham Young University. In 2023, Nelson was appointed Visiting Scholar at the University of California, Santa Cruz.

He began his career in 1982 as a Federal Banking Regulator. He also gained valuable experience in debt restructuring during the 1980s agricultural crisis. He held various management roles, including Senior Regional Commercial Banking Center Manager for Wells Fargo in a top-15 market. Later, he served as the Chief Credit Officer at a community bank. With extensive expertise in commercial finance, Nelson established a boutique commercial loan brokerage that specializes in syndicating loans for large multifamily projects.

Nelson's diverse background uniquely qualifies him for this comprehensive economic study. His career started as a Federal Banking Regulator, where he enforced key policies. He then served as a chief credit officer, developing critical policies. Subsequently, he worked as a lender and broker, specializing in financing large multifamily projects. This varied experience across sectors has given him a strong understanding of how different components interact to shape our data-driven rental industry. Today, he is known as the man behind the RealPage Lawsuits. [Franco Fraudo, "The Man behind the RealPage Lawsuit," Propmodo, January 19, 2023]

Nelson was raised on his family's farm near Tombstone, Arizona, and attended Eastern Arizona Junior College in southeastern Arizona before enrolling at BYU. Throughout his life, he has worked and lived in various Western states. He is a proud father of four and has eleven grandchildren. His passion for creating this work is driven by his profound concern for his grandchildren's future.

Endnotes

How References are Cited:

We utilized citations, endnotes, and a comprehensive bibliography to document our work, which is presented below. We used three citation styles for reference materials.

1. Standard citation for quotes
2. A citation may include multiple cited references. This method is used to encapsulate an entire concept. The industry releases valuable information; however, it is typically broken down into subparts and distributed through eBooks, articles, industry studies, and other channels. At times, we list various citations to group a conversation and form a comprehensive concept.
3. The citation may also include footnote information as needed to thoroughly cover the topic.

Many of the citations used are from the internet and are typically sourced from websites; however, over time, the website links become discontinued. Furthermore, when the reader attempts to verify the information by using the web link, the URL sometimes fails to work. Unfortunately, most links have a limited lifespan on the internet. Therefore, the reader has options.

- Search the remainder of the document for copies from the sites.
- Research the internet using parts of the text, then locate the new URL site.

Chapter 1 Endnotes

1. Herbert Bayard Swope, "The Government Accepts the Challenge of the Slums," *First Washington Conference on Public Housing*, January, 1934, https://www.huduser.gov/portal/sites/default/files/pdf/Speeches-Delivered-at-Washington-Conference.pdf

2. Moss, David A. and Bolton, Cole X. and Kintgen, Eugene, The Pecora Hearings (December 10, 2010). Harvard Business School General Management Unit Case No. 711-046, Available at SSRN: https://ssrn.com/abstract=2048500; and, "Financial Crisis Inquiry Commission is Biggest Financial Investigation Since 1930s' Pecora Commission," *ACFE (Association of Certified Fraud Examiners,)* November/December 2009, https://www.acfe.com/article.aspx?id=184.

3. John S. McCormick, "The Great Depression, *Utah History Encyclopedia*, 1994, https://historytogo.utah.gov/great-depression/.

4. Alison Collis Greene, "The Great Depression and Religion in Mississippi," *Mississippi History Now*, accessed August, 2019, http://www.mshistorynow.mdah.ms.gov/articles/413/the-great-depression-and-religion-in-mississippi.

5. Everman, Henry Esli, "Herbert Hoover and the New Deal, 1933-1940," *LSU Historical Dissertations and Theses*, 1918, digitalcommons.lsu.edu/gradschool_disstheses/1918.

6. Roosevelt, Franklin D., "ADDRESS AT OGLETHORPE UNIVERSITY IN ATLANTA, GEORGIA," May 22, 1932, https://fdrlibrary.wordpress.com/wp-content/uploads/2012/10/oglethorpe.pdf

7. Frederic C. Howe, Consumers' Counsel (Speech)," National Recovery Administration (NRA), Washington Conference On Public Housing, Willard Hotel, Washington D.C., January 27, 1934, New York, 728.1, W173, c.2.

8. Dr. Isadow Lubin, Commissioner Bureau Labor Statistics, *Washington Conference On Public Housing*, Willard Hotel, Washington D. C. January 27, 1934, National Public Housing Conference, New York, 728.1, W173, c.2. p. 15.

Chapter 4 Endnotes

1. Jon Bershad, "Warren Buffet on Class Warfare: If This is A War, My Side Has the Nuclear Bomb," *Mediaite.com*, January, 2012, https://www.mediaite.com/tv/warren-buffett-on-class-warfare-if-this-is-a-war-my-side-has-the-nuclear-bomb/ ; and, Greg Sargent, "There's Been Class Warfare for the Last 20 Years, and My Side Has Won," *The Washington Post*, September, 2011, https://www.washingtonpost.com/blogs/plum-line/post/theres-been-class-warfare-for-the-last-20-years-and-my-class-has-won/2011/03/03/gIQApaFbAL_blog.html?noredirect=on.

2. The New Deal: Three Foes and a Friend," *The New York Times*, April, 1983, https://www.nytimes.com/1983/04/10/business/the-new-deal-three-foes-and-a-friend.html .

3. "American Liberty League," *Encyclopedia.com*, encyclopedia.com/history/dictionaries-thesauruses-pictures-and-press-releases/american-liberty-league.and, Everman, Henry Esli, "Herbert Hoover and the New Deal, 1933-1940," *LSU Historical Dissertations and Theses*, 1918 digitalcommons.lsu.edu/gradschool_disstheses/1918.; and, ThoughtCo., Robert Longley, "America First—1940s Style," thoughtco.

com, https://www.thoughtco.com/america-first-1940s-style-4126686 ; or, The National WWII Museum, New Orleans, "American Nazism and Madison Square Garden," nationalww2museum.org, Accessed June 2020, https://www.nationalww2museum.org/war/articles/american-nazism-and-madison-square-garden

4. Douglas Martin, "Trammell Crow, Innovative Developer, Dies at 94," *nytimes*, Jan. 15, 2009, https://www.nytimes.com/2009/01/16/business/16crow.html

5. Understanding the Christian Conservative Coalition's influence is essential, as it played a pivotal role in shaping significant moments in American history, leaving a lasting mark on society and politics. To counter the Democrats and their connections to the working caste, the financial elite aimed to forge a strong alliance between the wealthy and the religious sector of the working class.

   The Republican Party collaborated with the Conservative coalition to enforce Prohibition, a misguided attempt by religious reformers to impose their values nationally, which banned alcohol. This sweeping measure arose from exaggerated fears of moral decay.

   The results empowered the wealthy, as Prohibition created a deep divide within the working class. This growing split, culminating in over 60% of Americans voting for Herbert Hoover in 1928, highlights how societal divisions can deepen under policy conflicts. This alliance ushered in the Roaring Twenties, an era marked by a stock market that surged over 400%, accompanied by a significant concentration of wealth and power.

   However, the real consequences were disastrous: liquor prices soared by about 400%, yet liquor consumption nearly doubled. By 1932, federal convictions related to alcohol surged by 561%, and the prison population increased by 366%. This period sparked widespread violence, organized crime, and corruption that infiltrated the government. The social fabric was strained as communities grappled with crime and lawlessness, illustrating Prohibition's profound societal impact. Ultimately, Prohibition was a colossal failure, leaving a legacy of dysfunction that troubled America for decades. Nevertheless, by creating a significant divide among the working class, the wealthy elites saw their wealth double by 1928.

   Volstead Act," Britannica.com, accessed July, 2019, https://www.britannica.com/topic/Volstead-Act; and, Warburton, The Economic Result of Prohibition; and, "The Chemist's War: The little-told Story of How The U.S. Government Poisoned Alcohol During Prohibition With Deadly Consequences," Slate.com, February, 2010, https://slate.com/technology/2010/02/the-little-told-story-of-how-the-u-s-government-poisoned-alcohol-during-prohibition.html; and, "Alcohol Prohibition Was a Failure," Cato.org, July, 1991, https://www.cato.org/policy-analysis/alcohol-prohibition-was-failure.

6. Stone Washington, "Originalism: The Supreme Legacy of Judge Bork," Ellis Washington Report, December 2016, elliswashingtonreport.com/2016/12/21/originalism-the-supreme-legacy-of-judge-bork/

7. Barak Orbach, *How Antitrust Lost Its Goal*, 81 Fordham L. Rev. 2253 (2013).
Available at: https://ir.lawnet.fordham.edu/flr/vol81/iss5/6

Chapter 5 Endnotes

1. CBRE Press Release, "CB Richard Ellis Group, Inc. Announces Agreement to Acquire Trammell Crow Company," ir.cbre.com, October 31, 2006, https://ir.cbre.com/press-releases/press-release-details/2006/CB-Richard-Ellis-Group-Inc-Announces-Agreement-to-Acquire-Trammell-Crow-Company/default.aspx

Chapter 7 Endnotes

1. RealPage News, "RealPage Announces Demandx, An AI-Powered Multifamily Demand Optimization Solution," realpage.com, August 7, 2023, https://www.realpage.com/news/realpage-announces-demandx/

Chapter 9 Endnotes

1. Deborah Nelson and M.B. Pell, "Ambushed at Home: Military Families Battle Mice, Mold and Powerful Private Landlords," *Reuters.com*, November, 2018, https://www.reuters.com/investigates/special-report/usa-military-contractors/.
2. "The Burden of Fees: How Affordable Housing Is Made Unaffordable," Urban Justice Center, https://cdp.urbanjustice.org/sites/default/files/The%20Burden%20of%20Fees_FINAL.pdf

Chapter 10 Endnotes

1. "Working Hard But Struggling to Survive," United for Alice, accessed September, 2019, https://www.unitedforalice.org/
2. Chris Glynn, Emily B. Fox, "Dynamics of homelessness in urban America," Cornell university, July 28, 2017, https://arxiv.org/abs/1707.09380
3. Joe Bousquin, "In the Back Office, Revenue Management Software is Causing a Revolution," Multifamily Executive, April, 2009,; and, Joe Bousquin, "Revenue Revolution: Pushing Rents Becomes the Norm," Multifamily Executive, February 13,2008, https://www.multifamilyexecutive.com/property-management/revenue-revolution-pushing-rents-becomes-the-norm_o?o=0
4. President George W. Bush, Address to the Joint Session of the 107th Congress, September 20, 2001. https://georgewbush-whitehouse.archives.gov/infocus/bushrecord/documents/Selected_Speeches_George_W_Bush.pdf
5. "The Gap: A Shortage of Affordable Homes," NLIHC.org, March, 2018, https://reports.nlihc.org/sites/default/files/gap/Gap-Report_2018.pdf;
6. Steven Q. McKenzie, & Andrew Dougherty, Fast Food Justice: The Denial of Tenants' Due Process Rights in Chicago's Eviction Courts, 9 Pub. Interest L. Rptr. 1 (2004). Available at: http://lawecommons.luc.edu/pilr/vol9/iss2/2

7. Tom Borgers, "Financial Crisis Inquiry Commission Is Biggest Financial Investigation Since 1930s' Pecora Commission," ACFE (Association of Certified Fraud Examiners), November/December 2009, https://www.acfe.com/article.aspx?id=184.

Chapter 11 Endnotes

1. Corynne Cirilli, "The US Chamber of Commerce Might Not Be What You Think," Racked.com, October, 2017, https://www.racked.com/2017/10/2/16370014/us-chamber-commerce-explainer.

2. The website for Department of Housing and Urban Development, "HUD History," accessed January, 2020, https://www.hud.gov/about/hud_history.

3. Stone Washington, "Originalism: The Supreme Legacy of Judge Bork," Ellis Washington Report, December 2016, elliswashingtonreport.com/2016/12/21/originalism-the-supreme-legacy-of-judge-bork/ ; and, Dylan Matthews, " 'Antitrust was defined by Robert Bork. I cannot overstate his influence' " Washington Post, December 2012, washingtonpost.com/news/wonk /wp/2012/12/20/antitrust-was-defined-by-robert-bork-i-cannot-overstate-his-influence/

4. Nikole Hannah-Jones, "Living Apart: How the Government Betrayed a Landmark Civil Rights Law," ProPublica.org, June, 2015, https://www.propublica.org/article/living-apart-how-the-government-betrayed-a-landmark-civil-rights-law

5. Daniel Beekman, "Discrimination alleged at 13 Seattle rental properties," seattletimes, June 13, 2015, https://www.seattletimes.com/seattle-news/13-rental-properties-in-seattle-accused-of-discrimination/

6. "Go Deeper: Where Race Lives," PBS.org, pbs.org/race/000_About/002_06-godeeper.htm.

7. Pedro da Costa, "Housing discrimination underpins the staggering wealth gap between blacks and whites," Economic Policy Institute, April, 2019, epi.org/blog/housing-discrimination-underpins-the-staggering-wealth-gap-between-blacks-and-whites/.

8. Pam Martens and Russ Martens, "Trump and Clarence Thomas Financial Disclosures Prove U.S. Is Officially a Kleptocracy," wallstreetonparade, May 20, 2018, https://wallstreetonparade.com/2018/05/trump-and-clarence-thomas-financial-disclosures-prove-u-s-is-officially-a-kleptocracy/; and, Campaign Finance Reports Show 'Super PAC' Donors," Jan 31, 2012, https://www.nytimes.com/2012/02/01/us/politics/campaign-finance-reports-show-super-pac-donors.html ; and, Danny Hakim and Jo Becker, "The Long Crusade of Clarence and Ginni Thomas," The New York times, September 1, 2022, https://www.nytimes.com/2022/02/22/magazine/clarence-thomas-ginni-thomas.html

9. David Grusky and Clifton B. Parker, "Stanford Report Shows that the US Performs Poorly on Poverty and Inequality Measures," Stanford News, February 2016, stanford.edu/2016/02/02/poverty-report-grusky-020216/.

Chapter 12 Endnotes

1. Bobby Allyn, "Justice Clarence Thomas Takes Aim At Tech And Its Power 'To Cut Off Speech'," npr, April 5, 2021, https://www.npr.org/2021/04/05/984440891/justice-clarence-thomas-takes-aims-at-tech-and-its-power-to-cut-off-speech
2. CIO New Zealand, "AI and price fixing: Collusion by machines," *cio.com*, March, 2019, https://www.cio.com/article/3491014/ai-and-price-fixing-collusion-by-machines.html
3. "Press Release: Forbes 33rd Annual World's Billionaires Issue Reveals Number of Billionaires and Their Combined Wealth Have Decreased For the First Time Since 2016," Forbes.com, March, 2019, https://www.forbes.com/sites/forbespr/2019/03/05/press-release-forbes-33rd-annual-worlds-billionaires-issue-reveals-number-of-billionaires-and-their-combined-wealth-have-decreased-for-for-first-time-since-2016/#670a16b245b9
4. Hospitalitynet, Press Release, "The Rainmaker Group Implements Revenue Management at Two Seminole Hard Rock Hotels and Casinos," June 9, 2010, https://www.hospitalitynet.org/news/4046951.html ; and. https://www.omnihotels.com/media-center/recent-news/2014/05/15/22/48/090129 ; and, https://hotelonline-assets1.nyc3.digitaloceanspaces.com/wordpress/hotelonline-News/News_posts/PR2010_1st/Feb10_RainmakerMicrosoftGold.html

Chapter 13 Endnotes

1. BERK analysis of Census LEHD Origin-Destination Employment Statistics, 2020. Ibid. www.seattle.gov/Documents/Departments/OPCD/OngoingInitiatives/HousingChoices/SeattleMarketRateHousingNeedsAndSupplyAnalysis2021.pdf ; and, Washington, The Joint Legislative Audit and Review Commission (JLARC), 19-08 Final Report, " Property Tax Exemption for Multifamily Housing in Urban Areas," December 2019, Accessed June 2020, https://leg.wa.gov/jlarc/taxReports/2019/MFTE/f_ii/print.pdf ; The Website of the Washington State Legislature, Joint Legislative Audit & Review Committee, Published Reports, Assessed 2019, https://leg.wa.gov/jlarc/AuditAndStudyReports/Pages/default.aspx ; and, Bob Young, Seattle Times, "Audit: Oversight lacking in tax breaks to Seattle housing developers," seattletimes.com, September 19,2012, https://www.seattletimes.com/seattle-news/audit-oversight-lacking-in-tax-breaks-to-seattle-housing-developers/ v ; and, Zack Freeman et al., "2019 Tax Preference Performance Reviews," Washington JLARC, July, 2019. http://leg.wa.gov/jlarc/AuditAndStudyReports/Documents/TaxPrelimRepPres.pdf\
2. Dees Stribling, "Build-To-Rent Developers See Opportunity In Growing Renter Class," bisnow.com, December 10 2020, https://www.bisnow.com/national/news/construction-development/build-to-rent-is-residential-real-estates-rising-star-107029

3. The White House Press Release, “The Accomplishments,” Accessed April 2021, https://georgewbush-whitehouse.archives.gov/infocus/achievement/chap7.html; and, The Website of The American Presidency Project, “Fact Sheet: President Bush Calls for Expanding Opportunities to Homeownership,” presidency.ucsb.edu , June 17, 2002, https://www.presidency.ucsb.edu/documents/fact-sheet-president-bush-calls-for-expanding-opportunities-homeownership

4. David L. Bahnsen, “Did The Financial Crisis End?” National Review, March 2019, https://www.nationalreview.com/magazine/2019/03/25/did-the-financial-crisis-end/

5. Frederic C. Howe, Consumers’ Counsel- (Speech) National Recovery Administration (NRA), Washington Conference On Public Housing, Willard Hotel, Washington D. C. January 27, 1934, National Public Housing Conference, New York, 728.1, W173, c.2.

Chapter 14 Endnotes

1. Constellis, formerly Blackwater, is an American private military contractor founded in 1997 by former Navy SEAL officer Erik Prince. It was renamed Xe Services in 2009 and again to Academi in 2011 after it was acquired by a group of private investors.

2. According to the Federal Reserve Bank of New York, household debt has more than doubled from $10 trillion in 2008 to $20 trillion by the end of 2024. The Federal Reserve System reports that the corporate and business sectors (excluding banks) also saw their debts more than double during this period, from just over $35 trillion to $80 trillion. According to the U.S. Treasury Department, total U.S. government debt increased by 370%, from $10 trillion to $37 trillion, during the same period.

Bibliography

The Six Independent Economic Impact Studies

The author, a former federal banking regulator with a degree in economics, conducted six independently financed economic impact studies completed over a five-year period to gain a deeper understanding of the housing crisis. This extensive research, spanning over 1,400 pages and supported by more than 3,500 cited references from over 10,000 pages of documents, along with nearly 500 quotes from industry insiders, provides readers with a comprehensive understanding of artificial intelligence-powered revenue management technology. The documents were prepared and are protected under the Attorney-Client Privilege.

Study 1—The Washington Study: The RealPage Platform Use in Washington—about 100 pages

To gain a deeper understanding of the housing crisis, we conducted a detailed rent analysis of the increase in rental rates for two Segments of the Washington State housing market from 2013 to 2018. To accomplish this, we compared rents in three metropolitan areas where Artificial Intelligence Technology was deployed (in King, Spokane, and Thurston County-Segment 1) to those where it was not (Franklin, Yakima, and Walla Walla-Segment 2). The study found no reasonable economic reasons for the skyrocketing rental rates of 96.24 percent in Segment 1 compared to the modest rental rate increase of 9.9 percent in Segment 2. Both control groups' economies were verified, and other contributing economic factors were eliminated. The study's Peer Reviewer, Fideres Partners, LLC., recommended expanding the study.

Study 2—Appendix 'A' The Pricing Concentration Study: Market Share Concentrations in Multifamily Property Management Companies Using a Common Pricing Platform—Metro, Seattle, WA—about 300 pages.

The second step included the Metro Seattle Market Concentration Study. The study focused on concentration analysis, which evaluates the competition among property management companies in the market, including their use of a shared pricing platform. The measurement of concentration level reveals market structure, behavior, and performance in the rental market industry. The first objective was to define the market, which included three ZIP codes. Rental unit data was obtained from the popular rental site Apartments.com, with CoStar providing the data. According to the Scope and Methodology, the first step involved determining the number of property managers using the technology. Our second objective aimed to establish when they acquired the technology. The third step of the process is to verify the number of rental units under management and the number of competitors in the defined market. By manual hand count, the studies confirmed that nearly 320,000 individual rental units were utilizing the technology for pricing. Explained more fully in Chapter 5.

Study 3—Appendix 'B' the Property Managers: —about 150 Pages

This study highlights the significance of a new breed of property managers and their changes to stay competitive. The survivors now function through vertical trust organizations that offer improved service arrangements for property owners. It outlines their adoption of the Manugistics standard of non-competition within the industry, allowing them to access and share data on tenants, applicants, and properties as if they were a single producer.

However, does the exchange of strategic information relating to pricing violate exclusionary conduct? Do they misuse the Platform through restraint of trade? To answer this question, an in-depth analysis of the top ten property management companies reveals their organizational structures, their massive size, and the significant interconnections they have formed within the industry. For example, roughly half of all rental units are priced by a small group of profoundly interconnected and interrelated managers who originate from or have deep roots in a single company.

Study 4—Appendix 'C' The Technology and the Technology Providers:—about 170 Pages

The primary goal of this study was to determine the nature and source of new Artificial Intelligence (AI)-driven technology. We detailed various IT programs and analyzed their contributions to the Platform, including a general understanding of their intended uses and predicted outcomes. We then focused on the industry's primary technology providers: RealPage, Yardi, and AppFolio. Their roles in deploying the technology were assessed.

Additionally, what are they promising for the billions of dollars they receive for their services? This technology was engineered to leverage the Manugistics standard of non-competition within the industry. Therefore, we researched and reported on the technology's deployment into the algorithms, its adoption of the Standard, and its impact on the pricing process.

Study 5—Appendix 'D' Experian RentBureau: —about 100 Pages

Of all the studies, this is one of the most critical because the Platform relies on Experian to provide vast amounts of tenant data. Additionally, the same group of institutional investors who financed the Platform's origination also funded and organized Experian RentBureau as a means to get to the tenant data. The study analyzed the overly close relationship between the common pricing platform, its member landlords, and Experian. It also exposes the various third-party connections that claim to have consumer-permissioned data and provide vast amounts of intimate details on their tenants. Although its original purpose was to gather and obtain tenant data, its relationship extends much deeper into all phases of the tenant life cycle. It could be argued that Experian, in conjunction with the Platform, has become the de facto co-gatekeepers to housing.

Study 6—Appendix 'E' How The Multifamily Tax Exemption (MFTE) Program Impacts the Affordable Housing Markets: —about 130 Pages

The MFTE programs to build affordable housing incentivize construction through property tax breaks. Yet, the program amounts to a tax burden shift. However, these taxes aren't discretionary; they include city services such as police, schools, firefighters, infrastructure, etc. For example, if the city needed $100 to operate, it would collect that amount. In short, the tax consequences are redirected to other taxpayers who already pay their fair share.

An economic impact study was conducted to assess whether the MFTE Program, as implemented in 2018 by Metro Seattle, achieved its objectives and program goals. The study included a cost-benefit analysis on four tax-exempt apartment properties closed in 2017 to determine if the program's annual cost of $137 million provides sufficient benefit for the lost tax revenues. In other words, does the cost of the program equal the benefits? The conclusion offers a warning to cities that are considering its use.

This study further highlights the larger problem of affordable housing: the builder's vertically integrated and interconnected management organizational structures that have become highly concentrated. Those overly close relationships have led to widespread fraud and abuse in the financing programs.

Summary of the Six Studies—Professional Legal Version—about 400 Pages

The six studies are summarized in "The New Landlord, Powered by Big Data and Artificial Intelligence," which also includes a legal analysis. This legal version, also known as a white paper, serves as the foundation for the legal cases against RealPage and the broader rental housing industry. Additionally, it underpins the second version, PRICED OUT BY DESIGN, which presents the study in layperson's terms, also known as the published book.

Used Source References

We reviewed thousands of pages of hard copy documents (including property management policy and procedure manuals) as well as numerous court cases. The industry provides its end users with massive amounts of information, keeping them informed about all the latest technological developments. I reviewed hundreds of e-books to gain a better understanding of their processes. Therefore, many of the cited references are e-books. Additional 3rd party studies that have been completed relating to the subject were used in this study, to name a few:

Experian Sources Used:

1. RealPage LeaseLabs Case Studies, "Customer Data Study, Revealing Lease conversion drivers for higher lead efficiency, yield and ROI," https://www.realpage.com/case-studies/want-better-leads-find-them/
2. Experian Case Studies, "The Power of Rental Payment Data," Experian, accessed November, 2019, https://www.experian.com/assets/rentbureau/product-sheets/experian-rentbureau-brochure.pdf
3. N. Henry and J. Morris, "Scaling Up Affordable Lending: Inclusive Credit Scoring," January 2018, https://www.researchgate.net/publication/342010616_Scaling_Up_Affordable_Lending_Inclusive_Credit_Scoring
4. U.S. GOVERNMENT PUBLISHING OFFICE 32–483 PDF WASHINGTON. HEARING BEFORE THE COMMITTEE ON BANKING, HOUSING, AND URBAN AFFAIRS UNITED STATES SENATE ONE HUNDRED FIFTEENTH CONGRESS SECOND SESSION ON EXAMINING THE CONSUMER REPORTING AGENCIES AND THE FAIR CREDIT REPORTING ACT, HRG. 115–361, "AN OVERVIEW OF THE CREDIT BUREAUS AND THE FAIR CREDIT REPORTING ACT," July 12, 2018, https://www.govinfo.gov/content/pkg/CHRG-115shrg32483/html/CHRG-115shrg32483.htm

5. Michael Turner and Patrick Walker, U.S. Department of Housing and Urban Development, Policy and Economic Research Council, "Potential Impact of Credit Reporting Public Housing Rental Payment Data," October 2019, https://www.huduser.gov/portal/publications/Potential-Impacts-of-Credit-Reporting.html

6. Kelly Thompson Cochran, Colin Foos, Michael Stegman, Urban Institute and FinRegLab, " Utility, Telecommunications, and Rental Data in Underwriting Credit," December 2021, https://www.urban.org/sites/default/files/publication/105282/utility-telecommunications-and-rental-data-in-underwriting-credit_1.pdf

7. Experian RentBureau publications, "Reporting rental payment data to Experian RentBureau," https://www.experian.com/rentbureau/renter-credit

8. Experian RentBureau publications, "Experian Access, User Guide," https://www.experian.com/consumer-information/access/help-center

9. Experian RentBureau publications, " eSolutions Credit Solutions Suite User Guide," https://www.experian.com/esolutions/docs/esolutions_user_guide.pdf

10. Experian RentBureau User guide, " Experian Access Prescreen suite—iScreen," https://www.experian.com/assets/access/iscreen/iscreen-user-guide.pdf

11. Experian RentBureau User guide, " Collection Advantage via Access," 2017, https://www.experian.com/assets/access/collection-advantage-access-user-guide.pdf

12. Experian RentBureau User guide, "Security Designate Guide Experian Web Access Control System," 2018, https://www.experian.com/content/dam/marketing/na/assets/bis/business-information/brochures/ewacs-security-designate-guide.pdf

13. Experian RentBureau Product Sheet, " Experian's Asset Verification," 2017, https://www.experian.com/assets/consumer-information/product-sheets/ps-voa.pdf

14. Experian RentBureau Publications, "Alternative Data Across the Loan Life Cycle: How FinTech and Other Lenders Use It and Why," 2018, https://www.experian.com/assets/consumer-information/reports/Experian_Aite_AltDataReport_Final_120418.pdf

15. Experian RentBureau publication, "IDC info snapshot: Modernizing employment and income verification in consumer lending," May 18, 2021, https://www.experian.com/innovation/thought-leadership/idc-snapshot-modernizing-employment-income-verification.jsp

16. Experian White Paper, "Getting in front of the shift of omnichannel collections," file:///J:/00000Research%20and%20Studies/0000Final%20New%20Landlord%20Documents/3_hard%20copy%20document/experian%20studies/1146-DA-Collections-WhitePaper-F.pdf

17. Experian White Paper, "Preparing for CECL and beyond," 2019, https://www.experian.com/innovation/thought-leadership/prepare-cecl-beyond.jsp

18. Experian Case Studies, "Preventing synthetic identity fraud," July 2020, https://www.experian.com/blogs/insights/2021/01/solving-fraud-problem-synthetic-identity-fraud/

19. The website for RealPage, Inc., "Knock Out Bad Debt," accessed September, 2019, https://www.realpage.com/lp/ai-screening/?utm_source=content-marketing&utm_medium=social&utm_campaign=social-ai-screening&utm_term=blog&utm_content=20190626-ai-screening

20. Experian Blogs, "How Paying Rent On Time Helps Build Your Credit History," Accessed 2020, https://www.experian.com/rentbureau/rental-payment

21. "Case study: MAA Rental payment data means big benefits for MAA and its residents," Experian.com, accessed December, 2019, http://www.experian.com/rentbureau/experian-rentbureau-testimonial-casestudies-maa.html

22. "Experian Rental Payment Data," Experian, accessed December, 2019, https://www.experian.com/rentbureau/rental-data

23. Maitri Johnson, "Big Data Minimize Evictions, Fraudulent Renters," Multifamily Executive, January, 2019, accessed November, 2019, https://www.multifamilyexecutive.com/property-management/big-data-minimize-evictions-fraudulent-renters_o

24. Michael Delgado, ed., "Experian RentBureau to Receive Rental Payment History from Riverstone Residential Group," Experian.com, May 2012, accessed November 2019. https://www.experian.com/blogs/news/2012/05/30/riverstone/

25. "Unlock the Power of Rental Payment Data," Experian.com, accessed November 2019, http://www.experian.com/rentbureau/rental-history.html

26. "Experian Rental Payment Data: Rental Tradelines Are Now Part of Experian Consumer Credit Files," Experian.com, https://www.experian.com/rentbureau/rental-data

27. "Case Study: Bad-debt recovery," Experian, accessed November, 2019, http://www.experian.com/rentbureau/experian-rentbureau-testimonial-casestudies-debt.html

28. "What Are Specialty Consumer Reporting Agencies and What Kind of Information do They Collect?" Consumer Financial Protection Bureau, updated March 2017, https://www.consumerfinance.gov/ask-cfpb/what-are-specialty-consumer-reporting-agencies-and-what-kind-of-information-do-they-collect-en-1813/

29. Experian RentBureau White Paper, "Risk versus reward," https://www.experian.com/assets/rentbureau/white-papers/experian-rentbureau-rental-history-analysis.pdf

30. Experian Case Studies, "Automating income verifications streamlines long approval times and mitigates rising fraud" https://www.experian.com/blogs/insights/2021/08/case-study-automating-income-verifications-streamlines-long-approval-times-mitigates-rising-fraud/

31. Experian, "Account Review Advantage," https://www.experian.com/assets/consumer-information/product-sheets/account-review-advantage.pdf

32. Experian publications, "True Credit Intelligence," file:///J:/00000Research%20and%20Studies/0000Final%20New%20Landlord%20Documents/3_hard%20copy%20document/experian%20studies/true-credit-intelligence-perspective-paper.pdf

33. Experian blogs, Brittany Ennis, "Case Study: Automating Income Verifications Streamlines Long Approval Times and Mitigates Rising Fraud," Experian.com, August 20, 2021, https://www.experian.com/blogs/insights/2021/08/case-study-automating-income-verifications-streamlines-long-approval-times-mitigates-rising-fraud/

34. Experian Reports, "Mastering the customer experience," 2018, https://www.edq.com/resources/data-management-whitepapers/mastering-the-customer-experience/

35. Experian White Paper, "Credit for renting," https://www.experian.com/assets/rentbureau/white-papers/experian-rentbureau-credit-for-rent-analysis.pdf

36. The Credit Builders Alliance White Paper, "The Power of Rent Reporting PILOT," 2015, https://www.creditbuildersalliance.org/wp-content/uploads/2019/06/CBA-Power-of-Rent-Reporting-Pilot-White-Paper.pdf

37. The website for Experian, Strengthen your debt recovery strategies, https://www.experian.com/business-services/debt-recovery

38. Experian Blogs, Gayle Sato, "What Do Landlords Look For in a Tenant?," Experian.com, April 29, 2021, https://www.experian.com/blogs/ask-experian/what-do-landlords-look-for-in-tenant/

39. Experian RentBureau, "Improving screening practices, reducing skips and bad debt," Experian.com, Accessed June 2020, https://www.experian.com/rentbureau/experian-rentbureau-testimonial-casestudies-amc

40. Website of Finicity, Accessed June 2020, https://www.finicity.com/supported-institution/

41. Experian RentBureau Press Release, "Experian® RentBureau® to present rental payment history data session at National Apartment Association 2013 Education Conference and Expo," Experian.com, June 11, 2013, https://www.experian.com/assets/rentbureau/news-releases/naa-session-announcement.pdf

42. National Apartment Association Press Release: "How to Eliminate the Burden of Manual Screening," naahq.org, Accessed June 2020, https://www.naahq.org/node/35985/article/how-eliminate-burden-manual-screening

43. Rachel Davidson, "It's Time to Make the Change to Automated Renter Screening," Multifamily Executive, January 2019, https://www.multifamilyexecutive.com/property-management/its-time-to-make-the-change-to-automated-renter-screening_o

44. Experian Website, "Collection Companies," Experian.com, Accessed June 2020, https://www.experian.com/rentbureau/rental-collection

45. Experian Press Release, "Experian RentBureau to receive rental payment history data from Riverstone Residential Group," experianplc.com, June 8, 2012, https://www.experianplc.com/media/latest-news/2012/experian-rentbureau-to-receive-rental-payment-history-data-from/

46. "Case study: MAA Rental payment data means big benefits for MAA and its residents," Experian.com, accessed December, 2019, http://www.experian.com/rentbureau/experian-rentbureau-testimonial-casestudies-maa.html

RealPage Publications

1. The website for RealPage, Inc., accessed September, 2019, https://www.realpage.com/

2. RealPage eBook, "Screening Strategies for an Evolving World," https://www.realpage.com/ebooks/screening-strategies-evolving-world/ ; or, https://www.realpage.com/ebooks/screening-strategies-evolving-world/&showPdf=true

3. RealPage White Paper, "AI Screening Performance Validation," re-issued February 2021, https://www.realpage.com/case-studies/ai-screening-performance-validation/&showPdf=true or, https://www.realpage.com/ebooks/screening-strategies-evolving-world/ or, https://www.realpage.com/case-studies/ai-screening-performance-validation/

4. RealPage e-book, "The Power of Payments: Turning Process Into Opportunity," Accessed June 2019, https://www.realpage.com/online-payments/?utm_source=pmi&utm_medium=bp&utm_campaign=EVG|Offer|Rent-Payments-Contact-Sales|0|RSCL&utm_term=blog&utm_content=20190411-residentservices

5. "RealPage AI Screening: A Seismic Leap Ahead," RealPage.com (eBook), https://www.realpage.com/ebooks/science-behind-solution/

6. The website for RealPage, Inc., "Support," accessed December, 2019, https://www.realpage.com/apartment-marketing/ai-screening/

7. RealPage eBook, "INTRODUCING AI REVENUE MANAGEMENT Next-Generation Price Optimization That Unlocks Hidden Yield," ASO-20-280-004, RealPage, Accessed April 2021, https://www.realpage.com/asset-optimization/revenue-management/?showPdf=true

8. RealPage eBook, "Know it All," September 2016, https://www.realpage.com/blog/know-it-all-multifamily-business-intelligence-software-ebook/

9. RealPage eBook, "Leveraging Lease Transactional Data," https://www.realpage.com/asset-optimization/market-analytics/

10. RealPage eBook, "Drive Better Deals with RealPage Market Analytics," https://www.realpage.com/ebooks/drive-better-deals-market-analytics/

11. RealPage e-book, "Proven in Any Market Cycle," Accessed April, 2019, https://www.realpage.com/ebooks/outperform-in-a-down-market/?utm_source=pmi&utm_medium=bp&utm_campaign=content-aso19163-revenue-management-in-a-downturn&utm_term=blog&utm_content=20190417-proven

12. RealPage eBook, "Proven, B & C Assets Ace the Market with RealPage," realpage.com, Accessed June 2019, https://www.realpage.com/ebooks/outperform-in-a-down-market/?utm_source=pmi&utm_medium=bp&utm_campaign=content-aso19163-revenue-management-in-a-downturn&utm_term=blog&utm_content=20190417-proven

13. RealPage e-book "Outperform In A Down Market," https://www.realpage.com/ebooks/outperform-in-a-down-market/

14. RealPage e-book, "Strength in Numbers," Assessed 2019, https://www.realpage.com/asset-optimization/market-analytics/

15. RealPage e-book, "Six Ways Revenue Management Software Benefits B and C Properties," RealPage, June 12, 2019, https://www.realpage.com/lp/revenue-management-b-c-assets/images/ASO-19-161_005_B-C-Assets_e-Book.pdf

16. RealPage eBooks, "Harness Data to Drive Results," realpage.com, Accessed June 2020, https://www.realpage.com/ebooks/harness-data-drive-results/&showPdf=true/

17. RealPage eBook, "5 Ways Revenue Management Elevates any Asset Strategy," https://www.realpage.com/blog/five-revenue-management-strategies-achieve-investment-goals/

18. The RealPage Blog, "Resident Screening Technology Helps You Say Yes," RealPage.com-Blog, March, 2017. https://www.realpage.com/blog/resident-screening-technology-helps-you-say-yes/

19. RealPage Website, "Resident Screening," realpage.com, Accessed 2020, https://www.realpage.com/apartment-marketing/resident-screening/

20. RealPage eBook, "3 Ways to Leverage AI for Maximum NOI," https://www.realpage.com/ebooks/leverage-ai-maximum-noi/

21. MultifamilyBiz Press Release, "YieldStar Offers Revenue Advisory Services," multifammilybiz, March 1, 2010, https://www.multifamilybiz.com/pressreleases/295/yieldstar_offers_revenue_advisory_services

22. David Polewchak, RealPage Blogs, "Unprecedented Times Call for Proven Solutions," realpage.com, May 21, 2020, https://www.realpage.com/analytics/unprecedented-times-call-proven-solutions/

23. RealPage News, "RealPage Presents New Data Reinforcing the Value of AI Screening," realpage.com, February 11, 2021, https://www.realpage.com/news/data-reinforcing-value-of-ai-screening/

24. "BH Management's Secret Weapons for Maximizing Revenues," accessed December, 2019, https://bhmanagement.com/documents/news/173.pdf

25. RealPage e-books, "Know What to Look for in a Business Intelligence Solution," realpage.com, February 11, 2021, https://www.realpage.com/ebooks/yieldstar-business-intelligence-know-it-all/
26. RealPage e-books, "Deposit Insurance, What You Need to Know Now," realpage.com, https://webassets.inman.com/wp-content/uploads/2021/07/Deposit-Insurance-eBook.pdf
27. RealPage e-books, "Resident Insurance: From Risk to Reward," realpage.com, 2021, https://www.realpage.com/ebooks/mitigate-risk-resident-insurance-solutions/
28. RealPage e-books, "The 5 Elements of a Successful Multifamily Learning Program," realpage.com, https://www.realpage.com/ebooks/multifamily-learning-management-systems/
29. RealPage e-books,"3 Strategies for Harnessing the Right Data the Drives Results," ASO-21-346_001 realpage.com, https://www.realpage.com/ebooks/
30. RealPage Rentlytics e-books, "Why you Need Business Intelligence," realpage.com, https://www.realpage.com/ebooks/yieldstar-business-intelligence-know-it-all/
31. RealPage e-books,"10 Ways RealPage Expense Management Helps You Cut Costs, realpage.com, https://www.realpage.com/ebooks/
32. Guy Lyman, RealPage Blog, "Don't Miss This! Unveiling of "AIRM" AI Revenue Management at RealWorld," realpage.com, September 8, 2020, https://www.realpage.com/blog/dont-miss-this-unveiling-of-airm-ai-revenue-management-at-realworld/
33. RealPage e-books," Open Platform, Your Route to More Residents, Retention and Productivity," realpage.com, www.realpage.com/apartment-marketing
34. RealPage e-books," Reach New Heights in Operational Excellence," realpage.com, https://www.realpage.com/ebooks/
35. RealPage e-books," 9 Ways to Accelerate Your Productivity," realpage.com, https://www.realpage.com/ebooks/; and, https://www.realpage.com/property-management-software/accounting-software/
36. RealPage LeasingDest Renters Insurance, "Welcome!, Renter's Insurance Property Training (for OneSite users) realpage.com, Dec. 2016, https://www.realpage.com/property-management-software/
37. RealPage e-books," Pump Up the Volume, the 3 Key Leasing Tools Proven to Optimize Occupancy," realpage.com, https://www.realpage.com/ebooks/three-essential-solutions-optimizing-occupancy/; or, https://www.realpage.com/ebooks/
38. RealPage e-books,"5 Sure Ways to get the Renter Love you Deserve," realpage.com, realpage.com/renter-engagement-suite/ ; https://www.realpage.com/ebooks/
39. RealPage User's guide, "Before you Begin," Release 3.0, Realpage.com, April 2006, Doc. ID OB58E.0

40. RealPage User Guide, "Lead2Lease," realpage.com, 2015, www.Lead2Lease.com

41. RealPage Propertyware User Guide, "New View Owner Portal," realpage.com, January 2020, Doc ID: 166453

42. RealPage User Guide, " Welcome Home Residential Portal Overview," realpage.com, 2019

43. RealPage User Guide, "P2 Peak Performance, Tech Stack," realpage,com, www.realpage.com/p2

44. YieldStar Best Practices," Sunridge Management Group PDF, http://www.sunridgemanagement.com/sites/180/siteFiles//Forms/OneSite/Yieldstar percent 20Best percent 20Practices.pdf

45. RealPage News, "LeasingDesk Launches New Web Site," RealPage, October 1, 2009, https://www.realpage.com/news/leasingdesk-launches-new-web-site/

46. Guy Lyman, RealPage Blog, "From "Ability to Pay" to "Willingness to Pay": AI-Based Tenant Screening is Boosting NOI," February 24, 2021, https://www.realpage.com/blog/ai-tenant-screening-is-boosting-noi/

47. RealPage News, "RealPage's YieldStar™ Revenue Management System Empowering On-site Staff, Managers at Camden," realpage.com, September 12, 2005, https://www.realpage.com/news/realpages-yieldstaramptrade-revenue-management-system-empowering-on-site-staff-managers-at-camden/

48. YieldStar Predicts Market Impact Down to Unit Type and Street Location," RealPage video, 2:00, https://www.realpage.com/videos/yieldstar-data-scientists-help-manage-supply-demand/4405965614001/

49. "YieldStar Calculates the Right Rent Price at the Right Time," RealPage video, 1:40, https://www.realpage.com/videos/yieldstar-measures-price-elasticity

50. RealPage eBook, "The Four Success Pillars of Commercial RealEstate," realpage.com, Accessed June 2021, https://www.realpage.com/ebooks/four-commercial-success-pillars/

51. Wang, Jian. (2008). A realization of an apartment dynamic pricing system. Journal of Revenue and Pricing Management. 7. 256-265. 10.1057/rpm.2008.11

52. Integrated Decisions and Systems, Inc. 2005, IDeaS, ID-MK-100102-v1-YMBasic, "The Basics of Revenue Management, Accessed 2020, https://www.hospitalitynet.org/file/152001833.pdf

53. van Ryzin and Talluri: An Introduction to Revenue Management, Tutorialsin OperationsResearch, © 2005 INFORMS https://www0.gsb.columbia.edu/mygsb/faculty/research/pubfiles/3958/Tutorials2005-chapter06.pdf

54. The Rainmaker Group, "Predicting Occupancy of Multi-family Apartments," https://www.crowdanalytix.com/

55. The Website of RealPage, "Resident Utility Billing Services," accessed September, 2020,https://www.realpage.com/utility-management/billing/

56. The website for RealPage, "Insights to Mitigating Risk in Affordable Housing," https://www.realpage.com/ebooks/affordable-housing-risk-management/

57. "RealPage Acquires YieldStar Multifamily Revenue Management System," RealPage News, July, 2002, https://www.realpage.com/news/realpage-acquires-yieldstar-multifamily-revenue-management-system/

58. Wang, Jian & Das, Murtaza & Duggasani, Amar. (2016). Predicting and measuring customer lifetime values for apartment tenants. Zeitschrift für Immobilienökonomie. 10.1365/s41056-016-0015-0. https://www.researchgate.net/publication/311527003_Predicting_and_measuring_customer_lifetime_values_for_apartment_tenants/citation/download

59. RealPage Blogs, "How Artificial Intelligence is Revolutionizing Resident Screening," realpage.com, June 26, 2019, https://www.realpage.com/blog/artificial-intelligence-revolutionizing-resident-screening/

60. RealPage Press Release, "RealPage Acquires EverGreen Solutions," RealPage, September, 23, 2009, https://www.realpage.com/news/realpage-acquires-evergreen-solutions/

61. Chris Wood, "RealPage Acquires EverGreen Solutions, A.L. Wizard," multifamilyexecutive, September 22, 2009, https://www.multifamilyexecutive.com/technology/realpage-acquires-evergreen-solutions-al-wizard_o

62. Tim Blackwell, RealPage Blog, "Changing the Way Multifamily Thinks About Apartment Market Research with Lease Transaction Data," realpage.com, September 21, 2020, https://www.realpage.com/blog/changing-the-way-multifamily-thinks-about-apartment-market-research-with-lease-transaction-data/

63. RealPage e-books, "Know What to Look for in a Business Intelligence Solution "https://www.realpage.com/ebooks/yieldstar-business-intelligence-know-it-all/

64. "Market Analytics," Realpage.com, accessed September, 2019, https://www.realpage.com/aim/

65. RealPage website, asset optimization, "YieldStar® Investment Analytics Powered by MPF Research," accessed June 2021, https://www.realpage.com/asset-optimization/investment-analytics/

66. Chris Wood, "Riverstone Moves to RealPage Cloud Computing Platform," multifamilyexecutive, July 21, 2010, https://www.multifamilyexecutive.com/technology/riverstone-moves-to-realpage-cloud-computing-platform_o

67. RealPage Press Release, "New RealPage Cloud Computing Division (the "Cloud") Formed," Assessed April 2021, https://www.realpage.com/news/new-realpage-cloud-computing-division-the-quotcloudquot-formed/

68. ANNUAL REPORT PURSUANT TO SECTION 13 OR 15(d) OF THE SECURITIES AND EXCHANGE ACT OF 1934, For the fiscal year ended December 31, 2012, RealPage, Inc., https://www.sec.gov/Archives/edgar/data/1286225/000119312513080071/d453457d10k.htm

69. RealPage Management Training, "AI Revenue Management, 6.2021, The Medve Group Inc," medve.com, June 23, 2021, https://medve.com/assets/airm-manager-training-medve-management-6.23.2021-(1).pdf

70. RealPage Compliance Services, "Compliance monitoring for all property types, taking the burden off of your staff, mitigating risk and keeping your properties in line with changing regulations," Assessed June 2021, https://www.realpage.com/compliance-services/

71. RealPage Press Release, "RealPage Reacts to Texas Governor Greg Abbott Signing Senate Bill 873 into Law," June 8, 2017, https://www.pressreleasepoint.com/realpage-reacts-texas-governor-greg-abbott-signing-senate-bill-873-law

72. RealPage Press Release, "RealPage Acquires Propertyware," realpage, November 10, 2009, https://www.realpage.com/news/realpage-acquires-propertyware/

73. Real Page Press Releases, "RealPage Releases AI Screening," realpage.com, June 26, 2019, https://www.realpage.com/news/realpage-releases-ai-screening/

74. Ryan Howard, "Increase Resident Collections with RealPage and BYL's OneSite Integration," March, 2016, accessed November, 2019, https://www.bylcollections.com/blog/5-ways-to-increase-tenant-collections-with-a-certified-onesite-app-partner and. https://www.cpexecutive.com/post/greystar-buys-riverstone-residential-group/

75. RealPage News, "RealPage Announces Demandx, An AI-Powered Multifamily Demand Optimization Solution," realpage.com, August 7, 2023, https://www.realpage.com/news/realpage-announces-demandx/

76. The RealPage Website, "RealPage, Inc. Corporate Privacy Policy updated February 10, 2020," Accessed June 2021, https://www.realpage.com/privacy-policy/

National Publications and Published Articles Used

1. "The State Of The Nation's Housing 2018," Joint Center for Housing Studies of Harvard University, accessed December, 2019, http://www.jchs.harvard.edu/sites/default/files/Harvard_JCHS_State_of_the_Nations_Housing_2018.pdf.

2. National Multifamily Housing Council, White Paper, "Automated Revenue Management: Opportunities and Challenges for Apartment Firms," nmhc.org, January 16, 2003, https://www.nmhc.org/research-insight/analysis-and-guidance/automated-revenue-management-opportunities-and-challenges-for-apartment-firms/

3. Working Hard but Struggling to Survive," Alice, accessed August, 2019, https://www.unitedforalice.org/home

4. "NLIHC Gap 2019 Report Calls for Significant Investments to Address Shortage of 7 Million Affordable and Available Homes for the Lowest-Income Households," NLIHC.org, March, 2019, nlihc.org/resource/nlihc-gap-2019-report-calls-significant-investments-address-shortage-7-million-affordable.

5. "Housing Finance At a Glance: A Monthly Chartbook," Urban Institute, June, 2018, urban.org/sites/default/files/publication/98669/housing_finance_at_a_glance_a_monthly_chartbook_june_2018_0.pdf.

6. Cosman, Jacob and Quintero, Luis, Market Concentration in Homebuilding (November 28, 2018). Johns Hopkins Carey Business School Research Paper No. 18-18. Available at SSRN: https://ssrn.com/abstract=3303984 or http://dx.doi.org/10.2139/ssrn.3303984

7. Chris Glynn and Emily B. Fox, "Dynamics of homelessness in urban America," arxiv.org, July 28, 2017, https://arxiv.org/abs/1707.09380v1 **(The Zillow Study)**

8. "The Burden of Fees: How Affordable Housing Is Made Unaffordable," Urban Justice Center, https://cdp.urbanjustice.org/sites/default/files/The%20Burden%20of%20Fees_FINAL.pdf

9. Jacqueline Rabe Thomas, "Separated by Design: Why Affordable Housing Is Built in Areas With High Crime, Few Jobs and Struggling Schools," Propublica.org, November, 2019, propublica.org/article/separated-by-design-why-affordable-housing-is-built-in-areas-with-high-crime-few-jobs-and-struggling-schools.

10. Noah Buhayar and Esme E. Deprez, "The Homeless Crisis is Getting Worse in America's Richest Cities," Bloomberg BusinessWeek, November, 2018, https://www.bloomberg.com/news / features/2018-11-20/the-homeless-crisis-is-getting-worse-in-america-s-richest-cities

11. Karen Weise, "Housing's 30-Percent-of-Income Rule Is Nearly Useless," Bloomberg.com, July, 2014, bloomberg.com/news/articles/2014-07-17/housings-30-percent-of-income-rule-is-near-useless.

12. Dan Kane and Ely Portillo, " 'It Wasn't Fair.' How Renters Are Battling Landlords over Eviction Fees," The News & Observer, May 2018, https://www.newsobserver.com/latest-news/article211154479.html

13. Go Deeper: Where Race Lives," PBS.org, pbs.org/race/000_About/002_06-godeeper.htm.

14. "The Case for Fair Housing 2017 Fair Housing Trends Report," National Fair Housing Alliance, April 2017, nationalfairhousing.org/wp-content/uploads/2017/04/TRENDS-REPORT-4-19-17-FINAL-2.pdf

15. Dan Gearino. "Shocking cost investigation: Utility middle men charge renters inflated prices," The Columbus Dispatch, October, 2013, accessed September, 2020, https://www.dispatch.com/article/20131020/NEWS/310209773

16. "The Financial Crisis Inquiry Report: Final Report Of The National Commission On The Causes Of The Financial And Economic Crisis In The United States," The Financial Crisis Inquiry Commission, February, 2011, https://www.govinfo.gov/content/pkg/GPO-FCIC/pdf/GPO-FCIC.pdf.

17. Michael Chui and James Manyika, "Competition at the digital edge: 'Hyperscale businesses,'" McKinsey Quarterly, March 2015, https://www.mckinsey.com/industries/technology-media-and-telecommunications/our-insights/competition-at-the-digital-edge-hyperscale-businesses.

18. Hsieh, Chang-Tai and Enrico Moretti, "Housing Constraints and Spatial Misallocation," Working Paper 21154, National Bureau of Economic Research May 2015.

19. Ganong, Peter and Daniel Shoag, "Why has regional income convergence in the U.S. declined? " Journal of Urban Economics, 2017, 102, 76-90.

20. Glaeser, Edward, and Joseph Gyourko, "The economic implications of housing supply," Journal of Economic Perspectives, 2018, 32 (1), 3-30.

21. Jung, Y.J., J.H. Kagel, and D. Levin (1994), "On the Existence of Predatory Pricing: An Experimental Study of Reputation and Entry Deterrence in the Chain-Store Game," Rand Journal of Economics, 25, 72-93.

22. Guiltinan, Joseph P. and Gregory T. Gundlach (1996), "Aggressive and Predatory Pricing: A Framework for Analysis," Journal of Marketing, 60 (July), 87–102.

23. Cross, Robert G (1998) "Revenue Management: Hard-core Tactics for Profit-making and Market Domination," Orion Business, 1998.

24. Tara Cookson, PhD, Margaret Diddams, PhD, Xochitl Maykovich, Edmund Witter, "Losing Home: The Human Cost of Eviction in Seattle," Seattle Women's Commission and the King County Bar Association, September, 2018, https://www.seattle.gov/documents/Departments/SeattleWomensCommission/LosingHome_9-18-18.pdf

25. Jayachandran, Satish, Javier Gimeno, and Rajan P. Varadarajan (1999), "The Theory of Multimarket Competition: A Synthesis and Implications for Marketing Strategy," Journal of Marketing, 63 (July), 49-66.

26. Gilo, D. (2000): \The anticompetitive effect of passive investment," Michigan Law Review, pp. 1-47.

27. Gilo, D., Y. Moshe, and Y. Spiegel (2006): "Partial cross ownership and tacit collusion," The RAND Journal of Economics, 37(1), 81-99.

28. O'Brien, D. P., and S. C. Salop (2000): "Competitive effects of partial ownership: Financial interest and corporate control, "Antitrust Law Journal, pp. 559-614.

29. Rotemberg, J. (1984): "Financial transaction costs and industrial performance," Cambridge, Mass. : Massachusetts Institute of Technology, Working paper (Sloan School of Management) ; 1554-84.

30. Texas Department of Housing and Community Affairs v. Inclusive Communities Project, Inc., 135 S. Ct. 2507, 2512 (2015).

31. Bilotkach, Volodymyr; Hüschelrath, Kai (2010) : Antitrust immunity for airline alliances, ZEW Discussion Papers, No. 10-080, https://econpapers.repec.org/paper/zbwzewdip/10080.htm

32. Military Family Advisory Network, "FINAL RESEARCH REPORT: LIVING CONDITIONS OF FAMILIES IN PRIVATIZED MILITARY HOUSING," May2019, https://www.mfan.org/blog/mfan-research-privatized-military-housing-survey-executive-summary/

33. David S Evans and Richard Schmalensee, Matchmakers: The New Economics of Multisided Platforms (Brighton, MA: Harvard Business Review Press, 24 May 2016), p. 210.

34. David S Evans and Michael D Noel, 'Defining Markets that Involve Multi-Sided Platform Business: An Empirical Framework with an Application to Google's Purchase of DoubleClick' (working paper No. 07-18, Reg-Markets Center November 2007), p. 3.

35. Marshall, Robert & Marx, Leslie. (2012). The Economics of Collusion: Cartels and Bidding Rings. 10.7551/mitpress/9011.001.0001.

36. Jayachandran, Satish, Javier Gibeon, and Rajan P. Varadarajan (1999), "The Theory of Multimarket Competition: A Synthesis and Implications for Marketing Strategy, "Journal of Marketing, 63 (July), 49-66.

37. Porter, Michael E. (1980), Competitive Advantage p.101 . New York: The Free Press.

38. Scherer, F.M., and D. Ross, 1990, Industrial market structure and economic performance (3rd ed. Houghton Mifflin, Boston, MA).

39. The 1929 Stock Market Crash," EH.net, eh.net/encyclopedia/the-1929-stock-market-crash/

40. "The U.S. Economy in the 1920s," EH.net, accessed July, 2019, https://eh.net/encyclopedia/the-u-s-economy-in-the-1920s/

41. "Subcommittee on Senate Resolutions 84 and 239 (The Pecora Committee), Notable Senate Investigations, U.S. Senate Historical Office, Washington, D.C." Accessed June 2020, March 2, 1932, https://www.senate.gov/about/powers-procedures/investigations/pecora.htm

42. "Great Depression Bank Crisis," United States History, accessed 2019, https://www.u-s-history.com/pages/h1525.html ; and, Ted Temzelides, "Are Bank Runs Contagious," Federal Reserve Bank of Philadelphia Business Review, November/December 1997, https://www.philadelphiafed.org/-/media/research-and-data/publications/business-review/1997/november-december/brnd97tt.pdf?la=en

43. FEDERAL RESERVE BULLETIN, "Recent Banking Developments Banking Act of 1933," fraiser.stlouisfed.org, June 1933, https://fraser.stlouisfed.org/files/docs/publications/FRB/1930s/frb_061933.pdf

44. David Moss, Cole Bolton, and Eugene Kintgen, "Pecora Hearings," Harvard Business School Case 711-046, December 2010 (revised June 2018).

45. Gilbert King, "The Man Who Busted the Banksters," Smithsonian.com, November 2011, https://www.smithsonianmag.com/history/the-man-who-busted-the-banksters-932416/

46. Larry Bumgardner, "A Brief History of the 1930s Securities Laws in the United States—and the Potential Lesson for Today," Pepperdine University, http://www.jgbm.org/page/5%20Larry%20Bumgardner.pdf.

47. "Banking Act of 1933," Federal Reserve History, June 1933.

48. Dustin Dunham, "Innovations in 'Big Data' Are Impacting Real Estate Investment," Cornell Real Estate Review, March 2018, https://blog.realestate.cornell.edu/2018/03/22/innovations-in-big-data/

49. James Bessen, Information Technology and Industry Concentration, Boston University School of Law & Economics Paper Series (2017). Available at: https://scholarship.law.bu.edu/faculty_scholarship/267

50. Chris Wood, Multifamily Executive, "Revenue Management's All Grown Up," multifamilyexecutive.com, March 20, 2012, https://www.multifamilyexecutive.com/technology/revenue-managements-all-grown-up-1_o

51. Press Release, the Auto Channel, "Talus Solutions Launches Talus Solutions Revenue Management Suite," February 8, 2000, Accessed June 2020, https://www.theautochannel.com/news/press/date/20000208/press007464.html

52. Press Release Bizjournals, "Talus Solutions gets $20 million investment," November 4, 1998, Accessed June 2020, https://www.bizjournals.com/atlanta/stories/1998/11/02/daily8.html

53. Mthink online Blog, "Manugistics: Collaboration and Optimization across Supply Chain, Demand Chain, and E-Markets," mthink.com, Accessed June 2020, https://mthink.com/legacy/www.ascet.com/content/pdf/ASC3_sp_manugistics.pdf

54. "Artificial Intelligence In Marketing," Lincoln Apartments (Infographic), https://www.lincolnapts.com/themes/lincoln-2015/infographic/trends-2020/default/images/titles/artificial-inteligence.svg

55. "Crow Holding Capital," crowholdings.com, June, 2020, https://www.crowholdings.com/chc

56. Testimony of Laura S. Wertheimer Inspector General, Federal Housing Finance Agency before the U.S. House Committee on Financial Services, September 27, 2018 https://financialservices.house.gov/uploadedfiles/09.27.2018_laura_s._wertheimer_testimony.pdf

57. "FHFA's Targeted Examinations of Fannie Mae: Less than Half of the Targeted Examinations Planned for 2012 through 2015 Were Completed and No Examinations Planned for 2015 Were Completed Before the Report of Examination Issued," Federal Housing Finance Agency OIG, AUD-2016-006, September, 2016, fhfaoig.gov/Content/Files/AUD-2016-006.pdf; and, OIG-2017-003, December 15, 2016). https://www.fhfaoig.gov/Content/Files/AUD-2016-006.pdf

58. "FHFA's Housing Finance Examiner Commissioning Program: $7.7 Million and Four Years into the Program, the Agency has Fewer Commissioned Examiners," Federal Housing Finance Agency OIG Compliance Review, September, 2018, fhfaoig.gov/Content/Files/Compliance%20Review%20COM-2018-006.pdf

59. RealPage News, "All Roads Lead to Vegas for RealPage Technology Conference 2002," RealPage.com, January 16, 2002, https://www.realpage.com/news/all-roads-lead-to-vegas-for-realpage-technology-conference-2002/

60. The website for RealPage, "In their own Words, Berkshire Communities Achieves Ideal Occupancy with Revenue Management," RealPage, Accessed April 2021, https://www.realpage.com/asset-optimization/revenue-management/?showPdf=true then at bottom of site, pull Berkshire communities

61. RealPage Blog, "Berkshire Communities Achieves Ideal Occupancy with Revenue Management, SO-17-035 e-Book.pdf," RealPage, 2017, https://www.realpage.com/asset-optimization/revenue-management/?showPdf=true

62. The Real Deal South Florida News, "Rent payment tracker to impact credit ratings," therealdeal.com, January 31, 2011, https://therealdeal.com/miami/2011/01/31/tracking-rent-payments-can-impact-credit-ratings/

63. Hospitalitynet News Release, "Seven Multifamily Housing Operators Tap Rainmaker LRO™ Revenue Optimization System," Accessed June 2020, https://www.hospitalitynet.org/news/4042573.html

64. Camden Property Trust, 2006 Annual Report, Accessed June 2020, https://s28.q4cdn.com/425223795/files/doc_financials/2006/ar/2006-Annual-Report.pdf

65. Michael Hoffman's LinkedIn page, accessed November, 2019, https://www.linkedin.com/in/michael-hoffman-5351474

66. Little Black Boxes," Multifamily Executive, July, 2007, https://www.multifamilyexecutive.com/property-management/apartment-trends/little-black-boxes_o

67. RealPage News, "Pinnacle Selects YieldStar® Price Optimizer," realpage.com, August 19,2010, https://www.realpage.com/news/pinnacle-selects-yieldstar-price-optimizer/

68. Kortney Balas, "YieldStar Accurately Forecasts Demand for Optimum Pricing," RealPage video, 0:48, https://www.realpage.com/videos/yieldstar-accurate-demand-forecasting/.

69. Noreen Seebacher, GlobeSt., "RealPage Exec: Software Boosts Rental Rates & Profit," globest.com, April 17, 2009, https://www.globest.com/sites/globest/2009/04/17/realpage-exec-software-boosts-rental-rates-profit/?slreturn=20211106120212

70. Joe Bousquin, Multifamily Executive, "Model World," multifamilyexecutive, September 29, 2008,; and, Wang, Jian & Das, Murtaza & Duggasani, Amar. (2016). Predicting and measuring customer lifetime values for apartment tenants. Zeitschrift für Immobilienökonomie. 10.1365/s41056-016-0015-0. https://www.researchgate.net/publication/311527003_Predicting_and_measuring_customer_lifetime_values_for_apartment_tenants/citation/download

71. Hospitalitynet News Release, "Waterton Residential Automates Forecasting and Community Pricing to Increase Revenue utilizing LRO and Yardi Systems," Hospitalitynet.org, September 16, 2009, https://www.hospitalitynet.org/news/4043401.html

72. Multifamily Biz Press Release, " Waterton Automates Forecasting," multifammilybiz, September 16, 2009, https://www.multifamilybiz.com/news/2207/waterton_automates_forecasting

73. Tammy Farley, "The Rainmaker Group Launches New Version of Multifamily Housing Revenue Management System, revolution LRO," Cision PRWeb, March, 2020, https://www.prweb.com/releases/rainmakergroup/therainmakergroup/prweb524795.htm.

74. John Egan, National Real Estate Investor, "Lift for Landlords," nreionline.com, Sept 1, 2008, https://www.nreionline.com/multifamily/lift-landlords

75. Experian media, "Experian Acquires RentBureau® Multifamily Division," experianplc, June 24, 2010, https://www.experianplc.com/media/latest-news/2010/experian-acquires-rentbureau-multifamily-division/

76. RealPage Press Release, "RealPage Announces "Front To Back" Integration Between Popular Third Party Back Office Accounting Systems and OneSite Front-Office Leasing & Rents," realpage, September 13, 2011, https://www.realpage.com/news/realpage-announces-front-to-back-integration-between-popular-third-party-back-office-accounting-systems-and-onesite-front-office-leasing-amp-rents-2/

77. Bendix Anderson, Multifamily Executive, "Multi-Tasking," multifamilyexecutive.com, March 20, 2012, https://www.multifamilyexecutive.com/technology/multi-tasking_o

78. Wendy Broffman, "Game Changer," yieldpro.com, August 1, 2014, https://yieldpro.com/2014/08/game-changer/

79. Justin Rubner, Atlanta Business Chronicle, "Startup will tract risky renters," Aug 28, 2006, https://www.bizjournals.com/atlanta/stories/2006/08/28/story2.html

80. Wendy Broffman, Yield Pro, "Taking chances," yieldpro, February 1, 2008, https://yieldpro.com/2008/02/taking-chances/

81. Experian Product Sheets, "the Power of rental payment data, Experian.com, Accessed June 2020, https://www.experian.com/assets/rentbureau/product-sheets/1018-CIS-Power-of-Rental-Payment-Data-Brochure-Final.pdf ; mostly, Experian then was able to share rental history about tenants in nearly real time with various screening services. Linsey Issacs, Multifamily Executive, "Data Mining Holds Great Promise for Multifamily," multifamilyexecutive.com, January 14, 2013, https://www.multifamilyexecutive.com/property-management/marketing/data-mining-holds-great-promise-for-multifamily_o

82. Stella Morrison, Business articles, "What Is Private Labeling, and How Does It Work?," business.com, April 17, 2023, https://www.business.com/articles/private-labeling-details/

83. Patrick Nelson, Algorithms for Rent: The Price Is Right, Tech News World, March, 2013, https://www.technewsworld.com/story/77498.html [states including vacancy loss and inventory hold periods.] ; and, RealPage eBook, "INTRODUCING AI REVENUE MANAGEMENT," ASO-20-280-004 10/28/2020, https://www.realpage.com/storage/files/pages/pdfs/2021/02/ai-revenue-management-lookbook-nov20.pdf [states: normalize demand based on unit days on market] ; and, The website for RealPage, "INTRODUCING AI REVENUE MANAGEMENT Next-Generation Price Optimization That Unlocks Hidden Yield," RealPage, Accessed April 2021, https://www.realpage.com/asset-optimization/revenue-management/?showPdf=true ; https://www.realpage.com/ebooks/outperform-in-a-down-market/ ; and Jerry Ascierto, "Revenue Management Market Heats Up," multifamilyexecutive, November 1, 2007, https://www.multifamilyexecutive.com/property-management/revenue-management-market-heats-up_o [shape by inputting parameters such as comparable rent analysis or the number of days a unit is vacant] Mostly use: Wang, Jian. (2008). A realization of an apartment dynamic pricing system. Journal of Revenue and Pricing Management. 7. 256-265. 10.1057/rpm.2008.11. Source: See details, [also Yardi discusses, Inventory Hold Days, at Yardi brochures, "Yardi RENTmaximizer," under Better Results, Accessed 2020, https://resources.yardi.com/documents/rentmaximizer-brochure/]; and, Bendix Anderson, Multifamily Executive, "Multi-Tasking," multifamilyexecutive.com, March 20, 2012, https://www.multifamilyexecutive.com/technology/multi-tasking_o

84. Washington, The Joint Legislative Audit and Review Commission (JLARC), 19-08 Final Report, " Property Tax Exemption for Multifamily Housing in Urban Areas," December 2019, Accessed June 2020, https://leg.wa.gov/jlarc/taxReports/2019/MFTE/f_ii/print.pdf ; The Website of the Washington State Legislature, Joint Legislative Audit & Review Committee, Published Reports, Assessed 2019, https://leg.wa.gov/jlarc/AuditAndStudyReports/Pages/default.aspx ; and, Bob Young, Seattle Times, "Audit: Oversight lacking in tax breaks to Seattle housing developers," seattletimes.com, September 19,2012, https://www.seattletimes.com/seattle-news/audit-oversight-lacking-in-tax-breaks-to-seattle-housing-developers/

85. Hotel Online Special Report, "Omni Hotels Reaps Revenue Increase with Manugistics and The Rainmaker Group," hotel-online.com, June 9, 2005, https://www.hotel-online.com/News/PR2005_2nd/Jun05_Omni.html

86. The Website of Agilysys Inc, "FAQ," Accessed July 2023, https://www.agilysys.com/en/faqs/

87. HotelExecutive News, "Casino Hotels Boost Profits with Rainmaker, Agilysys Tech Collaboration," hotelexecutive.com, October 14, 2008, https://www.hotelexecutive.com/newswire/5125/casino-hotels-boost-profits-with-rainmaker-agilysys-tech-collaboration

88. Hotel Online, News, "Casino Hotels Boost Profits with Rainmaker Group, Agilysys Tech Collaboration," hotel-online.com, March 27, 2007, https://www.hotel-online.com/News/PR2007_1st/Mar07_RainmakerAgilysys.html

89. RealPage Website, "Terms of Service for Rainmaker System Modules | Rainmaker - Industry-Leading Revenue Management Software," Accessed July 2021, https://www.realpage.com/rainmakermfh-terms/

90. LinkedIn Profile of Kristin Brown, Accessed June 2023, https://www.linkedin.com/in/kristin-brown-a851828

91. MultifamilyBiz News, "Rainmaker LRO Accomplishes Integration with Rent Manager Property Management Software," multifamilybiz.com, November 27, 2013, https://www.multifamilybiz.com/news/5191/rainmaker_lro_accomplishes_integration_with_rent_m...

92. Hospitality Updrade News, "Four Major Multifamily Housing Operators Select The Rainmaker Group for Revenue Management Pilot Launch," hospitalityupgrade.com, August 7, 2007, https://www.hospitalityupgrade.com/News/News-Article-Details/?docID=1575

93. Skift News, Sean O'Neill, "Rainmaker Group Sells Division for $300 Million to Focus on Hotel Revenue Management," skift.com, February 28, 2017, https://skift.com/2017/02/28/rainmaker-group-sells-division-for-300-million-to-focus-on-hospitality-revenue-management/

94. Archstone-Smith Operating Trust (2002) Form 10-K 2002. SEC.gov Archives. https://www.sec.gov/Archives/edgar/data/80737/000103570403000151/d03069e10vk.htm

95. Jerry Ascierto, "Revenue Management Market Heats Up," multifamilyexecutive, November 1, 2007, https://www.multifamilyexecutive.com/property-management/revenue-management-market-heats-up_o

96. Michael Singer, Internet News, "Intuit Gets Down To It With Acquisition," internetnews.com, June 4, 2002, https://www.internetnews.com/it-management/intuit-gets-down-to-it-with-acquisition/ ; and, The Wall Street Journal, Online News, "Intuit to Pay About $92 Million For Real-Estate Software Maker," June 4, 2002, https://www.wsj.com/articles/SB1023197436231373520

97. Emily Wells, MRI Software Blog, "Celebrating 50 years of MRI Software," mrisoftware.com, February 2, 2021, https://www.mrisoftware.com/blog/celebrating-50-years-mri-software/

98. Jarboe, Michelle (2010-01-19). "Private equity firm closes Intuit deal, renames real estate division MRI Software". Cleveland.com. Retrieved 14 April 2023.; and, Lightcast, "MRI (Property Management Software)," Accessed July 2023, https://lightcast.io/open-skills/skills/ESD74FDCC0D0A65E9D5D/mri-property-management-software

99. Website of GI Partners, News, "GI Partners to Acquire MRI Software," Accessed July 2023, https://www.gipartners.com/news/gi-partners-to-acquire-mri-software

100. Hospitalitynet Press Release, "The Rainmaker Group and Realty DataTrust Partner to Introduce Optimized," hospitalitynet.org, June 24, 2007, https://www.hospitalitynet.org/news/4032001.html ; and, Hotel Online Special Report, "The Rainmaker Group and Realty Data Trust Partner to Introduce Optimized Multi-Dimensional Online Pricing for the Apartment Industry," hotel-online.com, June 25, 2007, https://www.hotel-online.com/News/PR2007_2nd/Jun07_RainmakerRealty.html

101. The LinkedIn Profile of Mike Mueller, Accessed July 2023, https://www.linkedin.com/in/mikemuelleraz/ ;MRI Software News, CISION, "MRI Software Expands VaultWare Apartment Content Syndication Network," prweb.com, April 4, 2014, https://www.prweb.com/releases/mri_software_expands_vaultware_apartment_content_syndication_network/prweb11736778.htm; and, Website of MRI Real Estate Software, Multifamily, "4 VaultWare Apartment Marketing Tools You Should be Using," February 26, 2014, https://www.mrisoftware.com/blog/4-vaultware-apartment-marketing-tools-you-should-be-using/

102. Hotel-Online News, "The Rainmaker Group and Realty DataTrust Partner to Introduce Optimized Multi-Dimensional Online Pricing for the Apartment Industry," hotel-online.com, June 25, 2007, https://www.hotel-online.com/News/PR2007_2nd/Jun07_RainmakerRealty.html; and, Siegel Sez, HospitalityUpgrade, "REVENUE MANAGEMENT," hospitalityUpgrade.com, July12, 2007, https://www.hospitalityupgrade.com/_siegel_sez/siegel_sez_Detail.asp?ID=264

103. Chris Wood, Multifamily Executive, "Multifamily Operators Embracing New Lease Renewal, Lead Strategies," multifamilyexecutive, June 9, 2011, https://www.multifamilyexecutive.com/property-management/rent-trends/multifamily-operators-embracing-new-lease-renewal-lead-strategies_o

104. Jessica Fiur, Multi-Housing News, "MRI Software Announces Acquisition of VaultWare," multihousingnews.com, December 21, 2011, https://www.multihousingnews.com/mri-software-announces-acquisition-of-vaultware/

105. RealPage Publication, "ILM Lead Manager," Accessed July 2023, www.realpage.com/storage/files/pages/covid-19-resources/pdf/c19-ilm-lead-manager-lam-18-098.pdf

106. CISION News Release, "Multifamily's New Power Couple: Rainmaker's LRO and ILM Now Integrated to Optimize Multifamily Demand Management," prweb.com, March 9, 2017, https://www.prweb.com/releases/multifamily_s_new_power_couple_rainmaker_s_lro_and_ilm_now_integrated_to_optimize_multifamily_demand_management/prweb14135431.htm

107. MRI eBook, "MRI Contract Intelligence," accessed July 2023, file:///J:/000000The%20Final%20RealPage%20Product/Working%20Phases%20New%20Landlord/0000Release%20Draft/3_hard%20copy%20document/MRI/MRI_Contract_Intelligence.pdf

108. AppFolio News, "AppFolio Announces Two New Offerings for Property Management Customers," appfolioinc.com, September 19, 2016, https://www.appfolioinc.com/news/appFolio-announces-two_new-offerings-for-property-management-customers

109. Camden Property Trust, 2000 Annual Report, Accessed June 2020, [page 17] https://investors.camdenliving.com/investors/financials/annual-reports/default.aspx; and, Wendy Broffman, Yield Pro, "The bottom line on revenue management," April 1, 2007, Accessed 2020, https://yieldpro.com/2007/04/the-bottom-line-on-revenue-management/

110. RealPage Press Release, "RealPage Acquires RealHound.com and Announces OneSite© Portfolio," realpage.com, August 29, 2002, https://www.realpage.com/news/realpage-acquires-realhound-com-and-announces-onesite-portfolio/

111. RealPage News, "RealPage to Acquire On-Site," realpage.com, August 2, 2017 https://www.realpage.com/news/realpage-to-acquire-on-site/; and, Hospitality Technology News, "The Rainmaker Group to Sell LRO Multifamily Housing Assets to RealPage," hospitalitytech.com, February 27, 2017, https://hospitalitytech.com/rainmaker-group-sell-lro-multifamily-housing-assets-realpage; and, Website of Leaselabs, Products CRM, "content management system," leaselabs.com, Accessed July 2023, https://www.leaselabs.com/products/cms/

112. "YieldStar Calculates the Right Rent Price at the Right Time," RealPage video, 1:40, https://www.realpage.com/videos/yieldstar-measures-price-elasticity

113. Amruth Sivalenka, The Rainmaker Group, "Renewal Pricing and Expiration Management in the Apartment Industry," acsu.buffalo.edu, https://www.acsu.buffalo.edu/~batta/apartment.pdf

114. Blog, Invest Now LP, "INCREASE REVENUE THROUGH INTELLIGENT RENT RATE SETTING," campusadv.com, July, 2018, https://campusadv.com/increase-revenue-through-intelligent-rent-rate-setting/

115. Holly Caspar, "YieldStar™ Revenue Management Optimizes Rent Pricing," RealPage video, 2:13, https://www.realpage.com/videos/yieldstar-optimizes-rent-pricing/ ; RealPage Blog, "Six Ways Revenue Management Software Benefits B and C Properties," RealPage, June 12, 2019, https://www.realpage.com/lp/revenue-management-b-c-assets/

images/ASO-19-161_005_B-C-Assets_e-Book.pdf ; or, https://www.realpage.com/blog/six-ways-revenue-management-software-benefits-b-c-properties/ and, Patrick Nelson, Algorithms for Rent: The Price Is Right, Tech News World, March, 2013, https://www.technewsworld.com/story/77498.html ; and, Businesswire inline news, "HSL Properties Implements RealPage's YieldStar Revenue Management Solution, Anticipates 5% Income Boost," businesswire.com, January 10, 2018, https://www.businesswire.com/news/home/20180110005263/en/HSL-Properties-Implements-RealPage%E2%80%99s-YieldStar-Revenue-Management-Solution-Anticipates-5-Income-Boost

116. Chris Edwards and Vanessa Brown Calder, " Low-Income Housing Tax Credit Costly, Complex, and Corruption-Prone," The Cato Institute, November 13, 2017, https://www.cato.org/tax-budget-bulletin/low-income-housing-tax-credit-costly-complex-corruption-prone ; and, Government Accountability Office, "Federal Housing Assistance; Comparing the Characteristics and Costs of Housing Programs," GAO-02-76, January 2002, p. 18.

117. Gregory S. Burge, "Do Tenants Capture the Benefits from the Low-Income Housing Tax Credit Program?" Real Estate Economics (Blackwell Publishing Inc., December 2010), p. 95.

118. The website for MRI, "The Freedom to Choose," accessed September 2018, https://www.mrisoftware.com/products/property-management-software/

119. The website for MRI Software LLC, accessed December, 2019, https://www.mrisoftware.com/resources/mri-inspections-powered-happyco/

120. Chris Wood, Multifamily Executive News, "New Expectations in Multifamily Technology ROI: Q&A with RealPage's Steve Winn," multifamilyexecutive.com, July 15, 2009, https://www.multifamilyexecutive.com/technology/new-expectations-in-multifamily-technology-roi-q-a-with-realpages-steve-winn_o

121. RealPage Reports Second Quarter 2019 Earnings," Yahoo Finance, https://finance.yahoo.com/news/realpage-rp-q2-2019-earnings-092428152.html

122. RealPage Website, "User Group," RealPage, Accessed June 2020, https://www.realpage.com/user-group/

123. Joe Bousquin, Multifamily Executive, "Rental-History Technology Helps Nab Serial Skippers," multifamilyexecutive, July 12, 2012, https://www.multifamilyexecutive.com/property-management/rent-trends/rental-history-technology-helps-nab-serial-skippers_o

124. Hospitalitynet news release, "The Rainmaker Group Launches Revenue Management Pilots with Four Major Multi-Family Housing Operators," Hospitalitynet.com, January 11, 2007, https://www.hospitalitynet.org/news/4029890.html

125. Rachel Azoff, "New Dynamic," multifamilyexecutive, October 17, 2005, https://www.multifamilyexecutive.com/property-management/new-dynamic_o

126. Peggy Shaw, YieldPro, "Maximum occupancy," Accessed June 2020, December 1, 2013, https://yieldpro.com/2013/12/maximum-occupancy/

127. Jerry Ascierto, "Optimizing Opportunities," multifamilyexecutive.com, July 1, 2007, https://www.multifamilyexecutive.com/property-management/optimizing-opportunities_o

128. Kingkarn Amjaroen, The Motley Fool, "If You're Building a REIT Portfolio, Camden Property Trust Is a Top Choice," fool.com, July 11, 2014, https://www.fool.com/investing/general/2014/07/11/if-youre-building-a-reit-portfolio-camden-property.aspx

129. CISION PR Web News Release, "Four Major Multi-Family Housing Operators Select The Rainmaker Group for Revenue Management Pilot Launch," prweb.com, August 15, 2007, https://www.prweb.com/releases/rainmakergroup/therainmakergroup/prweb546813.htm

130. CISION Press Release, "Mid-America Apartment Communities Installs Rainmaker revolution LRO SM Revenue Management Throughout 140 Properties," prweb.com, August 1, 2007, https://www.prweb.com/releases/rainmakergroup/therainmakergroup/prweb543896.htm

131. Jerry Ascierto, Multifamily Executive, "Raising the Bar," multifamilyexecutive.com, May 1, 2007, https://www.multifamilyexecutive.com/property-management/raising-the-bar_o

132. Mid-America Apartment Communities, Inc. (NYSE: MAA) Second Quarter 2007 Earnings Release Conference Call August 3, 2007, Accessed June 2020, https://s1.q4cdn.com/498755859/files/doc_events/2007/08/Earnings-Call-Transcript-on-8-3-2007.pdf

133. Cision Press Release, "Multifamily Operator Julian LeCraw Implements Rainmaker Revolution LRO™ Revenue Optimization System," prweb.com, April 21, 2008, https://www.prweb.com/releases/rainmaker/letitrain/prweb873614.htm

134. CISION Press Release, "MEB Management Services Implements Rainmaker LRO Revenue Management," prweb, May 25, 2011, https://www.prweb.com/releases/therainmakergroup/revenuemanagement/prweb8486881.htm

135. "The Age of Analytics: Competing in a Data-Driven World," McKinsey Global Institute, December, 2016, https://www.slideshare.net/MichielNoij/mgi-theageofanalyticsfullreport-80712672.

136. Fran Worrall, Hospitality Upgrade, "HU Time Capsule: Robert Cross," hospitalityupgrade.com, June 18, 2018, https://www.hospitalityupgrade.com/_magazine/MagazineArticles/HU-Time-Capsule-Robert-Cross.asp/

137. Press Release, Hospitality Net, "Manugistics Completes Acquisition Of Talus Solutions - Supply Chain Management And Pricing And Revenue Optimization To Deliver Enterprise Profit Optimization™," hospitalitynet.org, January 5, 2001, https://www.hospitalitynet.org/news/4006776.html

138. Federal Trade Commission, 'Transcript of FTC Hearing 3: Oct. 15, Panel 1: The Current Economic Understanding of Multi-Sided Platforms', 15 October 2018, www.ftc.gov/system/files/documents/public_events/1413712/ftc_hearings_session_3_transcript_day_1_10-15-18_0.pdf, pp. 21–23.

139. Jeff Collins, The Orange County Register, "As apartment rents rise, landlords turn to software to set prices," March 15, 2105, https://www.ocregister.com/2015/03/15/as-apartment-rents-rise-landlords-turn-to-software-to-set-prices/

140. RealPage Press Release, "RealPage® to Acquire Lease Rent Options, LRO®," realpage, February 2017, https://www.realpage.com/news/realpage-to-acquire-lease-rent-options/

141. RealPage Press Release, "RealPage Receives $20 Million Private Investment for Continued Development of OneSite," Accessed April 2021, November 3, 2000, https://www.realpage.com/news/realpage-receives-20-million-private-investment-for-continued-development-of-onesite/

142. AppFolio Press Release, "AppFolio Announces Two New Offerings for Property Management Customers," AppFolio , September 19, 2016, https://www.AppFolio .com/news/AppFolio -announces-two-new-offerings-for-property-management-customers

143. The Website of AppFolio, "About Us," Accessed June 2021, https://www.AppFolio .com/about-us

144. Business Wire—RealPage Press Release: "RealPage Closes Acquisition of Lease Rent Options, LRO®," businesswire, December 4, 2017, https://www.businesswire.com/news/home/20171204006136/en/RealPage-Closes-Acquisition-of-Lease-Rent-Options-LRO%C2%AE

145. Brian O'Keefe and Nicolas Rapp, "Finance has usurped tech among the 100 Fastest-Growing Companies," fortune.com, October 29, 2020, https://fortune.com/2020/10/29/fastest-growing-companies-AppFolio -tech-finance-industry-tech-company-growth/

146. Tim Blackwell, RealPage Blog, "Benefits of Using a Regulated Money Services Business for Online Payments," realpage.com, September, 29, 2021, https://www.realpage.com/blog/benefits-of-using-a-regulated-money-services-business-for-online-payments/

147. The LinkedIn Profile of "Andrew Blount," Accessed June 2020, https://www.linkedin.com/in/andrewblount

148. Brad Berton, Los Angeles Times, "CoStar Loses in Software Dispute," latimes.com, May 14, 2002, https://www.latimes.com/archives/la-xpm-2002-may-14-fi-costar14-story.html

149. John Salustri, Globe St., "Jennifer Nevitt of Bravo Strategic Marketing," globest.com, May 23, 2002, https://www.globest.com/sites/globest/2002/05/23/jennifer-nevitt-of-bravostrategic-marketing/

150. The Website of The MKTG Dept., "brandi bailey," accessed June 2021, https://themktgdeptblog.wordpress.com/about/the-talent/

151. Matt Hudgins, New York Times, "When Apartment Rents Climb, Landlords Can Say 'The Computer Did It'," nytimes.com, Nov., 29,2011, https://www.nytimes.com/2011/11/30/realestate/commercial/landlords-use-computers-to-arrive-at-the-right-rental-fee.html

152. Yahoo! Money, blog, "RealPage to Present at J.P. Morgan 41st Annual Technology, Media and Telecom Conference," March 8, 2013, https://money.yahoo.com/2013-05-08-realpage-to-present-at-jp-morgan-41st-annual-techn.html

153. Erika Schnitzer, "Planning for a Sunny Forecast," multifamilyhousingnews, June 2010, https://www.multihousingnews.com/planning-for-a-sunny-forecast/

154. National Apartment Association, Instructor Guide, "Module 3: IMPROVING ASSET PERFORMANCE," Accessed June 2020, https://www.naahq.org/sites/default/files/naa-documents/education/caps_mc3_instructor.pdf

155. Amruth Sivalenka, The Rainmaker Group, "Renewal Pricing and Expiration Management in the Apartment Industry," acsu.buffalo.edu, https://www.acsu.buffalo.edu/~batta/apartment.pdf

156. Website of Leaselabs, 'flex," accessed 2021, https://www.leaselabs.com/products/flex/#:~:text=empower%20your%20decision%20making%20with%20GoDirect%20%2B%20flex&text=This%20eliminates%20guesswork%20that%20results,strategies%20with%20robust%20data%20analytics

157. Website of Leaselabs, 'flex," accessed 2021, https://www.leaselabs.com/

158. The Website of Leaselabs, Assessed June 2020, https://app.leaselabs.com/products/flex

159. Brian Croce, Multifamily Executive, "Willett: Analytics Focus Drives RealPage's Acquisition of Axiometrics," multifamilyexecutive.com, January 24, 2017, https://www.multifamilyexecutive.com/business-finance/transactions/willett-analytics-focus-drives-realpages-acquisition-of-axiometrics_o

160. RealPage News, "RealPage® to Acquire Axiometrics®," realpage.com, January 24, 2017, https://www.realpage.com/news/realpage-to-acquire-axiometrics/

161. The website for Axiometrics, "AXIOAparment," accessed December, 2019, https://www.axiometrics.com/axioapartment/

162. RealPage event brochure, "RealPage® Axiometrics® Major Enhancement Update," eventson24.com, Accessed June 2021, https://event.on24.com/eventRegistration/

163. The Website of Apartments.Com, "Apartments.com Listings Feed Program," Apartments.com, Accessed June 2021, https://www.apartments.com/advertise/resources/listings-feed-program

164. Joe Bousquin, "Institutional Investors Hot on Revenue Management Adoption," multifamilyexecutive, January 10, 2012, https://www.multifamilyexecutive.com/technology/institutional-investors-hot-on-revenue-management-adoption_o

165. David Lee, "American Airlines Fined $45 Million in Antitrust Case," courthousenews.com, June, 2018, https://www.courthousenews.com/american-airlines-fined-45-million-in-antitrust-case/

166. From the Website of National Apartment Association, "What's Revving Revenue Management?," www.naahq.org, September, 2016, https://www.naahq.org/news-publications/units/september-2016/article/whats-revving-revenue-management

167. "Regional Affordable Housing Task Force Five-year Action Plan," KingCounty.gov, updated December, 2018, https://kingcounty.gov/~/media/initiatives/affordablehousing/documents/report/RAH_Report_Final.ashx?la=en

168. Paul R. Bergeron III, National Apartment Association, "Revenue Management: Why It Works," naahq.org, July 30, 2015, https://www.naahq.org/revenue-management-why-it-works

169. NBC News Release, "RealPage Announces That Wilkinson Selects YieldStar(R) Price Optimizer," nbcnews, June, 2011, https://www.nbcnews.com/id/wbna43480582

170. The standard for unfairness in the Dodd-Frank Act has the same three-part test as the FTC Act. This standard was first stated in the FTC Policy Statement on Unfairness (Dec. 17, 1980), available at: http://www.ftc.gov/bcp/policystmt/ad-unfair.htm. Congress later amended the FTC Act to include this specific standard in the Act itself. 15 U.S.C. § 45(n). See Credit Practices Rule, 49 Fed. Reg. 7740, 7746 (1984).

171. "CFPB and the New York Attorney General Settle with Debt Collection Group," Consumer Financial Protection Bureau, July 2019,https://www.consumerfinance.gov/about-us/newsroom/cfpb-and-new-york-attorney-general-settle-debt-collection-group/

172. "World's Largest Debt Collection Operation Settles FTC Charges, Will Pay $3.2 Million Penalty," FTC Bulletin, https://www.ftc.gov/news-events/press-releases/2013/07/worlds-largest-debt-collection-operation-settles-ftc-charges-will

173. Warren, Samuel D., and Louis D. Brandeis. "The Right to Privacy." Harvard Law Review 4, no. 5 (1890): 193–220. https://doi.org/10.2307/1321160. https://www.jstor.org/stable/1321160

174. Les Shaver, "When To Walk Away From A Client," Naahq.org, March, 2018, https://www.naahq.org/news-publications/when-walk-away-client

175. "NLIHC Gap 2017 Report Calls for Significant Investments to Address Shortage of 7 Million Affordable and Available Homes for the Lowest-Income Households," NLIHC.org, March, 2017, https://nlihc.org/sites/default/files/Gap-Report_2017.pdf

176. Website of the Federal Trade Commission (FTC), "Monopolization Defined," Accessed June 2021, https://www.ftc.gov/tips-advice/competition-guidance/guide-antitrust-laws/single-firm-conduct/monopolization-defined

177. Website of Apartments.com, "2900 on First," Accessed June 2021, https://www.apartments.com/2900-on-first-seattle-wa/6bc5xqv/ also, Per their Resident Portal, they now use RealPage, The Website of 2900 on First, "Resident Portal," accessed June 2021, https://www.realpage.com/privacy-policy/

178. See, e.g., Rebecca Haw Allensworth, The Commensurability Myth in Antitrust, 69 VAND. L. REV. 1, 5 n.7 (2016) ("The Rule of Reason . . . [is] a standard that balances pro- with anticompetitive effects . . . ."). But see Michael A. Carrier, The Real Rule of Reason: Bridging the Disconnect, 1999 B.Y.U. L. REV. 1265 (finding that actual balancing is quite rare); D. Daniel Sokol, The Transformation of Vertical Restraints: Per Se Illegality, the Rule of Reason, and Per Se Legality, 79 ANTITRUST L.J. 1003, 1008 (2014) (arguing that some types of vertical restraints, including maximum resale price maintenance and territorial restrictions, have effectively become per se legal).

179. Neither Congress nor the U.S. Supreme Court have clearly articulated the goal(s) of antitrust law. See, e.g., Roger D. Blair & D. Daniel Sokol, The Rule of Reason and the Goals of Antitrust: An Economic Approach, 89 ANTITRUST L.J. 471, 473 (2012). That said, the modern consensus—which the present analysis joins—is that antitrust should seek to maximize the economic conception of consumer welfare, though some argue instead for a total-welfare standard. See, e.g., id

180. Mike Kingsella, "The First Step in Solving Washington's Housing Crisis Is Preserving Existing Affordable Housing Programs," Upforgrowth.org, March 2019, https://www.upforgrowth.org/news/first-step-solving-washingtons-housing-crisis-preserving-existing-affordable-housing-programs

181. Seattle's 2020 homelessness budget shows that approximately 80 percent of spending goes to crisis management and supportive services and only about 20 percent to housing for extremely low-income households. Based on discussion with the county, estimates suggest that approximately 55 percent of its spending goes to crisis management and supportive services, and 45 percent of its spending is housing related. "Citywide homelessness response: 2020 proposed budget," Seattle Office of the City Clerk, October 2, 2019, seattle.legistar.com.

182. The Business Journal, "The Price of Homelessness: Humanitarian crisis costs Seattle area more than $1B, bizjournals, November 16, 2017, https://www.bizjournals.com/seattle/news/2017/11/16/price-of-homelessness-seattle-king-county-costs.html?s=print

183. Benjamin Maritz and Dilip Wagle," Why does prosperous King County have a homelessness crisis?," mckinsey.com, January 22,2020, https://www.mckinsey.com/industries/public-and-social-sector/our-insights/why-does-prosperous-king-county-have-a-homelessness-crisis

184. Gene Balk, "No Major City has Enough Affordable Housing to Meet Demand, but How does Seattle Stack up?," The Seattle Times, February, 2018, https://www.seattletimes.com/seattle-news/data/no-major-city-has-enough-affordable-housing-to-meet-demand-but-how-does-seattle-stack-up/

185. Becca Savransky. Seattle P-I, "What will it cost to solve the homelessness crisis in King County? New report says up to $11 billion," seattlepi.com, February 5, 2022, https://www.seattlepi.com/seattlenews/article/what-it-costs-to-end-homelessness-in-King-County-15008905.php

186. Josh Cohen, Crosscut, "New King County homelessness authority kicks off with $170M budget," crosscut.com, January 27, 2022, https://crosscut.com/politics/2022/01/new-king-county-homelessness-authority-kicks-170m-budget

187. Washington Joint Legislative Audit and Review Committee Report, "2019 TAX PREFERENCE PERFORMANCE REVIEWS Property Tax Exemption for Multifamily Housing in Urban Areas," December 2019, (page 12),

188. The longstanding debate about whether antitrust should aim to prevent wealth transfers or allocative efficiency losses is surveyed critically in Jonathan B. Baker, Economics and Politics: Perspectives on the Goals and Future of Antitrust, 81 Fordham L. Rev. 2175, 2176-80 (2013).

189. Brummet, Quentin and Reed, Davin, The Effects of Gentrification on the Well-Being and Opportunity of Original Resident Adults and Children, July 2019, Federal Reserve Bank of Philadelphia White Paper WP 19-30, https://www.philadelphiafed.org/-/media/research-and-data/publications/working-papers/2019/wp19-30.pdf

190. As measured by the Center for Housing Policy for the period 2008 to 2011.; and, Data for the nation, the four geographic regions of the U.S., and 22 metropolitan areas nationwide are available at www.bls.gov/cex/tables.htm. Metropolitan definitions used in the survey are available at www.bls.gov/cex/ce_msa_201516.htm. The metropolitan area discussed in this release is the Seattle-Tacoma-Bellevue, WA Metropolitan Statistical Area which comprises King, Pierce, and Snohomish Counties in Washington. Metropolitan area news releases for the Consumer Expenditure Survey are available at www.bls.gov/regions/subjects/consumer-spending.htm.

191. WASHINGTON CENTER FOR REAL ESTATE RESEARCH, Housing Affordability Index, http://realestate.washington.edu/wp-content/uploads/2020/05/2020Q1HousingMarketReport.pdf

192. Wade Wetherington, The District of Columbia Rental Housing Act of 1977: The Effect of Rent Control on the Rental Housing Market, 27 Cath. U. L. Rev. 607 (1978). Available at: https://scholarship.law.edu/lawreview/vol27/iss3/7 ; and, Housing and Land Use—Lindsey v. Normet: A Supreme Court Refusal to Federalize Oregon's Landlord Tenant Procedure, 1973 URB. L. ANN. 309 (1973) Available at: https://openscholarship.wustl.edu/law_urbanlaw/vol1973/iss1/17

193. J. BLACK, PROSPECTS FOR RENTAL HOUSING PRODUCTION UNDER RENT CONTROL: A CASE STUDY OF WASHINGTON, D.C. 7 (ULI Research Report No. 24, 1976).

194. Aaron Glantz, "America's Largest Private Landlord Faces Civil Rights Lawsuit," Revealnews.org, December, 2017, https://www.revealnews.org/blog/americas-largest-landlord-faces-civil-rights-lawsuit/

195. "Consumer Financial Protection Bureau Settles with Employment Background Screening Company," Consumer Financial Protection Bureau, November, 2019, https://www.consumerfinance.gov/about-us/newsroom/bureau-settles-employment-background-screening-company/

196. "Texas Company Will Pay $3 million to Settle FTC Charges That it Failed to Meet Accuracy Requirements for its Tenant Screening Reports," Federal Trade Commission, October, 2018, https://www.ftc.gov/news-events/press-releases/2018/10/texas-company-will-pay-3-million-settle-ftc-charges-it-failed .

197. Lesley Fair, "FTC's AppFolio case: The Fair Credit Reporting Act does more than just abide," ftc.gov, December 8, 2020, https://www.ftc.gov/news-events/blogs/business-blog/2020/12/ftcs-AppFolio -case-fair-credit-reporting-act-does-more-just

198. Press Release KIRO 7 News, "$150,000 settlement in tenant lawsuit may affect hundreds of people," kiro7, September 19, 2013, https://www.kiro7.com/news/150000-settlement-tenant-lawsuit-may-affect-hundre/246463008/

199. Dees Stribling and Bianca Barragán, "Bisnow: These Developers Have Built Up America. Their Executives Are 93% White," bisnow, February 25, 2021, https://lusk.usc.edu/news/bisnow-these-developers-have-built-america-their-executives-are-93-white

200. Kriston Capps, "How HUD Could Dismantle a Pillar of Civil Rights Law (CityLab)," Poverty and Race Research Action Council, August 2019, prrac.org/how-hud-could-dismantle-a-pillar-of-civil-rights-law-citylab/

201. The Federal Register, "HUD's Implementation of the Fair Housing Act's Disparate Impact Standard," federalregister, September 20, 2020, https://www.HUD's Implementation of the Fair Housing Act's Disparate Impact standardfederalregister.gov/documents/2020/09/24/2020-19887/huds-implementation-of-the-fair-housing-acts-disparate-impact-standard

202. ABBY LIVINGSTON AND ANNIE DANIEL, Texas Tribune, "The Top GOP Donors and Bundlers in Texas," March 1, 2015, https://www.texastribune.org/2015/03/01/texas-donors/ ; and, Stephanie Kirchgaessner, the Guardian, "Billionaires backed Republicans who sought to reverse US election results," theguardian.com, January 15, 2021, https://www.theguardian.com/us-news/2021/jan/15/trump-republicans-election-defeat-club-for-growth ; and, Brian Slodysko and Kevin Freking, "President Trump Gets in a Few Digs at California During West Coast Fundraising Blitz," NBC Los Angeles, September 2019, nbclosangeles.com/news/local/President-Trump-California-Fundraising-Visit-Los-Angeles-Beverly-Hills-Politics-560568751.html.; and, Sarah K. Burris, Raw Story, "Kyrsten Sinema now getting bankrolled by major GOP donors after helping spike Biden agenda," January 31, 2022, https://www.rawstory.com/republican-donors-fund-kyrsten-sinema/ ; and Kenneth P. Vogel and Shane Goldmacher, New York Times, "An Unusual $1.6 Billion Donation Bolsters Conservatives," nytimes.com, August 22, 2022, https://www.nytimes.com/2022/08/22/us/politics/republican-dark-money.html

203. Arizona Multihousing Association, Courtney LeVinus, "Members Will Save Nearly $600,000 in Rent Taxes; Cities Prohibited from Increasing the Regressive Tax Due to New State Law," pages 30-31, February 12, 2013, https://www.azmultihousing.org/

204. Kayla Devon, "NMHC 50: Managers Follow the Opportunity," Multifamily Executive, April, 2016, https://www.multifamilyexecutive.com/business-finance/top-50/nmhc-50-managers-follow-the-opportunity_o.

205. Jon Banister, "Greystar CEO Bob Faith On $4.6B EdR Acquisition And His Outlook For Multifamily," Bisnow.com, November 2018, https://www.bisnow.com/national/news/multifamily/greystar-ceo-bob-faith-on-46b-edr-acquisition-and-his-outlook-for-multifamily-95183.

206. "The Financial Crisis Inquiry Report: Final Report Of The National Commission On The Causes Of The Financial And Economic Crisis In The United States," The Financial Crisis Inquiry Commission, February 2011, govinfo.gov/content/pkg/GPO-FCIC/pdf/GPO-FCIC.pdf.

207. Hui-yong Yu and John Gittelsohn, "Blackstone Makes Foray Into Houses for Rent: Mortgages," Bloomberg, July 3, 2012, https://www.bloomberg.com/news/articles/2012-07-03/blackstone-makes-foray-into-houses-for-rent-mortgages ; and, Teresa O'Dea Hein, "BlackRock Realty Signs Riverstone Residential to Manage 62-Property Portfolio," multihousing, December 1, 2008, https://www.multihousingnews.com/post/blackrock-realty-signs-riverstone-residential-to-manage-62-property-portfolio/

208. National Multifamily Housing Council (NMHC). "NMHC 50 largest apartment owners, 2018." https://www.nmhc.org/research-insight/the-nmhc-50/top-50-lists/2018-owner-list/

209. Julie Segal, "Large Investors Will Be the Most At Risk in the Next Bond Sell-Off," Institutional Investor, November 2018, institutionalinvestor.com/article /b1c0x7kq08z5fs/Large-Investors-Will-Be-the-Most-At-Risk-in-the-Next-Bond-Sell-Off.

210. "Multifamily Market Commentary – July 2019 Multifamily Supply and Demand Varies by Metropolitan Areas," Fanniemae.com, https://multifamily.fanniemae.com/news-insights/multifamily-market-commentary/multifamily-supply-and-demand-varies-metropolitan-areas

211. "What Are Vertical Restraints," Anti-trust laws, December 2019, https://anti-trust.laws.com/vertical-restraints/vertical-restraints

212. Carl Cronan, "Greystar Acquires JPI Management Services," globest.com, January 05, 2009, https://www.globest.com/sites/globest/2009/01/05/greystar-acquires-jpi-management-services/; and, https://www.cpexecutive.com/post/bob-faiths-mission-to-buy-build-manage-drives-greystar/

213. Jerry Ascierto, "Seattle's Apartment Market Heats Up," multifamilyexecutive, July 21, 2011, https://www.multifamilyexecutive.com/property-management/apartment-trends/seattles-apartment-market-heats-up_o

214. Data Source: Gail Kalinoski, "Greystar Buys Riverstone Residential Group," commercialsearch, June 6, 2014, https://www.cpexecutive.com/post/greystar-buys-riverstone-residential-group/

215. Testimony of Laura S. Wertheimer Inspector General, Federal Housing Finance Agency before the U.S. House Committee on Financial Services, September 27, 2018 https://financialservices.house.gov/uploadedfiles/09.27.2018_laura_s._wertheimer_testimony.pdf

216. "FHFA's Targeted Examinations of Fannie Mae: Less than Half of the Targeted Examinations Planned for 2012 through 2015 Were Completed and No Examinations Planned for 2015 Were Completed Before the Report of Examination Issued," Federal Housing Finance Agency OIG, AUD-2016-006, September, 2016, fhfaoig.gov/Content/Files/AUD-2016-006.pdf; and, OIG-2017-003, December 15, 2016). https://www.fhfaoig.gov/Content/Files/AUD-2016-006.pdf

217. "FHFA's Housing Finance Examiner Commissioning Program: $7.7 Million and Four Years into the Program, the Agency has Fewer Commissioned Examiners," Federal Housing Finance Agency OIG Compliance Review, September, 2018, fhfaoig.gov/Content/Files/Compliance%20Review%20COM-2018-006.pdf

218. RealPage Press Release, "Research From RealPage Shows Mandatory Renters Insurance Does Not Negatively Impact Revenue Performance," pressreleasepoint.com, April 11, 2016, https://www.pressreleasepoint.com/research-realpage-shows-mandatory-renters-insurance-does-not-negatively-impact-revenue-performance

219. The King County Executive, "Executive, Seattle Mayor declare emergencies, announce new investments to respond to homelessness," November 2, 2105, https://kingcounty.gov/en/dept/executive/governance-leadership/king-county-executive/news/archive/2015/November/02-homeless-emergency.aspx

220. Aaron Kunkler, Bothell-Kenmore Reporter, "King County considers building 44,000 affordable housing units by 2024," bothell-reporter.com, January 21, 2019, http://www.bothell-reporter.com/news/king-county-considers-building-44000-affordable-housing-units-by-2024/

221. Ryan Briggs, PBS WHYY, "A Philly lawyer evicts people for city courts. She's married to a judge who presides over evictions," why.org, https://whyy.org/articles/philly-lawyer-collects-millions-evicting-people-for-city-courts-shes-married-to-an-eviction-judge/

222. Sandra Park and John Pollock, "Tenants' Right to Counsel is Critical to Fight Mass Evictions and Advance Race Equity During the Pandemic and Beyond," aclu.org, January 12, 2021, https://www.aclu.org/news/racial-justice/tenants-right-to-counsel-is-critical-to-fight-mass-evictions-and-advance-race-equity-during-the-pandemic-and-beyond/

223. We Are Apartment Management Consultants," Apartment Management Consultants, LLC, accessed September 2019, https://www.amcllc.net/amcrfp.pdf ; and, The website for American Management Consultants, LLC, accessed December, 2019, https://www.amcllc.net/about.asp#

224. Dallas News Administrator, "History Abounds inside Harlan Crow's home," dallasnews, March 21, 2014, https://www.dallasnews.com/arts-entertainment/2014/03/21/history-abounds-inside-harlan-crows-home/

225. News Blog, "FDIC Selects CB Richard Ellis as Advisor," multifamilybiz, November 28, 2008, https://www.multifamilybiz.com/news/1417/fdic_selects_cb_richard_ellis_as_advisor

226. Wtopstaff Blog, "Firm chaired by Sen. Feinstein's husband cashes in on another federal crisis," wtop, May 31, 2013, https://wtop.com/news/2013/05/firm-chaired-by-sen-feinsteins-husband-cashes-in-on-another-federal-crisis/

227. The Website of Federal Deposit Insurance Corporation, Office of Inspector General Report, "The National Owned Real Estate Management and Marketing Services Contract with CB Richard Ellis, Inc.," dated March 2012, Accessed April 2021, https://www.fdicoig.gov/publications/national-owned-real-estate-management-and-marketing-services-contract-cb-richard-ellis

228. Douglas Martin, "Trammell Crow, Innovative Developer, Dies at 94," nytimes, Jan. 15, 2009, https://www.nytimes.com/2009/01/16/business/16crow.html

229. Jeanne B. Pinder, "END OF AN EMPIRE," chicagotribune, November 14, 1993, https://www.chicagotribune.com/news/ct-xpm-1993-11-14-9311140221-story.html

230. EMILY FREEMAN PINKSTON, "The Men Who Left the Crow's Nest," dmagazine, May 1984, https://www.dmagazine.com/publications/d-magazine/1984/may/the-men-who-left-the-crows-nest/
231. CBRE Press Release, "CB Richard Ellis Group, Inc. Announces Agreement to Acquire Trammell Crow Company," ir.cbre.com, October 31, 2006, https://ir.cbre.com/press-releases/press-release-details/2006/CB-Richard-Ellis-Group-Inc-Announces-Agreement-to-Acquire-Trammell-Crow-Company/default.aspx
232. The Website of Trammell Crow Company, "Corporate Information," Accessed April 2021, https://www.trammellcrow.com/en/about/corporate-information
233. Texas Department of Housing and Community Affairs v. Inclusive Communities Project, Inc., 135 S. Ct. 2507, 2512 (2015).
234. UCPcouncil News, "Trump Administration Launches Long-Promised Challenge to Fair Housing Law," www.ucpcouncil.com, August, 2019, https://www.ucpcouncil.com/trump-administration-launches-long-promised-challenge-to-fair-housing-law/
235. "History of Fair Housing," HUD.gov, hud.gov/program_offices/fair_housing_equal_opp /aboutfheo/history
236. Michael Rudy, YieldPro, "Yardi steps onto the path to machine learning," yieldpro.com, June 7, 2018, https://yieldpro.com/2018/06/yardi-incorporate-machine-learning/
237. PressRelease News, "Tom Walker Returns to The Rainmaker Group to Help Drive Revenue and Profitability for Casino Hotel Operators," pressrelease.com, January 25, 2012, https://www.pressrelease.com/news/tom-walker-returns-to-the-rainmaker-group-to-help-drive-revenue-and-107050; and, travel communication news, " Tom Walker Returns to The Rainmaker Group," January 25, 2012, https://travelcommunication.net/people/tom-walker-returns-to-the-rainmaker-group/
238. Archstone-Smith Operating Trust (2002) Form 10-K 2002. SEC.gov Archives. https://www.sec.gov/Archives/edgar/data/80737/000103570403000151/d03069e10vk.htm
239. HotelExecutive News, "Casino Hotels Boost Profits with Rainmaker, Agilysys Tech Collaboration," hotelexecutive.com, October 14, 2008, https://www.hotelexecutive.com/newswire/5125/casino-hotels-boost-profits-with-rainmaker-agilysys-tech-collaboration
240. Hotel-Online News, "The Rainmaker Group and Realty DataTrust Partner to Introduce Optimized Multi-Dimensional Online Pricing for the Apartment Industry," hotel-online.com, June 25, 2007, https://www.hotel-online.com/News/PR2007_2nd/Jun07_RainmakerRealty.html; and, Siegel Sez, HospitalityUpgrade, "REVENUE MANAGEMENT," hospitalityUpgrade.com, July12, 2007, https://www.hospitalityupgrade.com/_siegel_sez/siegel_sez_Detail.asp?ID=264 ; and, Hospitalitynet Press Release, "The Rainmaker Group and Realty DataTrust Partner to Introduce Optimized," hospitalitynet.org, June 24, 2007, https://www.hospitalitynet.org/news/4032001.html

241. HospitalityUpgrade News, "The Rainmaker Group Brings Revenue Management Discipline to Hoteliers at Agilysys 2011 Users Conference," hospitalityupgrade.com, January 25, 2011, https://www.hospitalityupgrade.com/News/News-Article-Details/?docID=4485

242. Linnell Taylor Marketing, CISION News, "Rainmaker ILM Announces Integration with MRI Software," prweb.com, October 16, 2017 https://www.prweb.com/releases/rainmaker_ilm_announces_integration_with_mri_software/prweb14806370.htm

243. CISION News Release, provided by On-Site, "On-Site Integrates With MRI Software," prweb.com, February 29, 2016, https://www.prweb.com/releases/on_site_integrates_with_mri_software/prweb13238093.htm

244. Anuradha Kher, Multi-Housing News, "White Paper Shows Archstone Increased Revenue by 1.5% from Call Center's Capture of Incremental Leads," multihousingnews.com, March 26, 2010, https://www.multihousingnews.com/white-paper-shows-archstone-increased-revenue-by-1-5-from-call-centers-capture-of-incremental-leads/

245. NBC news, GlobeNewswire, "RealPage Online Renewals Reduces Turnover by 2 Percent and Increases Asking Rents by 3 Percent at UDR," May 2, 2011, https://www.nbcnews.com/id/wbna42862409

246. eBook, REDIRECT, "The Year in MRI, 2017 Edition," Accessed July 2023, www.redirectconsulting.com/hubfs/eBooks/2017/mri%202017/redirect_ebook_This-Year-in-MRI_2017-06-22.pdf

247. MRI Website, "MRI Products," Accessed June 2023, https://www.mrisoftware.com/products/

248. MRI Real Estate Software Website, Multifamily, "Take better care of residents, business, and yourself," Accessed July 2023, https://www.mrisoftware.com/multifamily/?creative=637893796951&keyword=multi%20family%20property%20management&matchtype=p&network=g&device=c&utm_source=Google+Ad&utm_medium=Website&utm_campaign=MRI+NA+Website+PPC+2023&utm_content=637893796951&utm_term=multi%20family%20property%20management&gad_source=1&gclid=CjwKCAjw-eKpBhAbEiwAqFL0mphHMCQzyLnBuSYfp1yVOBIRo9jlnJRS0n9yH8AegR9R_HamoSc52hoCj-oQAvD_BwE ; specifically https://www.mrisoftware.com/products/residential-management/

249. Wendy Broffman, YieldPro, "Tech wars," yieldpro.com, April 2, 2018, https://yieldpro.com/2018/04/tech-wars/

250. Chris Wood, "RealPage Countersues Yardi," multifamilyexecutive, March, 31, 2011, https://www.multifamilyexecutive.com/technology/realpage-countersues-yardi_o

251. Tim Blackwell, RealPage Blog, "Changing the Way Multifamily Thinks About Apartment Market Research with Lease Transaction Data," realpage.com, September 21, 2020, https://www.realpage.com/blog/changing-the-way-multifamily-thinks-about-apartment-market-research-with-lease-transaction-data/

252. Nat Kunes, AppFolio Blogs, "Utility Billing: Growing Trend That's Not Just for the Big Guys," appfolio.com, March 29, 2019 https://www.appfolio.com/blog/utility-billing-growing-trend-that%E2%80%99s-not-just-for-the-big-guys/

253. GLOBE NEWSWIRE, "AppFolio Expands Real Estate Product Capabilities," globenewswire.com, September 17, 2018, https://rss.globenewswire.com/en/news-release/2018/09/17/1571792/36405/en/AppFolio-Expands-Real-Estate-Product-Capabilities.html; or, Kelsi Maree Boreland, Globest News, "AppFolio Boosts Property Management Technology," globest.com, September 25, 2018, https://www.globest.com/2018/09/25/appfolio-boosts-property-management-technology/

254. Yardi News, "Yardi Unveils New Solution to Optimize Asset Performance for Commercial Real Estate," yardi.com, May 31, 2018, https://www.yardi.com/news/yardi-unveils-new-solution-to-optimize-asset-performance-for-commercial-real-estate/

255. Guy Lyman, RealPage Blogs, "Don't Miss This! Unveiling of "AIRM" AI Revenue Management at RealWorld," realpage.com, September 6, 2020, https://www.realpage.com/blog/dont-miss-this-unveiling-of-airm-ai-revenue-management-at-realworld/

256. Wendy Broffman, YieldPro, "Same assets. Better performance," yieldpro.com, October 16, 2022, https://yieldpro.com/2022/10/same-assets-better-performance/

257. RealPage News, "RealPage Announces Demandx, An AI-Powered Multifamily Demand Optimization Solution," realpage.com, August 7, 2023, https://www.realpage.com/news/realpage-announces-demandx/

258. Wendy Broffman, YieldPro, "Same assets. Better performance.," yieldpro.com, October 16, 2022, https://yieldpro.com/2022/10/same-assets-better-performance/

259. RealPage News, "RealPage to Acquire On-Site," realpage.com, August 2, 2017, https://www.realpage.com/news/realpage-to-acquire-on-site/

260. RealPage News, "RealPage Presents New Data Reinforcing the Value of AI Screening," realpage.com, February 11, 2021, https://www.realpage.com/news/data-reinforcing-value-of-ai-screening/ and, RealPage Blog., "Screening Strategies for an Evolving World," e-book, realpage.com, Accessed 2021, https://www.realpage.com/ebooks/screening-strategies-evolving-world/&showPdf=true

261. The Website of AppFolio, articles, "Unlock new levels of success with AppFolio Property Manager Max," Accessed—updated, October 2023, https://www.appfolio.com/articles/appfolio-property-manager-max

262. Jorge Mercado, Pacific Coast Business Times, "AppFolio lays off 62 people," pacbiztimes.com, May 27, 2023, https://www.pacbiztimes.com/2023/05/27/appfolio-lays-off-62-people/

263. AppFolio Website, customer stories, "Evernest," Accessed July 2023, https://www.appfolio.com/customer-stories/evernest

264. Hina Navin, Gulf News, "How Artificial Intelligence and IoT are transforming real estate," gulfnews.com, September 24, 2019, https://gulfnews.com/business/property/how-artificial-intelligence-and-iot-are-transforming-real-estate-1.66641869

265. Hotel Online, News, "Boyd Gaming Hits Jackpot With Revenue Management Strategy," hotel-online.com, September 7, 2006, https://www.hotel-online.com/News/PR2006_3rd/Sep06_TheRainmakerGroup.html

266. Hotel Online, News, "The Rainmaker Group to Share Expertise at Revenue Management and Pricing Conference," hotel-online.com, August 23, 2006, https://www.hotel-online.com/News/PR2006_3rd/Aug06_Rainmaker.html

267. Chris Woods, Multifamily Executive, "Combining Multifamily Technologies Leads to Revenue Lift," multifamilyexecutive.com, March 10, 2010 https://www.multifamilyexecutive.com/technology/combining-multifamily-technologies-leads-to-revenue-lift_o

268. John M. Newman, "Procompetitive Justification in Antitrust Law," University of Memphis Cecil C. Humphreys School of Law, and NYU Law, Accessed June 2021, https://www.law.nyu.edu/sites/default/files/upload_documents/John%20Newman.pdf

269. The Smithsonian Magazine, Alice George, "The 1968 Kerner Commission Got It Right, But Nobody Listened," smithsonianmag.com, March 1, 2018, https://www.smithsonianmag.com/smithsonian-institution/1968-kerner-commission-got-it-right-nobody-listened-180968318/

270. Margaret C. Levenstein, Valerie Y. Suslow, "What Determines Cartel Success," Journal of Economic Literature, Vol. 44, No. 1 (Mar. 2006), https://www.jstor.org/stable/30032296.

271. The Website for Justia US Law, Jeff Persigehl and Samone Bodley, individually and on behalf of the putative classes, Respondents (A14-0027),Appellants (A14-0123), vs. American Utility Management, Inc., ETAL No. 27-CV-13-13415., https://cases.justia.com/minnesota/court-of-appeals/2015-a14-27.pdf?ts=1422904069

272. Office of Karl A. Racine, "Complaint Alleges Affordable Units Prevented from Being Available to District Residents," oag.dc.gov, April 25, 2017, https://oag.dc.gov/release/attorney-general-racine-sues-company-offers-rent

273. "Amber Nicole Lompe v. Sunridge and AMC, Case No. 2:12-cv-00088-ABJ (UNITED STATES COURT OF APPEALS FOR THE TENTH CIRCUIT)" Chamberlitigation.com, April, 2015.; and, Amber Lompe, "Lompe: Poisoned by indifference," Casper Star Tribune, October, 2016, https://trib.com/opinion/columns/lompe-poisoned-by-indifference/article_e175b3fc-1982-5ae0-be59-8be3d77aec5e.html

274. "Broderick v. Apartment Mgmt. Consultants, LLC Justia Opinion Summary," Justia US Law, accessed September, 2020, https://law.justia.com/cases/utah/supreme-court/2012/20100276.html.

275. The Website of The American Presidency Project, "Fact Sheet: President Bush Calls for Expanding Opportunities to Homeownership," presidency.ucsb.edu , June 17, 2002, https://www.presidency.ucsb.edu/documents/fact-sheet-president-bush-calls-for-expanding-opportunities-homeownership

276. David L. Bahnsen, "Did The Financial Crisis End?" National Review, March 2019, nationalreview.com/magazine/2019/03/25/did-the-financial-crisis-end/

277. Karl E. Case, "Housing, Land, and the Economic Crisis," lincolninst, January 2010, https://www.lincolninst.edu/publications/articles/housing-land-economic-crisis

278. "The State Of The Nation's Housing 2007," Joint Center for Housing Studies of Harvard University, https://www.jchs.harvard.edu/sites/jchs.harvard.edu/files/son2007.pdf

Websites

We also gathered substantial amounts of information from more than 500 company and industry websites.

www.ingramcontent.com/pod-product-compliance
Lightning Source LLC
LaVergne TN
LVHW052245200926
848481LV00002B/277
9781734641820